MANNERHEIM, MARSHAL OF FINLAND

HENRIK MEINANDER

Mannerheim, Marshal of Finland

A Life in Geopolitics

HURST & COMPANY, LONDON

First published in the United Kingdom in 2023 by
C. Hurst & Co. (Publishers) Ltd.,
New Wing, Somerset House, Strand, London, WC2R 1LA
© Henrik Meinander, 2023
All rights reserved.

Distributed in the United States, Canada and Latin America by
Oxford University Press, 198 Madison Avenue, New York, NY 10016,
United States of America.

The right of Henrik Meinander to be identified as the author
of this publication is asserted by him in accordance with the
Copyright, Designs and Patents Act, 1988.

A Cataloguing-in-Publication data record for this book
is available from the British Library.

ISBN: 9781787389373

This book is printed using paper from registered sustainable
and managed sources.

www.hurstpublishers.com

Printed and bound in Great Britain by Bell and Bain Ltd, Glasgow.

CONTENTS

LIST OF MAPS

LIST OF ILLUSTRATIONS

LIST OF ILLUSTRATIONS

LIST OF ILLUSTRATIONS

LIST OF ILLUSTRATIONS

FOREWORD

Every book has its own history. This particular one has its origin at a lunch in the mid-2010s at the Helsinki Bourse Club with the *grand seigneur* of the Finnish book trade, Professor Heikki A. Reenpää (1922–2020). Before we had even begun the main course, he had proposed that I should write a new concise biography of Gustaf Mannerheim, Marshal of Finland, and one of the few Finns renowned internationally. The idea had certainly crossed my mind before, since I had spent almost three decades researching, writing and lecturing about the Marshal. Until that point, however, I had always put it off, as I had not felt ready for such a demanding undertaking.

In all probability, I would have gone on putting it off for the rest of my life, if the suggestion had not come from Heikki A. Reenpää himself. It was he who had helped bring out the Finnish edition of the Marshal's memoirs in the early 1950s, published by Otava. Reenpää had afterwards nurtured a great number of other Mannerheim books to fruition at Otava, which meant that his proposal was too tempting to resist. To put it simply, I wanted to join the publisher's long line of Mannerheim authors, the first of whom had been no less than the Marshal himself.

Writing a biography of Mannerheim (1867–1951) was therefore both a rewarding and a demanding task. It was not only that his impressive life's work as an Imperial Russian officer, a Finnish military commander and head of the state covered a crucial era in the formation of modern Europe. It was also the way Mannerheim conducted this journey—so dramatically and sometimes even unpredictably that, to keep the grip concise, I tried to follow Lytton Strachey's advice, in the foreword to his classic study *Eminent Victorians*: the first duty of the biographer is to preserve "a brevity which excludes everything that is redundant and nothing that is significant".

Another challenge, of course, was to keep a balance between critical distance and empathic understanding, not least because Mannerheim still can inspire either unconditional admiration or deep irritation among many of my countrymen. It is inevitable that my perspectives and conclusions bear the imprint of my own background and career. Particularly relevant here is the fact that I was curator of the Mannerheim Museum in Helsinki in the 1990s, which taught me much about both the panegyric and demonising tendencies in the politicisation of Mannerheim's story, whether in historical research or popular commemoration.

Mannerheim was born into one of Finland's leading noble families, which lost all its fortunes due to his father's fatal shortcomings. After these and some other early difficulties, he forged a splendid career in the Russian Army, coming into close contact with the Imperial family and serving for three decades. That fascinating chapter in his life ended abruptly when the Russian Revolution of late 1917 brought him back to Finland, which declared its independence after 108 years as a Russian Grand Duchy. When the revolution spread to Finland in 1918, Mannerheim was appointed Commander-in-Chief of the counter-revolutionary Finnish White Army, which ultimately triumphed over the Finnish Red Guards.

After a short period as interim regent of the newborn Finnish state, Mannerheim retreated into a comfortable life as a national hero, living off a fund raised by the people for his income—until the Second World War saw him return to the heart of power, picking up where he had left off two decades earlier. Now in his seventies, he once again took to the world stage, now as Commander-in-Chief of the Finnish Army; and, for the second time, steered his country through the Armageddon of European war with its independence intact. The price Finland paid for its survival was harsh: the death of almost 100,000 soldiers, and a military alliance with Hitler's Third Reich between 1941 and 1944, for which Mannerheim held responsibility as commander-in-chief. Not surprisingly, the Marshal has been both adulated and vilified for the decisions taken during these troublesome years.

Mannerheim's life and legacy are thus closely intertwined with the dramatic twists and turns of Finland's history as an independent state. For a long time, the concept of geopolitics as a meaningful way to understand events was severely tarnished by the experiences of the two world wars. But, gradually, the concept has become relevant again. As we have seen in Ukraine, geography, along with the control of strategically important territories and trade routes, simply continues to be a decisive factor in international politics. Mannerheim seems almost an embodiment of this truth. Finland's border with Russia constitutes the longest and, in some senses, the sharpest frontier between civilisations in Europe; as such, the country has often been a pawn on the international chess board. Even to this day, geopolitics still has a considerable impact on Mannerheim's reputation in Finland: how the Second World War is commemorated and how the Marshal is viewed often go hand in hand.

The first editions of this book were published in Finnish and Swedish in June 2017 for the 150th anniversary of Mannerheim's birth. Foreign interest in the Marshal has only grown since then, with the biography brought out in Estonian and Russian in 2018 and 2020, respectively. With this English translation, it has now been published in five languages, which I am naturally proud of and thankful for.

I warmly thank Dr Richard Robinson for his precise and nuanced English translation of the manuscript. I am indebted to my editor Lara Weisweiller-Wu for her thorough and engaged editing of the manuscript, which made it more accessible for Western readers. I must also express my gratitude to Dr Hannu Linkola, who draw the six maps that so vividly uncover the different geopolitical contexts of Mannerheim's career. This translation has been funded by the Mannerheim Foundation, for which I am also grateful.

Henrik Meinander
Helsinki, January 2023

1

CHILDHOOD AND ADOLESCENCE

Unrest and Upheaval

"At a ¼ past 7 in the evening Hélène had a healthy baby boy." So reported Louise von Julin to a close relative on 4 June 1867, after she had assisted in the birth of her stepdaughter's third child. The grandmother had washed the newborn, and described him as "kind and jolly", which were not exactly qualities for which the boy would always come to be known later in life, serving as a reminder that we all start out as blank slates. The birth took place in Louhisaari Manor in Southwest Finland, a stately stone mansion from the seventeenth century which had been a home for the noble family since its purchase by Carl Erik Mannerheim in the 1790s. While the baby's delivery went smoothly, the mood was sombre, for the newborn's aunt had only recently died in childbirth. Hence the christening, held three weeks later on Midsummer's Eve, was solely for the immediate family, with the grandmother as the only godmother in attendance.

In a letter to her sister in Sweden, Hélène Mannerheim complained that "not a single person was glad about" the boy's arrival. He would, however, go on to become more famed and fêted than anyone else in twentieth-century Finland. He was baptised Carl Gustaf Emil, but was usually called Gustaf. The first two names had been borne by many of his forefathers; the last came from his oldest uncle, ironmaster Emil Lindsay von Julin, who would later try to guide his nephew down the right path with the help of moral insights from British literature. While Mannerheim could have arrived into the world at a more propitious moment in history, there is no doubt

1

Willnäs.

Fig. 1.1: Louhisaari Manor, Gustaf Mannerheim's birthplace and childhood home.

that he was born with a silver spoon in his mouth. On numerous
occasions in his early career, he would get himself out of a tight spot
with the aid of his uncles' money and his noble relatives' contacts,
above all those in the centre of the Russian Empire, St Petersburg.

But let's not jump forward in Mannerheim's life without first
examining how the world and Finland looked in the mid-1860s.
Tired truism it may be, but these years really were a time of
upheaval in many respects. The Crimean War of the 1850s had
resulted in Great Britain surpassing Russia as Europe's leading
Great Power. Over the next two decades, and thanks to its tech-
nological and military advantages, the British Empire expanded
faster than any other before or since, in the process spreading its
innovations and the British social ideal to other parts of Europe. As
the world's leading industrial and colonial power, it stood to reason that Britain was the foremost advocate of a liberalised global
trade and a free civil society, one that not only gave its citizens

freedom of speech and association, but also the right for a growing number of them to vote.

In the same year that Mannerheim was born, a parliamentary reform was implemented in Britain that significantly broadened the franchise. The reform did not seem to impress Karl Marx in the slightest, for 1867 was also the year when the socialist, who had moved from Germany to England in 1849, published the first—and certainly the most influential—part of his work *Das Kapital*. Due to the boom in newspaper publishing, the 1860s witnessed a formidable eruption of ideas and ideologies about what the future of society could and should look like. The majority of those seeking reform had freedom as their common cause, but they became increasingly fractured as to whether the freedom should be individual, national or economic in nature.

Across Europe and North America, more and more resources were being invested in railways, industry and steamboats. In February 1867, the first ships sailed through the French-built Suez Canal. The canal company was soon purchased by the British, and the European colonial powers tightened their grip over East Africa and Asia via this new waterway. Also noteworthy is the 1867 International Exhibition, held in Paris and opened in April, which even featured a Finnish exposition in the Russian pavilion. On the very date of Mannerheim's birth, *Helsingfors Dagblad* featured a long report from the exhibition, which paid special attention to the public demonstrations of "improvements in the social, moral and physical standing of the working class in France".

The modest Finnish products and artworks told a very different story. In the mid-1860s, Finland was one of Europe's poorest countries, and the plight of its inhabitants was heightened by the succession of extremely cold summers that struck the northernmost parts of Europe between 1865 and 1868. These led to crop failures, famines, epidemics and, ultimately, to high death tolls, not least in the isolated and capital-poor Finland, where more than 100,000 people died. So, while the display cases at the world fair were abundant with culinary delicacies, food shortages in the Finnish countryside were degenerating into a humanitarian catastrophe. The spring of 1867 came extremely late, and by August the arable land was again being assailed by hard frosts at night. Although the Senate had, at long last, taken foreign loans to buy grain from abroad, the early onset of winter meant there was no time for it to arrive before the sea froze and put a stop to all shipping traffic.

The irony of fate was that, in this case, ultimate responsibility for the government's fatal procrastination lay with J. V. Snellman, a member of the Senate's Department of Finance. He was at the vanguard of the burgeoning Finnish nationalist movement—Fennomania—and in previous years he had succeeded in forcing through a number of decisions and reforms that were extremely important for Finland's development. In 1863, after a 54-year wait, the Russian Emperor had agreed that the Diet of Finland, the country's chief legislative body, could begin to meet regularly. Also in 1863, an imperial edict was issued—on Snellman's initiative—declaring that Finnish would gain equal status with Swedish as an official language within twenty years. In the same period there began a comprehensive modernisation of the country's education system, and the recently introduced Finnish currency (*markka* and *penni*) was tied to the silver standard rather than to the rouble.

All these reforms caused cracks to emerge in the established social order, within which many previous generations of the Mannerheim family had reached high positions. The family's progenitor was the merchant Henning Marhein from Hamburg: his son Hinrich, born in 1618, was drawn north to Sweden, which was a Great Power at the time. He settled first in Gävle, where he worked as a merchant, before later moving to Stockholm and earning his living as a bookkeeper. The following two generations climbed rapidly up the social ranks. Hinrich's son Augustin was ennobled in 1693 for his contribution to Charles XI's Great Reduction (in which the Swedish Crown reclaimed land from the high nobility) in the Baltic provinces. In 1768, Augustin's son, Colonel Johan Augustin Mannerheim, was made a baron. The two generations that followed also included high-ranking officers.

An integrated part of Sweden since the twelfth century, Finland was brought under Russian rule following the Finnish War of 1808–09. The country was designated an autonomous Grand Duchy of the Russian Empire as a result of negotiations in which Carl Erik, Johan Augustin Mannerheim's grandson, played a central role. As a consequence he was appointed a member of the country's first Senate, originally called the Governing Council, and received the title of count in 1824. This title was subsequently held by the head of the family: that is to say, the eldest male family member of each generation. Hence the Mannerheim dynasty became one of the high-ranking families that led the Grand Duchy, in part through high office and in part through many mutually beneficial marriages. This continued until the 1860s, when the aforementioned Diet of Finland began to assemble and the nobility's privileges were slowly eroded.

As the winds of change sweeping across Europe were finally felt in Finland, one after another of the well-to-do noble families lost

Fig. 1.2: Brothers Count Carl and Baron Gustaf Mannerheim posing cheerfully, 1884.

their social status and financial fortunes. Carl Erik Mannerheim's son, Carl Gustaf, became a provincial governor and the President of Viipuri's Court of Appeal, but his grandson, Carl Robert, did not fare so well. In the late 1850s, he ruined his reputation among the powers that be in St Petersburg by joining a clique of liberals critical of the regime, thereby losing all prospects of a successful career in the Russian bureaucracy. Instead, Carl Robert tried his luck as an entrepreneur in the nascent forestry industry.

But in common with many of his standing, Carl Robert completely lacked the necessary qualities to prosper as a capitalist and industrialist. His childhood friend, the upper-class liberal Anders Ramsay, would candidly recall in his memoirs, *Från barnaår till silfverhår* (1904–07; From Child's Play to Going Grey), how he himself managed to bankrupt not one but two large businesses. In Carl Robert's case, his unsuccessful investments and half-baked ventures were exacerbated by his accumulation of gambling debts. By 1866, straitened circumstances compelled him to begin selling his and his wife's shared heirlooms one after another. Fourteen years later this culminated in a catastrophe that would leave its mark on the whole family.

Hélène von Julin's brothers and relatives could surely not have imagined that everything would end so badly when the young Count Mannerheim eagerly proposed to her in autumn 1862, even though they were somewhat hesitant in approving the couple's marriage. Carl Robert was undeniably handsome and charming, but also notorious for his outspoken political views and lavish lifestyle. This contrasted with the Julins' frugal existence, which was more in keeping with that of merchants or industrialists than the upper class. Indeed, although the family had been ennobled in the late 1840s, the railways, mechanical workshops and estates that they ran in Länsi-Uusimaa continued to prosper, to the benefit of the whole region. In spite of her family's doubts, Hélène got her way, and the couple's wedding was celebrated at Fiskars's factory on New Year's Eve 1862, with guests including a number of high-ranking officials and liberal cultural personalities.

Unions of this kind between ancestry and money were customary at this time in Finland, as elsewhere in Europe, and if everything went well they could work to the advantage of both sets of relatives.

Hélène and Carl Robert's matrimony initially appeared to have fulfilled the young couple's romantic expectations. As the family grew, Hélène was increasingly tied to the Louhisaari Manor, which became a meeting place for the Mannerheim clan. It often proved attractive to her relatives, too, such as when Grandma Louise helped with the birth of Gustaf during the exceptionally cold early summer of 1867. The eldest child of the brood was Sophie, who was born in 1863 and who shouldered a large responsibility for her younger siblings from an early age. Two years later, their son Carl was born, who inherited his father's countship; then came Gustaf and after him a further four children between 1868 and 1873: Johan, Eva, Annica and August.

Mannerheim's early years at Louhisaari are described in idyllic terms in just about all his biographies. But what did his boyhood surroundings actually look like? The stone manor that housed the large family, its guests and servants comprised three storeys, plus attic and cellar spaces. The interior was fairly typical for a manor of the period. The accumulated furniture, pictures and other household paraphernalia of past generations were interspersed with the occasional object that reflected the current inhabitants' interests and characters. In Carl Robert's case, his personal additions included a choice art collection of the period's foremost Finnish painters. The strict symmetry of the main building's north-easterly entrance hall contrasted with the English park that stretched out to the southwest. Behind the park could be spied Louhisaari Bay, a broad archipelago where the children spent their summers happily swimming, rowing and sailing.

There are numerous anecdotes detailing the young Gustaf's wild nature and his almost foolhardy bravery. Yet it is pertinent to consider the extent to which he greatly differed from other healthy and boundary-testing boys of his age. Perhaps his unruliness was a way for him to assert himself in the shadow of his elder brother, Carl, who was often praised for his level temperament. Perhaps he took the lead from his father, whose vivacious but unstable nature stood in contrast to his mother's steady and discreet disposition. Or perhaps it was simply that his father was far too rarely at home to instil discipline in him.

The Mannerheim siblings would later reminisce about their childhood at Louhisaari with gratitude, always emphasising the memory of their mother, whose love and devotion they all attested to. In contrast, their father's contribution was typically and tellingly absent from such recollections. It is no accident that Mannerheim chose to start his memoirs from the year 1882, when his career in the military began. Much later, Gustaf's younger brother Johan wrote to his fiancée that his parents' marriage during his childhood had been a horrible failure: "I would in no way induce myself to experience all the misery, that I, as a child, have witnessed." Johan and his betrothed kept this in mind and went on to spend a con tented life together in a manor in Östergötland in Sweden. The other children were not quite as successful in shaking off the traumatic experiences of their parents' abrasive marriage, not least because Carl Robert's gross mismanagement of many generations' accumulated fortune and reputation caused the family to fall apart. This left the deepest impression on Sophie and Gustaf, who would themselves both enter into a short-lived wedlock and never remarry.

In autumn 1879, the bankrupt Carl Robert, together with his lover Sofia Nordenstam, fled to Paris. True to form, he did not bother to enquire about the mess that he had left behind. A year later, all his remaining property was sold at auction to cover at least some of his creditors' claims. Fortunately, Carl Robert's sister, Eva Vilhelmina Mannerheim, was able to buy Louhisaari, which allowed the family to continue to spend their summers at the manor, although this was, of course, scant comfort. Hélène and the younger children were compelled to move to their grandmother's manor house, Sällvik, in Pohja, while the older children continued their schooling in Helsinki and Hamina.

Gustaf had begun his schooling in Helsinki in 1874, and while there his unruly conduct had continued to attract attention. A few years later, in autumn 1879, he was expelled from the prestigious Helsingfors Lyceum—sometimes also called the *Böökska lyceet*—for having broken a number of windows in the city with some friends. As a consequence he was sent instead to Hamina, the home of the Finnish Cadet Corps; he passed its entrance exam in summer 1882, after a couple of years in the local grammar school. This was neither an unusual nor an ignominious solution for a Finnish noble family in the nineteenth century; especially not if the family had a military history or was in straitened circumstances, and even less so if the boy had shown himself to be too disorderly for a civil education. Around 3,000 sons of the nobility passed through the corps during its years of operation between 1818 and 1903, and so made up the majority of its 4,000 graduates. Around 500 Finns reached the rank of general or admiral in the Imperial Russian Army and Navy.

Since autumn 1879 was also when his bankrupt father left the family high and dry, it was hardly a coincidence that Gustaf's bad behaviour degenerated and led to his expulsion from Helsingfors Lyceum at that particular moment. And as the family's possessions were sold off and rumours spread of Carl Robert's exploits in Paris, the social pressure became too much for Hélène, who died in January 1881 from a heart attack. It has been reported that the children welcomed Carl Robert with open arms when he came back to attend her funeral. However, when he married his mistress a few years later and returned with her to Finland, their disappointment with him hardened into a lifelong contempt, not least in the case of his eldest boy, Carl. According to hearsay, his sons took to calling him "Count Swine" behind his back.

It should, however, be noted that Gustaf's relationship with his tarnished father was less condemnatory. It seems the fact that they had both slipped up and suffered setbacks made them more prepared to forgive each other. Upon his return home, his father founded a new business specialising as agents of office supplies, which gradually came to provide him with a modest standard of living. Both father and son were happy to meet when Gustaf was in Helsinki, and they maintained a regular correspondence. As the letters make clear, Carl Robert accepted his son's career in the Russian military, even though it was increasingly at odds with his own and his other sons' liberal and constitutional attitudes.

The Cadet in Hamina

In his expansive biography of Mannerheim, Stig Jägerskiöld advances the idea that Gustaf was his father's son, in the sense that he remained, at heart, a constitutional and liberal patriot throughout his life, even as he later expressed an unwavering loyalty to the Russian Emperor. John Screen, who has likewise written a splendid biography of Mannerheim, is not so convinced that this was the case. That said, he also does his utmost to demonstrate that the ideological tension within the Mannerheim family was handled rationally and analytically. Perhaps both Jägerskiöld and Screen try too hard to find a coherent ideological explanation for Mannerheim's imperialistic outlook and career choice that is consistent with his future role as the foremost defender of independent Finland.

A more down-to-earth interpretation is that the young Mannerheim stumbled into a military career for want of a better alternative. In common with most people who possess a typical level of self-preservation and ambition, he was thinking first and foremost about his own career and future. His uncle Emil Lindsay von Julin, who was prone to moralising, urged Mannerheim to approach his fresh start at Hamina with this in mind: "You must not forget that you must earn your keep early on, and try to make the best use of the training you get."

When his career continued in Russia and the constitutional conflict heightened between Finland and the empire, Mannerheim followed the dispute guardedly, if not indifferently. Over time he was afflicted by a scepticism that became increasingly difficult to conceal. His main consideration seemed to be whether committing to Finland's autonomy would help further his career. His father and his brothers evidently knew that it was unlikely to, and they therefore had to accept his reluctance to get involved with the issue. Their disagreement with Mannerheim was, in other words, one of principle that could not be resolved. Finland's cause would only become Mannerheim's cause much later on.

The educational programme at the Finnish Cadet Corps in Hamina, a fortress and port town in the Eastern Gulf of Finland, had a well-established form by the time the 15-year-old Mannerheim began his studies there in autumn 1882. The roughly 120 cadets were quartered in barracks with large dormitories that allowed little space for a private life. The studies took seven years, and, besides the military drills, field training and gymnastics, they mostly encompassed the same subjects taught in the civilian grammar schools: languages, mathematics, religion, history and natural sciences. Academic instruction mainly took place in Swedish, but also partly in Russian, since the aim was to cultivate an accomplished officer corps for the whole empire. The cadets were also frequently drilled in the use of Russian commands and forms of address, in addition to which the programme included fairly extensive Russian language classes.

All the uniforms, teaching plans and daily routines were, of course, the same as in any other Russian officer school. Yet Finland's increasing separatism meant that the Cadet Corps gradually developed into something of a hybrid between a native Finnish and a generic Russian institution. Especially after Finland established its own army in 1878, expectations rose that the Cadet Corps would train both regular and reserve officers for domestic use. This ran entirely contrary to the Russian military authorities' rational aim of consolidating and modernising officer training in order to better centralise power and strengthen the empire, and in 1903 the corps was closed down.

Mannerheim was not exactly enthusiastic about his new life course. As his stubborn nature began to collide with the spartan and rigid military regime of the corps, he received repeated reprimands

Fig. 1.3: Homework test in Hamina Cadet Corps.

and punishments, which, in turn, increased his disillusionment and created new problems. Nonetheless, during his first years in Hamina he gradually improved on his initially modest school performance, showing a particular interest in French, history and gymnastics. Except for occasional balls and military feasts, life in the corps was mostly monotonous and spent in the company of his course comrades at the barracks, where the internal hierarchy was maintained through a variety of informal rituals which were tantamount to systematic bullying. The well-built and self-assured Mannerheim appears to have got on well in these rugged games, and would later often deploy such mild forms of sadism to keep his colleagues on their toes.

Hugo Backmansson—officer, artist and former student of the corps—did an excellent job of depicting everyday life at Hamina. His illustrated book from 1892 on the cadets' daily duties gives a vivid portrayal of how they were under constant and collective supervision. Each newly enrolled student would serve an older cadet, who was expected to act as a guardian in return. Mannerheim's first guardian was Ernst Löfström, who would, like him, reach the rank of general and play an important role on the frontline in Finland in 1918. Such ceaseless surveillance did not suit Mannerheim, and his reports from Hamina to his siblings were full of biting observations and barbs which laid bare the fact that he almost never got used to this stifling existence.

At the same time, the collective made his distinctive character and individual strengths visible. Poor and unruly noblemen, as has already been noted, were in abundance in the Cadet Corps. Few, however, were quite so physically imposing: as a fully grown adult, Mannerheim measured 1.87 metres tall, approximately 20 centimetres more than the average Finnish man at that time. Through physical training and, later, above all through horse-riding, his naturally slender physique developed a splendid posture and a lithe mobility which he would maintain into his old age. In his youth, Mannerheim's regular and composed features most resembled those of his mother, but over the years his face's increasing tautness bore a closer likeness to his father or grandfather.

The cadets were constantly drilled to adhere to the military dress code, which instilled in many of them a lifelong inclination to be well groomed, even in civilian life. In Mannerheim's case this developed into such a studied sense of style that it inspired both admiration and jealousy over the years. It also put considerable strain on his personal finances. Without a doubt, this costly quirk was partly a consequence of his aesthetic sensibility, but also of the example set by his perniciously wasteful father. Already, during his time as a cadet, Mannerheim displayed clear difficulties in managing his finances, and so he learnt fast how to write effective entreaties for more money to his wealthy uncles.

How did Mannerheim speak? Here it is certainly worth differentiating the vocabulary and playful diction of the unconstrained young man from the oratory of the urbane Field Marshal. Nonetheless, we all carry particular linguistic mannerisms and intonations with us throughout our lives, and Mannerheim was no exception. His Swedish mother tongue—the Finnish upper class's *lingua franca* long into the twentieth century—was the language he used most growing up, and in which he continued to best express himself throughout his life in both spoken and written form. His latter-day radio speeches, of course, give some indication of his turn of phrase, but such public speaking is also misleading, in the sense that its articulation is exaggerated to clearly convey its message. Mannerheim's contemporaries, with an ear for class-based and phonetic distinctions, have characterised his spoken language in the 1940s as typical of the Swedish that was used by the old upper class in nineteenth-century Finland. It bore traces of the epoch when the ruling elite lived principally in Southwest Finland and were in close contact with Sweden. Certain speech sounds were sharper and more distinct than the more bourgeois Swedish of Helsinki, which, with its frequent broad l-sounds and abrupt consonants, is now the norm in Swedish-speaking Finland.

Mannerheim's upbringing and character could also be heard in the other languages that he acquired and used over the years. He learnt French, Russian and English best, and in that chronological order, while his early knowledge of Finnish ebbed away due to the years he spent in Russian service. In later years, his Finnish was gradually reactivated, but could, at best, be described as adequate, even though he used it actively. German was also in his linguistic repertoire, but it was not a language that he favoured. One overlooked dimension of language use is that it is greatly dictated by a person's company: in Mannerheim's case, this meant that he could switch between many different variants of spoken Swedish, Russian and French.

It is difficult to judge the extent to which Mannerheim's clear and concise written prose reflected his manner of speaking, although many have indicated that it very much did. What we do know with certainty, however, is that he started to pay attention to his handwriting at a young age, and it became extremely distinct over the years. In a letter from the mid-1880s, he advised his younger brother August against developing an overly convoluted calligraphy: "because a simple style is good, much better than one which is full of flourishes that run into each other, and which give the handwriting the impression of a tangled reel of twine". Such skeins are not to be found in the letters and other handwritten documents that are in abundance in the large Mannerheim collection at the National Archives in Helsinki, although he did purge many of his papers after some dramatic twists in his private life and career. His younger relative G. A. Gripenberg, a diplomat and Mannerheim's close collaborator during the Second World War, later wrote that Mannerheim "had steady, smooth, calligraphic handwriting, which appeared carefully printed". Another interesting, if immaterial, detail is that Mannerheim started to hold his pen behind his right index finger after he broke it, which perhaps contributed to him writing slowly and legibly.

Graphologists are certainly prone to offer a psychological interpretation of Mannerheim's somewhat angular and uniformly economic handwriting as an expression of the strong need for external order and internal control that he came to exhibit as an adult. In fact, at the Cadet Corps he was so lacking in these qualities that he was dismissed after four years in April 1886, following a string of rule infractions. The last straw was when the 18-year-old youth defied a curfew and snuck off to visit a tavern in Hamina. The following morning, according to the corps' teaching committee, Mannerheim was found unconscious in the out-of-town drinking den of a generally "ill-reputed person" in the region, the local tax inspector Hugo Elfvengren. As a consequence he was forced to leave the corps two days later. The corps' director made reference to Mannerheim's many serious rule violations and demanded a standard dismissal. This would, however, have prevented Mannerheim from gaining admission to any other educational institution in Finland, and so, after a vote, the committee decided instead to request that his guardian apply for his dismissal. This charitable arrangement was carried out.

This incident has been investigated in minute detail by Teemu Keskisarja in his engaged work on Mannerheim's youth. According to Keskisarja, some of Mannerheim's denigrators would much later let it be understood that the harsh punishment was because one of the drunken revellers at Elfvengren's home was Agathon Lindholm, the head of the town's telegraph station and the subject of vague rumours of homosexuality. The disciplinary committee established that Mannerheim was guilty of a "demeaning indecency". Keskisarja does not exclude the possibility that this signalled that it was highly detrimental to the Cadet Corps' reputation that Mannerheim had passed out in such company. He does add, however, that Mannerheim had amassed such a multitude of misdemeanours and rule breaches by that point that, most likely, the committee simply wanted rid of the corps' rotten apple.

Whatever the truth of such conjecture may be, it is clear that the interest in and interpretations of Mannerheim's sexuality have reflected, in one way or another, the significance that people have sought to attribute to his role in Finland's history. His growing number of admirers and panegyric biographers over the years have willingly emphasised or subtly hinted at the handsome Mannerheim's successes as a seducer. His critics, for their part, have readily interpreted his aesthetic temperament, his failed marriage and the long bachelorhood that followed as indicators of his sexual instability and repressed homosexuality. This is a classic tactic when seeking to tarnish the heroic reputation of an adversary.

It is natural that future generations are curious about the sexuality of famous historical figures. Consider, for example, the interest in the libido of Adolf Hitler, Henry VIII or indeed Urho Kekkonen, Finland's longest-serving president (in power from 1956 to 1982). Yet to understand how they perceived their own lives, it is wise not to draw too far-reaching conclusions about their sexuality, since these can so easily be exaggerated or directly misleading. In any case, it is clear that Mannerheim himself felt no need to comment on the matter, and, in common with the majority of his military colleagues of the time, took a straightforward approach to fulfilling his sexual needs. That is to say, he frequented bordellos and kept mistresses, even when he was married.

According to the memoirs that Mannerheim allowed to be chronicled later in life, he was almost relieved when he left the Cadet Corps. This reaction was probably in part connected to the rejection of his application for a transfer to the Imperial Corps of Pages a month prior to his dismissal. The career-oriented young Mannerheim realised that this would have facilitated his ascent to the more senior officer positions, and it is often suggested that this particular setback drove him to deliberate rebellion. His memoirs recount that, at his point of departure, he boldly informed his cadet colleagues: "Now I will travel to St Petersburg and enlist in the Nicholas Cavalry School to become an officer in the Chevalier Guards." These last words were either remarkably prescient or born of hindsight, since this was the exact path his life would take next.

Mannerheim decided to apply to the Nicholas Cavalry School in St Petersburg on the advice of his uncles' contacts in the Russian Army, after having failed to gain admission to a Russian grammar school. The cavalry school's two-year training offered excellent opportunities for a future career in one of the metropole's guards regiments. Before enrolling, however, he had spent two summers in Russia studying the language and pondering his future. He had also taken the opportunity to pass his public examination, in spring 1887, as a private pupil at his old grammar school, Helsingfors Lyceum. In July that year, his uncle Albert von Julin informed him that he could take the entrance examination for the Nicholas Cavalry School, which is exactly what he did. By 15 September 1887, Mannerheim had passed the exam, donned his new cavalry uniform, sworn the military oath and written a letter to his siblings in which he resigned from civilian life in Finland with a sanguine last remark: "Thanks for the dress coat, Carl. Hopefully it didn't get damaged. Farewell: Gustaf, apostate."

Mannerheim the apostate, the defector from the Fatherland, had come to the conclusion that he wanted to continue his military career in Russia, after little more than sixteen months spent there as a civilian. This was despite the fact that he had followed the political debate in Helsinki during the preparations for his public examination in spring 1887, when many in his social circles took an increasingly critical attitude towards Russia and its representatives in Finland. One of his close friends in the school year 1886–87 was George Schauman, who was to become a fearless liberal politician and head librarian at the University of Helsinki. George was probably already heavily influenced by his father, August Schauman, during his grammar school years. Besides being an old friend of Mannerheim's own father, August was also the founder and recently departed editor-in-chief of *Hufvudstadsbladet*, the biggest-selling newspaper in late nineteenth-century Finland. His tireless campaign for a more westernised civil society resulted in the essayistic collection *Nu och förr* (Now and Then), in which he commented astutely and acerbically on the news in the Grand Duchy in 1886, the year of its publication.

In September 1886, August Schauman praised the publication of the liberal senator Leo Mechelin's French-language report on Finland's constitution, in which Finland's status in relation to Russia was described as a personal union, with the Emperor as the common monarch. This obviously conflicted with the Russian authorities' view of their Finnish neighbour's status, and marked the birth of the protracted constitutional struggle that continued until Finland's ties to Russia were finally severed in autumn 1917. In November 1886, Schauman wrote enthusiastically about the opening of the new railway to Oulu, which reached further north than any other track in the world, and which united Finland "as *one* more closely than ever before".

True to form, Schauman neglected to mention that the new trunk line also strengthened the whole Russian Empire. It made the transportation of troops to the Swedish-Norwegian border significantly easier, thereby increasing the region's strategic importance in the process. Indeed, the expanding railway network was the most important instrument for the consolidation of the Emperor's central power at the end of the nineteenth century. This was also noticed in Finland after the rail connection to St Petersburg was opened in 1870, for the country's southern regions, in particular, became increasingly closely tied to the empire, both economically and militarily.

The Up-and-Coming Cavalryman

Fig. 1.4: The 20-year-old civilian, Gustaf Mannerheim, between military schools in 1887.

The young Mannerheim became something of a regular fixture on the Helsinki–St Petersburg line, when he, like tens of thousands of other Finns, sought his fortune in the imperial capital. St Petersburg was booming at this period, with its population growing to over one million inhabitants in the 1890s. The training at the Nicholas Cavalry School, founded in 1823, was held in very high esteem among cavalrymen and took place in a large building complex in the middle of the city. The location was not especially practical, but, on the other hand, it allowed the school's aspiring officers to quickly participate in the manoeuvres and parades organised by the city's garrison troops. In spite of the school's packed programme, the young cavalrymen had plentiful opportunities to become acquainted with the capital's magnificent architecture, bustling trade and glittering entertainments, as well as with its teeming mass of people and languages from all parts of the empire.

It is no surprise that Mannerheim, in his memoirs, lists all the metropole's sights without the slightest mention of the psychological effect that his immersion in the heart of the empire must have had on his geopolitical outlook and his general attitude towards Russia. The memoirs were composed a long time later, and with the overarching purpose of strengthening the Finnish populace's willingness to defend their country. Understandably enough, this did not allow for the inclusion of a wider perspective on Russia's role in European security politics. Nevertheless, Mannerheim's

Fig. 1.5: Mannerheim (on the right) and a young cadet colleague at the Nicholas Cavalry School, 1888.

initial impression of St Petersburg must surely have had a profound effect both on his opinion of Russia in general and on Finland's real significance to the whole empire in particular.

Mannerheim's education at the Nicholas Cavalry School naturally also influenced his imperialistic outlook on the world, for it was, in most respects, of a better quality than that offered at the Finnish Cadet Corps. Alongside military training and natural sciences, the students were taught military history, political science, Russian and other modern languages. Mannerheim would later appreciatively remember his teacher in military tactics, Colonel Alekseyev, who rose to be Chief of General Staff of the whole Russian Army in the First World War. Undoubtedly the most demanding challenge for Mannerheim was to become sufficiently proficient in Russian to cope with the teaching and to be able to communicate unimpeded with his course colleagues and superiors. He was apparently fairly successful in this, even if his vocabulary was limited and he was never able to get rid of his Swedish accent, which was "horrible", according to the blunt recollection of one of his last Russian aides-de-camp.

Thick accents, however, were hardly unheard of in the multicultural empire's officer corps, in which a significant number of recruits came from the so-called Baltic provinces and Finland in the late nineteenth century. Although the cavalry school was commonly seen as the first step in the career of the sons of the Russian high nobility, its recruitment base was, in practice, more geographically and socially diverse. Of course, the large majority of aspiring officers were Russian, but Mannerheim also had, for example, another Finn and a few Baltic Germans in his year group. To some extent, they served to soften the "coarse" Russian atmosphere that he felt prevailed at the school. Above all, however, he seemed to have been annoyed that the same kind of bullying that he had previously encountered in the Finnish Cadet Corps also ran rampant in the cavalry school.

As a counterbalance to these irritations, the 20-year-old Finn appeared to have learnt from his previous indiscretions and displayed a growing self-control, faring increasingly well in the tightly packed schedule of exams and physical tests that the officer cadets had to endure. He also displayed a clear talent for horse-riding: in late autumn 1887, he was honoured as the best rider in his year group by becoming the first of his squadron to obtain spurs. As was the tradition in Russia at the time, riding practice included a lot of dressage, which entailed precision movements and parade training, with an eye on the magnificent imperial changing of the guards and reviews that even first-year students at cavalry school took part in. During the summer months, the instruction took place south of the city on the large training ground in Krasnoye Selo. This location provided much better opportunities than the city centre for practising modern battle skills of the type that had risen to prominence in the Franco-Prussian War of 1870–71, such as cross-country riding and racing.

This intensive training on horseback finally convinced Mannerheim that he had found the right profession and branch of service. When he was expelled from the Finnish Cadet Corps, he had contemplated the possibility of going to sea or becoming a naval officer. But the more evident it became that he was born to be a cavalryman, the more he sought leaves of absence to return to the imperial stables and riding halls. "The horse, the ride, the horse-breeding, everything concerning horses, could count on my undivided interest from that point on", commented Mannerheim in his memoirs. Over time, it is evident that his passion began to stand out as old-fashioned and out of place in military circles, even though horses still played an important role as draught animals during the Second World War. On the other hand, it was a reminder of chivalrous times when nobility was earned expressly as a horseman and when generals commanded whole armies from horseback. It was no coincidence that Mannerheim readily used the adjective "chivalrous" when he wanted to underline that someone had acted in an uncommonly upright and consistent manner.

So, even after warfare had begun to mechanise in earnest, Mannerheim still usually appeared before troops and paraded on horseback. It is entirely appropriate that the most well-known of all his portraits and monuments is the grand equestrian statue that was unveiled in Helsinki in 1960. This was erected on almost exactly the same spot where he had marched into the city in the victory parade of spring 1918, having led the Whites to victory over the Reds in the Finnish Civil War. On top of the ceremonial importance,

Mannerheim's proficiency as a rider stood him in good stead in other respects too. It contributed to him being selected for a demanding espionage assignment in Central Asia, and it came to stimulate his apparent innate need for high speed and dangerous situations that required both power and precision. His composure under pressure was reflected by his fearless conduct on the battle-field, which earned him respect among his troops.

Mannerheim was not, moreover, the only adept cavalryman who played a notable role in the political machinations of the Great Powers in twentieth-century Europe. Winston Churchill, seven years Mannerheim's junior, had a similarly action-packed start to his career: he, too, came from one of his country's leading families, and there were no signs in his youth that he would go on to have a bright future. Churchill's makeshift solution was a career in the British cavalry, one that proved so expensive that he was soon forced to supplement his meagre finances as a war correspondent in different parts of the world. While Churchill was enormously fasci-nated by modern military technology, the cavalryman in him rose to the fore at regular intervals. A telling example comes from his own memoirs, where he recalled the Battle of Omdurman and described the distance to the murderous charging dervishes as the length of half a polo field. He had, as a young hussar in 1890s Bombay, become such an avid polo enthusiast that he would later facetiously describe the sport as "the serious purpose of life".

The two men, future icons of their respective nations, would later meet each other on a few occasions in London. Their first encounter occurred in the aftermath of the First World War, when both were fervently trying to mobilise counter-revolutionary forces against the Bolsheviks. Their fierce anti-communism would also bring them together twice in the 1930s. Those days, however, were still far beyond the horizon in the late nineteenth century, when Mannerheim was winning prizes and trophies as a polo player and steeplechaser on the large training ground south of St Petersburg.

This success came at a cost, however, since life as a cavalryman in the capital was an expensive business. In cavalry school, Mannerheim had already had difficulty keeping his spending in check, even though his uncle Albert von Julin paid the tuition fees and other relatives had arranged a rolling stipend for him from the

Emperor's Finnish discretionary fund. Many costs were unavoidable, such as all the military equipment, the private tuition in a number of demanding subjects, and the sundry expenses that were obligatory for all students. In addition, there was a succession of extra costs that students were expected to cover by their own means, since it was presumed that they came from well-to-do homes. As a result, Mannerheim was forced to regularly request more money from his uncle, and soon began to calculate how he could advance in his career to become economically independent.

He made some of these calculations while on his holidays in Finland. Just as his grades were starting to improve in his academic subjects, in spring 1889 he set his sights on a career in the Chevalier Guards, Empress Maria Feodorovna's personal Life Guards in St Petersburg. The Life Guards were one of the empire's most distinguished cavalry regiments, principally comprising recruits from its leading noble families. Even more importantly for Mannerheim, being on duty at the court offered these guards officers the realistic prospect of a fast track to the Russian military academy and its General Staff training, which was, in principle, a prerequisite for entry into the higher officer ranks.

Mannerheim was careful to mention all of this in his correspondence with his uncle Albert, probably with a view to securing his relative's continued financial support. His uncle, however, does not appear to have been convinced that Mannerheim had the capacity and motivation to reach the higher ranks of the military. In the background there also flickered suspicions that he would be incapable of keeping his spending in check as a young guards officer in the vibrant metropolis. After Mannerheim vowed to do his utmost to gain admission to the Russian military academy after his three years in the Chevalier Guards, he and Albert finally reached an agreement. Mannerheim would receive an annual loan to finance his time in the Life Guards. The money would come from the inheritance that he and his sister were to receive from their grandmother.

This, however, did not solve all his problems. The application to the royal guards was processed by many authorities, and had to be submitted before Mannerheim would receive his diploma from cavalry school. He passed his final and decisive exams with flying colours in April 1889, and had success in the shooting and riding competitions that were held that summer on the training ground in Krasnoye Selo. The one blot on his copybook was when he appeared heavily intoxicated on the return train from leave and then subsequently insulted the duty officer, for which he was placed under arrest and demoted. After that his conduct was irreproachable and he quickly regained his previous rank, but the misstep did result in him only coming second in his year group, which many have interpreted as having contributed to his Chevalier Guards application being rejected.

Mannerheim's first military appointment was, therefore, to take him to Poland: more precisely, to a cavalry regiment in the small garrison town of Kalisz, a little over 200 kilometres west of Warsaw, near the border with the German Empire. There is no doubt that Mannerheim was deeply dissatisfied with this posting. In his very first letter back to Finland, sent to his uncle Albert von Julin at the beginning of October 1889, he made sarcastic comments about the place and his colleagues, disparaging their military ability, educational level and social circle:

> The regimental commander is a nobody, whom the officers take very little notice of. One scandal follows another and arrest at the main guard is a daily routine. There is no social life to speak of. Most of the regimental wives are of inferior lineage with a rather ambiguous reputation and upbringing. The occupations of the regiment constitute attending to duties in the morning and hanging around the town's taverns for the rest of the day.

A short visit to the considerably better-kept Prussian side of the border only reinforced his dismissive attitude. This drove Mannerheim to appeal to his uncles with even greater energy than before, urging them to use their contacts in the Russian court to arrange for his transfer to the Chevalier Guards. His campaign would continue for the whole of the following year, which meant that he remained in Poland long enough to take part in a number of large-scale field exercises. During one of these, in the summer of 1890, he was introduced to the Emperor's nephew and the regiment's honorary commander, Grand Duke Nicholas Nikolaevich, whom Mannerheim, many years later, brought up as his model soldier in conversation with fellow Finnish officers.

It was in October 1890 that Mannerheim was finally admitted to the Chevalier Guards, thanks to the Baroness Alfhild Scalon de Coligny, who lived in St Petersburg and was the sister of Mannerheim's godmother, general's wife Louise Aminoff (née Cedercreutz). By means of a highly placed lady friend in the court, the Baroness successfully entreated the Empress, or rather, her husband Alexander III, to detail Mannerheim to the regiment. In and of itself, the decision was hardly unprecedented, since Mannerheim, in spite of his petty misdemeanours, more than met the requirements that were set for the Empress's Life Guards. Hailing from a Finnish noble family which had loyally served its emperors carried weight, as did the family's significant contacts with the court and the Minister-Secretary of State for Finland in St Petersburg. Mannerheim's stately appearance was one added boon; another was his first-rate riding ability, which he would continue to develop and refine with enthusiasm in the future.

He began his service with the Chevalier Guards in January 1891, and it marked, in many respects, the end point of his transformation into a disciplined and loyal career officer in the Imperial Army. While his route to the Life Guards had been facilitated by his relatives' contacts, the selection process had involved an assortment of exams, aptitude tests and inspections, in any one of which he could have failed to make the grade. Each success in this sorting process honed his professional identity, which did not pass unnoticed by his male relatives back home in Finland. According to his elder sister Sophie, they felt a touch offended by the way he had started to look "down with disdain on all 'civilian loafers', as befits a real soldier".

It just so happened that Mannerheim's professional consolidation took place in the same year that European great power politics took a new turn. In spring 1890, the Chancellor of Germany Otto von Bismarck resigned after a dispute with the new Kaiser, Wilhelm II. The Kaiser's expansionist demands were not at all compatible with Bismarck's long-practised balance-of-power diplomacy, a cornerstone of which had been the maintenance of good international relations, particularly with Russia. As a consequence, Germany decided not to renew its alliance with Russia in 1890. The very next year this resulted in the thawing of Franco-Russian relations, with the two countries entering into an official treaty in 1894. Thereafter the European Great

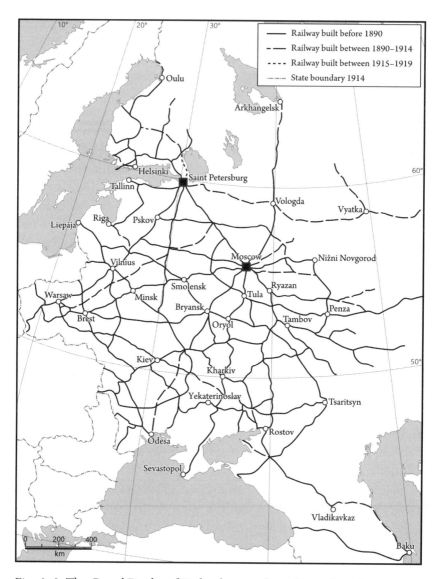

Fig. 1.6: The Grand Duchy of Finland strengthened its political autonomy in the late nineteenth century; all the while Finland's expanding railway network tied its economy increasingly tightly to the Russian Empire. Map by Hannu Linkola.

Powers aligned themselves increasingly rigidly into two camps: once Great Britain joined the Franco-Russian alliance in 1907, the countdown to the First World War began in earnest.

It was not until much later that Mannerheim would be privy to the secrets that lay behind this geopolitical chess game. Nevertheless, he naturally paid attention to the way Russia's military and economic relationship with France strengthened, just as the Russian Army's leadership began to make increasingly overt preparations to ward off a German war of aggression. In a letter to his uncle Albert von Julin at the end of July 1891, Mannerheim described the great enthusiasm caused by the French naval visit that had just taken place in St Petersburg. It was evident that this indicated a shift of political alliances, but, as Mannerheim stated, it was not unequivocally beneficial to Russia: "From a purely military perspective I have to say, that what I have now seen of the French Army seems to be far inferior to that of the Germans, with which I am of course more familiar."

One concrete manifestation of these military preparations was that the Russian central authorities undertook a systematic effort to tie the empire's western regions ever more tightly to the realm in the 1890s. However, this led to a nationalist backlash in many quarters, not least in Finland, where the social elite to which the Mannerheim family belonged had already grown accustomed to conceiving of the Grand Duchy as a state within a state.

2

THE EMPIRE'S MAN

Life Guard and Father of the Family

Early in the morning of 19 January 1891, the 23-year-old Mannerheim donned his regulation dress and kit at the Chevalier Guards' head-quarters, a grand administrative building in the Empire style on Shpalernaya Street in the centre of St Petersburg. Mannerheim reported to the regiment's commander, Major-General Nikolay Timiryazev, and was detailed to the first division of the Life Guard Squadron, where he was introduced to his unit chief and his new offi-cer colleagues. The Life Guard Squadron was the regiment's model unit, with 190 cavalry-men on its register, of whom a dozen were officers like Mannerheim.

Mannerheim's admission into the Chevalier Guards was the product of many weeks' preparation. The Life Guard officers had to procure and pay for all their outfits and accoutrements themselves: seven different uniforms, each with its own boots, buckles

Fig. 2.1: Chevalier Guards' officer Mannerheim in full dress uniform, 1892.

and belts; the guards' gilded helmet, with its double-headed eagle crest to be screwed on for parades; copper armour and a sabre; spurs and saddles; and, finally, a bay horse that met particular measurements and the correct breed characteristics. Mannerheim sourced his equipment from St Petersburg's well-stocked specialist shops. His horse, however, proved to be too small and completely the wrong colour, so just before departing from Poland for the final time, he made a brief trip to Breslau in Germany to buy a Hungarian mare that would suffice. Six months later he bought a high-class gelding for a good price; the horse was ill disciplined, but Mannerheim soon managed to bring him under control.

Given all these expenses, it is little wonder that Mannerheim's relatives were uneasy. And their fears were well founded: although his uncle had arranged a loan for him, Mannerheim appealed to them for more money immediately upon his return to St Petersburg. At least they could be satisfied that his accommodation was organised fairly quickly and cheaply. While he was waiting to enter service, Mannerheim had lodged both with his godmother's sister, Alfhild Scalon de Coligny, and with the Finnish courtier Hjalmar Linder. Just before his duty began, he was given the use of two rooms at the residence of his old acquaintance from the Nicholas Cavalry School, the wealthy Prince Elim Demidov, who had begun a diplomatic career. At the start of December 1891, Mannerheim moved into a three-room apartment with a very reasonable rent in the vicinity of the barracks.

Service in the Empress's Life Guards followed a long-established pattern. Its heritage could be traced back to the late 1600s, and it gained its reputation as one of the most distinguished guards regiments while Catherine the Great was on the throne. It became known as the "Chevalier Guards" in the relatively short reign of her son Paul I, and thereafter its function remained largely unchanged until the outbreak of the First World War, save for some minor adjustments to the uniforms and diurnal routines. Alongside the Life Guards' daily duties in the neighbourhood of the palace and their frequent parades in the heart of the city, they also took their place at the head of imperial coronation processions. Since Paul I's reign, the Life Guard officers had taken an oath in which they swore to serve their country and their Emperor loyally and honourably. They also promised to give their life for him if necessary.

Such promises do not always count for much: Paul I ended up being murdered by his own officers in 1801, and in the twentieth century too, the Chevalier Guards were unfortunately found lacking when it really mattered. In March 1917, when revolution broke out in St Petersburg, most of the regular Life Guard officers were fighting at the front, and the few units assigned as their replacements actually took part in the uprising. This amounted to a gross dereliction of their duty to protect the imperial family, who were captured by the Bolsheviks and taken to the Alexander Palace in Tsarskoye Selo. According to the British Ambassador to Russia, George Buchanan, whose 1923 memoirs detail his dramatic years in the post, a makeshift squadron of the remaining loyal Chevalier Guards did ride through swirling snow to the palace to try to rescue the Emperor's family. However, the riders were stopped by revolutionary troops at the palace gates, who coldly announced that the empire had been abolished. Realising that the situation was lost, the squadron chief gave the order to retreat, and so the last remnants of the Life Guards rode slowly away.

No one, of course, could have imagined that this would be the end of the proud Chevalier Guards' story when Mannerheim joined the regiment. In the 1890s, Russia was still a mighty empire. Its expansion east towards the Pacific Ocean continued apace, and its economic outlook was bright in spite of various social problems. Its fledgling alliance with France lowered the threshold for Western European investment in the country. Over the following two decades the Russian economy grew faster than ever before, which resulted in large industries establishing themselves in St Petersburg, Moscow and other well-located cities in the empire. At the same time, this growth also demanded increasing state supervision and a social elite fit for the purpose.

Standing at the head of the empire was the physically imposing Alexander III, who appointed the enterprising Baltic German, Sergei Witte, as Minister of Finance in 1892. Witte's extensive modernisation of the empire's economic policies and investment in Siberia raised expectations that Russia, in the long term, could draw level with the other Great Powers. Other officials were, like Witte, granted positions in the central administration after rising through the ranks on their own merits, but these were the exception, rather than the rule. Until the revolution in 1917, the highest offices and posts in the empire were dominated by the old social elite. This comprised a number of intermarried noble families, for whom the continuation of the Emperor's autocracy was naturally in their best interests. The same closed conditions prevailed in the other European empires, a state of affairs which ultimately contributed to the outbreak of the First World War, as there were not enough officials with a modern education and a rational mindset to stop events from escalating.

Mannerheim's career in Russia was a fairly typical example of how the old elites of European empires succeeded in maintaining their standing in spite of rapid social upheaval. It was, of course, largely thanks to his noble lineage and his relatives' close connections at court that he advanced to the Chevalier Guards. And, thanks to their exclusivity and court duties, the guard officers enjoyed the vibrant milieu of high society, into which Mannerheim was immediately initiated. A mere week after he had entered the guards' service he was invited, together with a few colleagues, to a large ball at the home of one of the city's richest men, where he was introduced to his future wife, the 19-year-old noblewoman Anastasia Arapova, a general's daughter with a considerable fortune behind her. Similar parties would also be held in the future, the most grandiose of which was the Emperor's ball at the Winter Palace that same spring, which Mannerheim, along with a few other Chevalier Guards, was instructed to attend.

Between these tastes of court life, Mannerheim quickly settled into his new military post. His duties initially consisted of developing recruits into accomplished cavalrymen, while at the same time sharpening his own riding and fighting skills. The daily programme included demanding riding exercises and stable care, along with a range of other drills. Mannerheim's exceptional drive to advance in his career—a consequence of having far more meagre finances than his fellow officers—was swiftly noted. One of Mannerheim's younger colleagues at the Life Guards, Count Aleksei Ignatiev, remembered him many years later as a "model mercenary", whose attitude to the service was more professional than that of the other officers: "He could perform everything in an exemplary manner and even drank in such a way that he remained sober."

One reason for Mannerheim's moderation was that he did not initially have the means for extravagant parties; another was that, as Ignatiev added, in his heart he probably despised his *bon vivant* colleagues. His sense of superiority and innate self-centredness were fed by the fact that he was undeniably a better rider and a more imposing officer than the majority of them. There might well also have been a cultural rift between Mannerheim and his fellow officers. His upbringing had certainly not instilled any great affection for Russia in him; rather, a cold acceptance that Finland was attached to the empire and that it was best to take full advantage of the situation.

Perhaps this also explains why his colleagues interpreted his sarcastic sense of humour as a sign of his "well-meaning but limited" character. His middling Russian was best suited to short and cutting criticisms, and it also served as excellent camouflage for his detached bearing. The language was, incidentally, less of a problem when Mannerheim communicated socially with his peers. As was so elegantly put in Leo Tolstoy's classic *War and Peace*, since the eighteenth century the Russian social elite had readily switched into speaking French when they wished to express themselves wittily and in a sophisticated fashion. Mannerheim, too, adopted this practice in his free time, whether meeting with friends or seeking to charm ladies at balls and parties.

One of the ladies with whom he probably spoke French from the outset was the aforementioned Anastasia Arapova. According to Mannerheim's Russian biographer, Leonid Vlasov, whose vivid accounts are certainly prone to embellishment, they met each other at three parties in spring 1891. Even if this is an exaggeration, by the end of December that same year the youngsters' relationship had developed to the point that Mannerheim proposed to Anastasia. More accurately, he approached her guardian to ask for her hand in marriage. As both Anastasia's parents were dead, this was her maternal aunt, Vera Zveginzeva, whose husband was a colonel in the Chevalier Guards. The young Mannerheim, then a low-ranking cavalry officer, had nevertheless apparently made a good impression on her, for his request was immediately accepted.

It probably did not hurt that Alfhild Scalon de Coligny, a long-time acquaintance of the Arapov family, had already broached the topic with them. It is possible that she made her enquiries without

Fig. 2.2: Anastasia Mannerheim, née Arapova, in the mid-1890s.

Mannerheim's knowledge, but it is more likely that he had agreed to her plans, viewing the marriage as an excellent opportunity to align himself with the Russian high nobility and to solve his financial problems. For Anastasia had inherited two estates, the assets of which, if sensibly managed, were more than sufficient for a comfortable life. According to Mannerheim family legend, Anastasia gave her instant consent to the marriage, exclaiming: "who wouldn't want to have the handsome Mannerheim, who is so *à la mode*".

The engagement came into effect in March 1892, and the wedding was celebrated on 2 May that same year, once the Arapov family had agreed, after some hesitation, that Mannerheim did not need to convert to the Orthodox faith. In spite of the obvious advantages of the marriage, it did not arouse any enthusiasm among Mannerheim's relatives, as demonstrated by the fact that only his father and eldest brother took part in the wedding. This took place at the Chevalier Guards' Orthodox chapel in the presence of Russian high nobility and Mannerheim's closest colleagues in the guards' officer corps. Thereafter the celebration continued at the home of Anastasia's relatives, as was the Lutheran fashion. Despite his relations' evident reservations, Mannerheim himself appears to have been pleased with the arrangement. In a letter to his aunt he described his bride-to-be in the following words: "She is 20 years old, entirely blonde, a little over average height, full-figured, robust and vivacious."

Studies on Mannerheim have typically placed emphasis on the fact that this was an arranged marriage and that the groom saw it solely as an advantageous transaction. This is quite true, but it should also be noted that this was most often the case with marriages of the European high nobility well into the twentieth century. It was important for them to avoid so-called misalliances, that is, marriages in which the spouses had different backgrounds and where the union strengthened neither the family's standing nor its means. The marriage with Anastasia lasted, in practice, for only eight or nine years, even if the couple only officially got a divorce in autumn 1918, when Mannerheim returned to Finland. Consequently, many have interpreted the marriage as having been ill fated from the start, but during their first years together the young couple lived a fairly typical private life for a noble family in St Petersburg, trying to get to know each other as well as possible. They celebrated their honeymoon at Anastasia's mansion in Uspenskoye, and upon their return to St Petersburg they moved into a spacious apartment on the waterfront street by the River Moyka in the city centre. In April 1893, Mannerheim's wife gave birth to a daughter, named Anastasia after her, and a little over two years later she had a second daughter, christened Sophie (most often spelt Sophy). According to some sources, Anastasia also gave birth to a stillborn son.

As time went by, however, the couple's different interests and dispositions began to create problems. Anastasia was happiest as a society lady, while Gustaf preferred to occupy himself with various equestrian and hunting sports. This drove them apart, to the extent that they could not even agree on how their daughters should be raised. Long after their marriage had gone to pieces, Gustaf would continue to characterise Anastasia as work-shy and disorganised. She, for her part, had good grounds for accusing him of being unfaithful. One of Gustaf's longest affairs probably began in spring 1894, when his success in a riding competition led him to make the acquaintance of the spirited and intelligent Countess Elizaveta Shuvalov. His frequent visits to "Betsy's" place on the Fontanka River in the late 1890s are well documented, since officers had to state where they were staying when they were on duty. Another indication of their intimate relationship is Mannerheim's calendar from this period, on which he had noted only three birthdays: two were those of his daughters, while the third was Betsy's.

One jealous drama followed another until finally, in 1900, Anastasia left without warning for the Far East to work as a nurse in a Russian Red Cross field hospital. There she looked after Russian troops who had been injured while participating in an international effort to quell the Boxer Rebellion in China. Anastasia returned to St Petersburg a year later after breaking her leg in a carriage accident, but in 1902 she moved to France with her daughters for good. Two years later, Mannerheim made arrangements to sell her property in Russia, ensuring that the proceeds were passed on to her. They would meet again only once, in Paris during autumn 1936, just before Anastasia died.

All these developments in Mannerheim's personal life lay, of course, far beyond the horizon in the early 1890s. His original plan was to use his service with the Chevalier Guards as a springboard to the Russian military academy, from where he could ascend further to higher officer ranks and better annual incomes. This path was prematurely blocked, however, at the end of August 1892, when Mannerheim failed the preliminary Russian language test of the academy's entrance examination. Still, this was no great catastrophe, since both his military status as a Chevalier Guard and his personal finances remained secure. Instead, he directed his energy and attention into his existing post and into his great passion for various equestrian sports.

Over the following decade, Mannerheim won a number of prizes and trophies in many of St Petersburg's most prestigious equestrian competitions. These successes were often recorded in the daily press. In March 1893, he pulled off one of his finest show-jumping triumphs in front of a sizeable crowd of high-ranking dignitaries from the court and the officer corps. The following day his victory occasioned effusive praise in the press: "Baron Mannerheim is truly a peerless rider. Poise, grace, extraordinary forbearance—these are his qualities. It was as though he had cleared all the obstacles effortlessly."

His reputation also spread to his homeland, where in 1906 one sporting omnibus described Mannerheim as one of the few Finns "who, like the very finest riders in the empire, has acquired world renown and is adjudged an expert in all cavalry and sports circles".

Mannerheim's interest in horses also extended to breeding them at Apriki Manor in Courland, in modern-day Latvia. This had been procured in 1901 as a replacement for one of Anastasia's two estates in the Moscow region that had been sold a few years previously, in 1894. With its 6,000 hectares of farmland, suitable building stock and a more diligent staff than at the Russian estates, Apriki offered Mannerheim every opportunity to become an old-fashioned lord of the manor. But since he had neither sufficient time nor interest to keep abreast of the manor's affairs, many of his projects there came to nothing and it was ultimately sold in 1912, along with the rest of Anastasia's assets.

Coronation and Crisis

As a break from routine duties, not to mention the ups and downs of their private lives, the Chevalier Guards had special assignments at imperial parades, festivities and ceremonies. The greatest honorary role given to Mannerheim as an officer of the Imperial Life Guards was in May 1896, when his regiment took part in the coronation of Nicholas II and Empress Alexandra in Moscow. Together with three other Life Guard officers, Mannerheim stood in the guard of honour at the throne during the entire coronation ceremony, which was held within the walls of the Kremlin at the Dormition Cathedral. Mannerheim described the atmosphere in the following terms in his memoirs: "The air was stifling from incense. With a heavy rapier in the one hand and 'the dove' [the double-eagle helmet] in the other we stood motionless from half past eight in the morning until half past one in the afternoon."

The coronation was followed by a magnificent procession from the church out into Red Square and then on to the Imperial Palace, in which the young Lieutenant Mannerheim and the Baltic German Under Rittmeister, Andrei von Knorring, marched side by side in front of Emperor Nicholas II in his imperial crown. The freshly anointed Emperor advanced under a large baldachin carried by thirty-two adjutant generals in white lambskin caps. Hemmed in among the thousands of spectators stood one of Mannerheim's compatriots, the noted painter Albert Edelfelt. He had spent the preceding weeks in St Petersburg painting an imperial portrait of the soon-to-be monarch, and was now tasked with immortalising the coronation procession across Red Square. In a letter to his mother, illustrated with vibrant watercolours of the newly crowned Emperor, Edelfelt attested that Mannerheim looked "most impressive". That same evening, Mannerheim again stood in the guard of honour at a magnificent dinner for the Emperor and Empress in the Palace of Facets, which had the air of an enormous show, such were all the traditional rituals, courtesies and costumes that were on display.

Fig. 2.3: Nicholas II's coronation in May 1896. Mannerheim is on the right, parading ahead of the Emperor.

No other Russian coronation has been so well documented and analysed as this one, which is partly a consequence of the fact that it turned out to be the last. A little over twenty-two years later, the Emperor, Empress and their five children were killed by a heavily intoxicated firing squad in a storeroom outside the Siberian city of Yekaterinburg. The execution was so carelessly conducted that the commander had to finish off Alexei, Nicholas II's only son and heir to the throne, by firing two extra shots into his skull. After this, paraffin and sulphuric acid were poured on what remained of the bullet-torn bodies before they were burnt and tossed into a mineshaft.

The Bolsheviks' desecrations were in dizzying juxtaposition to the imperial pomp that preceded them, but there are, in fact, numerous examples of similarly morbid regime changes in the history of both Russia and the other European Great Powers. In Russia, however, these cruel seizures of power occurred more frequently and continued long into the twentieth century. The rulers of this vast realm have, therefore, been forced to take concerted measures to protect themselves, while at the same time emphasising their own irreplaceability. This has meant that, to the present day, they have inspired something that could be characterised as a combination of religious devotion and oppressed veneration.

This sort of cult of personality also sprang up around Nicholas II and his family. The Empress Dowager's former Life Guard Mannerheim was one of their sworn lifelong admirers. In common with other eyewitnesses, he remembered a tragic sequel to the coronation as a "sinister omen". Four days after the ceremony, chaos had broken out when a huge crowd gathered to see the new Emperor on a drill ground, and nearly 1,400 people were trampled to death. However, as so often happened in this immense empire, attention soon drifted to other sensational happenings in public life. Over his years in Russian service, such events offered Mannerheim a number of opportunities to meet and make the personal acquaintance of the innermost circle of the imperial family.

The first and, as it happens, also the last of Mannerheim's intimate acquaintances within the family itself was Alexander III's Danish-born wife, Maria Feodorovna, often called Empress Dagmar in Finland. In spring 1892, Mannerheim performed extraordinarily well at a large riding competition in St Petersburg and was presented with various prizes by the Empress, who even addressed him in Swedish. And since Mannerheim served in what were her own Life Guards, he also had many other opportunities to exchange a few words with her. This familiarity probably contributed to the young Mannerheim being selected for the guard of honour at the coronation of her son in 1896.

One sign of their intimacy was that only a few weeks before the outbreak of the March Revolution in 1917, he received an audience with the Dowager Empress. He later recalled that they conducted a lively discussion about the war situation: "The 13-year-old successor to the throne, Alexei, had climbed up on a sofa nearby, from where he listened attentively to what I had to tell." Unlike Alexei and his parents, the Dowager Empress escaped the revolution and returned to Denmark, where she was visited by Mannerheim on a number of occasions during his travels in the 1920s.

Mannerheim showed the same unwavering, life-long loyalty towards Nicholas II, even though the Emperor became deeply unpopular in Finland because of his Russification measures. In the historiography, he would come to be seen as partly culpable for the fact that the situation in the empire degenerated into revolution and Bolshevik rule. Such hindsight was alien to Mannerheim. He conceded in his memoirs that Nicholas had been a weaker leader than his father, Alexander III, but characterised him otherwise as simple, unpretentious and brave. Accordingly, Mannerheim always had photographs of the former emperors on display at his home in Helsinki. Until his death he also maintained contact with many exiled Russians in different parts of Europe, all of whom lived in hope of one day restoring the empire.

Many of these emigrants were already Mannerheim's friends and colleagues in the late 1890s, when he found himself enticed by the chance to work at the Royal Stables. The proposal came from his previous regiment commander, General Arthur von Grünewaldt, who, in 1897, had been appointed chief of the Imperial Stables' administration. Mannerheim was widely recognised as a distinguished rider and connoisseur of horses, and von Grünewaldt soon realised that he would be the right man to take responsibility for the Imperial Stables' extensive equine purchases, which were often made in Central Europe. He was appointed in autumn 1897. In addition to trips to the Continent on business, the post also included a spacious and high-class official residence in the vicinity of the Imperial Stables. Besides these perks, Mannerheim was doubtless also induced to take the role out of concern for his career. As has been noted, his dream of General Staff training had gone to pieces in 1892: in spite of his promotion to lieutenant the next year and his good contacts with the court as a Life Guard, his position at the time did not indicate a brilliant military future.

Over the next seven years, Mannerheim frequently travelled to stud farms and horse markets in different parts of the Russian Empire, Austro-Hungary, Germany, Belgium and France. More than anything this deepened his knowledge of horses, while also giving him the opportunity to get to know the social elite and the cultural life of the Great Powers in Central Europe. The turn of the twentieth century has often been seen as the high point of La Belle Epoque, the golden age of continental high culture and aesthetics, in which the old and the new were brought together in an unprecedented and perhaps still unparalleled way. The old consisted of highly contrived quality expectations and refined tastes, which were given sustenance by the growing prosperity and concentrations of capital in Europe. And the new consisted of the outpouring of original ideas and technical innovations, which gave the impression that the rhythm of life was accelerating.

St Petersburg was one of the most dynamic centres of this golden age. As such, the only slightly Russified Mannerheim had no difficulties asserting himself when he arrived in the Central European metropoles and mixed with the officers and courtiers there. Generally speaking, they were of the same background as himself, that is to say a cosmopolitan upper class who for reasons of both etiquette and convenience usually socialised in French. During this period Mannerheim also gained a good knowledge of English. This was no doubt partly to do with his closest relatives being pronounced liberals and Anglophiles, but the main reasons for his language studies were his great admiration for English horse culture and the business he did, on behalf of his post, with British stud farms. Mannerheim could also practise English during the riding lessons he regularly took at this time with the English instructor James Fillis, who had been employed at the Officers' Cavalry School in St Petersburg because of a pioneering dressage technique that had given him international renown. Added to all this, English was often the internal language of the Russian imperial family, since Empress Alexandra was Queen Victoria's grandchild.

Mannerheim further honed his spoken English by means of conversation lessons which he took in spring 1906, during an extended stay in Helsinki. His tutor was John Dover Wilson, a visiting language lecturer at the University of Helsinki, who referred to Mannerheim in his memoirs as his most famous pupil. Mannerheim had rooms at the Society House, a fashionable hotel facing the Market Square, which today functions as Helsinki City Hall. "There I visited him for a series of conversation lessons", Wilson recalled, "just to polish up the English of which he already had a pretty good command."

It is unknown what language Mannerheim spoke when he had the honour of dining with the Emperor and Empress of Germany during a trip to Berlin in December 1898: presumably French, although it could quite conceivably have been English, for Wilhelm II's mother "happened" to be Queen Victoria's eldest daughter, and she had ensured that her son had learnt impeccable English. The invitation for dinner came because Mannerheim had suffered a serious injury while visiting the Royal Stables in the German capital, where a powerful kick from a horse had cracked his kneecap. The Kaiser had heard about the accident and arranged first-class treatment for the Imperial Life Guard, as the injury potentially threw Mannerheim's future as a cavalryman into doubt. Thanks to a prompt operation by an eminent German surgeon, Mannerheim gradually recovered and returned to his service again in autumn 1899, when he almost immediately went off to Central Europe to purchase new horses.

In spite of these interesting and sometimes highly exclusive experiences in the line of duty, Mannerheim's officer career advanced at a fairly sluggish pace. He was promoted in summer 1899 to Under Rittmeister, and three years later to Rittmeister (cavalry captain), but these steps up the ladder took two or three years longer than was usually the case. There are many indications to suggest that while his commanders valued his riding skills and abilities as an instructor, they remained sceptical as to whether he had the potential to reach the rank of general. That he had failed the military academy's entrance exam was undoubtedly a disadvantage. On the other hand, as the court's favourites, the Life Guards had good opportunities to advance, even ahead of officers who had received General Staff training. Understandably enough, Mannerheim did not divulge a word in his memoirs about this lull in his career. Perhaps his civil assignment at the Royal Stables also meant that there was little impetus to nudge him up the ranks more quickly. Or perhaps his British biographer John Screen was right when he supposed that, as a Finn, Mannerheim faced discrimination due to the increasingly Slavophile attitude of Russia's military elite.

Whatever the reason for this slow progress, the unwaveringly career-oriented Mannerheim returned to an out-and-out military post in spring 1903. In April that year he was appointed commander of the Model Squadron of the Officers' Cavalry School, which signified a real rise in status and required close collaboration with the head of the school, the esteemed General Aleksei Brusilov. The General's training programme was known for being both demanding and of high quality. The new post immediately involved intensive field training and a lengthy autumn exercise in Lithuania. There, Mannerheim nearly broke his neck in a dangerous somersault off his horse, but luckily only came away with minor injuries.

In late winter 1904, however, something happened that was to have decisive consequences for both Mannerheim and the Russian Empire. On 8 February, a squadron of Japanese destroyers attacked the Russian naval base at Port Arthur on the Pacific coast. The incident quickly escalated into a full-blown war between the two expanding empires. The Japanese would have contented themselves with Russia keeping control of Manchuria if, in return, the Russians had accepted that the Korean Peninsula fell within the Japanese sphere of interest. However, the Russian administration's presumptuous attitude and slow response caused the Japanese to go on the attack, for they had wrongly concluded that Russia was unwilling to comply. It soon became clear that the modernised Japanese Army was more effective than the Russian one, for the latter's logistics and reinforcements had to be conducted, in the main, along the unfinished Trans-Siberian Railway. Any concession, however, would have signified an all too great loss of prestige for Russia. Therefore, the Emperor gave orders for a large-scale mobilisation of both the army and the navy.

News of the outbreak of war brought about a patriotic frenzy and imperialistic warmongering in St Petersburg. Only a few weeks later, Mannerheim began to contemplate the possibility of heading out east to fight as a volunteer. This did not fill his relatives in Finland with great enthusiasm, for many of them were involved in the passive resistance against Russia's efforts to tie the Grand Duchy more closely to the empire. Almost as discouraging was Mannerheim's commander at the Officers' Cavalry School, General Brusilov, who tried to convince him that his ability ought to be saved for the war between Europe's Great Powers that many were already predicting. But the more the conflict in Manchuria escalated, the greater Mannerheim's desire to fight became. Once he had taken out a considerable amount of life insurance as a precaution against his outstanding debts, Mannerheim submitted his application for frontline service in late summer 1904. In mid-October he received his orders and was immediately transported to the battlefields of Asia.

Mannerheim's decision stemmed from both personal and professional considerations. There is no doubt that his private life in St Petersburg had become even more precarious after his separation from his wife. His rather hopeless situation was not only due to his disorderly bachelor's lifestyle but also to the gambling debts that he had incurred, which he could no longer cover with his wife's money since the breakdown of their marriage. When his relatives' energetic attempts to dissuade him from departing intensified in June 1904, Gustaf wrote a long letter to his elder brother Carl in Stockholm. In this he spoke unflinchingly about his debts and his diminished lust for life that drove his desire to leave St Petersburg: "I often feel so melancholy & downhearted, that I have to force myself to keep going with this life."

In the same letter, sent from the training camp in Krasnoye Selo on 28 June, Gustaf also gave a thorough explanation of his professional motives. He did so out of necessity, for his opinions on the Russian Empire were in complete opposition to those of his brother. Indeed, Carl had been deported the previous year by the Russian authorities for his role in the leadership of the Finnish passive resistance. He was active in a group that has gone down in history under its unofficial name, the Kagal (*Kagaali*). Mannerheim's brothers and father had long been critical of Russia, but their attitude had hardened further when Governor-General Nikolay Bobrikov introduced his robust integration measures in 1899. These were interpreted in Finland as a programme of Russification, and they ultimately led to Bobrikov's murder on 16 June 1904, only twelve days before Gustaf's report to Carl.

It is clear that Gustaf's brothers had demanded, in unusually strong terms, that Gustaf should not only refrain from participating in the Russo-Japanese War, but also that he should resign from the Russian Army. His counterargument was that this would in no way have improved Finland's situation. On the contrary, such protests would only result in the Imperial Army being increasingly commanded only by officers who supported the suppression of "weaker opinions". If one wanted to fight against this, it was better to strive for the greatest possible professional success, in order to be in a better position to influence developments.

At the same time, he conceded that his almost twenty years of military service had inevitably strengthened his sense of duty to the Russian Army and its men: "The individual does not fight in a foreign war for a regime, but instead for the country of the army to which he belongs." Mannerheim consciously avoided using emotionally charged expressions of loyalty or allegiance here, since these would only have infuriated his brothers, who were by this time fervently anti-Russian. Nonetheless, everything suggests that these principles also lay behind his desire to go off to war. Rather than dwell on them, Mannerheim advanced a less controversial, but no less honest, argument, that he had to participate in the war to keep his career on track:

> If I am not a part of this, there is every chance that I will never be anything other than a tin soldier and will have to hold my tongue when my more experienced brothers-in-arms call upon their war stories to support them. After a war like this the number of these "more experienced" will rise to the thousands.

And sure enough, Mannerheim would have cause to return to his experiences in the Russo-Japanese War on many occasions in his life. One well-known case occurred four decades later, on 7 October 1944, when, as President of Finland for the first time, he met the Chairman of the Allied (Soviet) Control Commission,

Colonel-General Andrei Zhdanov. The latter sent an amused report home to Stalin declaring that Mannerheim, to lighten the mood, had mentioned that his order of the day to the frontline commanders in the war against the Germans up in Lapland had had the same message that Nicholas II gave to his commanders-in-chief in the Russo-Japanese War: "Patience, resourcefulness, learn from the enemy!"

The Russo-Japanese War

On the evening of 22 October 1904, Lieutenant-Colonel Mannerheim departed from St Petersburg's Nicholas Railway Station, as it was then known, for the Manchurian Front on the coast of the Pacific Ocean. His stylish Chevalier Guards uniform had been left behind. Instead, he was clad in the considerably coarser dress of the 52nd Nezhin Dragoon Regiment, which included a frieze jacket and a tall black goatskin cap. His old rank had been left behind, too, since guards officers received an automatic promotion when they were transferred to a line regiment.

Mannerheim was accompanied by a large collection of luggage. Besides his kit, there were necessities that he had promised to take to his comrades at the front, while his three newly purchased horses were sent east in another train. Also neatly packed were a selection of items that he had bought from Nordiska Kompaniet, a fashionable department store in Stockholm, on a personal trip he made to Sweden while awaiting his departure to Manchuria. This extra attire was of the highest quality, but not at all regulation. It would later lead to Mannerheim being mistaken for a Japanese spy during a reconnaissance mission at the front. According to reports intercepted by the *Hufvudstadsbladet* correspondent, Mannerheim's yellow leather spats had been a source of particular suspicion. From Mannerheim's own account it is clear, however, that the misunderstanding was sooner caused by his "English variety of sabre scabbard and perhaps the tad extravagant fur coat".

Mannerheim's train journey along the Trans-Siberian Railway totalled over 9,000 kilometres and took a month to complete. By the time he arrived at the scene of action in the Far East in late November 1904, the Japanese Army had already intensified its siege of the Port Arthur naval base, which was located at the south-western cusp of the Manchurian Liaodong Peninsula. From this position, the Japanese would have little trouble moving their troops eastwards to invade the Korean Peninsula, from where they could also direct their attack northwards against the Russian forces in Manchuria. The decisive land battles were, however, initially for control of Port Arthur. After the naval base capitulated in early January 1905, the fighting continued in a northerly direction along the Liaodong Peninsula's railway to the city of Harbin, one of the last junctions on the Trans-Siberian Railway before the eastern terminal station of Vladivostok.

Both sides suffered large losses, but the superior operational capability of the Japanese was decisive overall. Little by little they succeeded in driving the recalcitrant and unmotivated Russian troops northwards. To counter this, the Russian military command sent their Baltic Fleet on a 29,000-kilometre voyage over the oceans to the Pacific Front. This was to incur a catastrophic defeat of the Russian fleet by the Japanese at the Battle of Tsushima Strait at the end of May 1905, after which both sides were ready to resolve the conflict at the negotiating table. The Treaty of Portsmouth, signed in September 1905, stipulated that Japan got control of Port Arthur, the Liaodong Peninsula, the Kuril Islands and the southern two fifths of Sakhalin, as well as a firm hold on Korea. The Japanese, however, regarded the peace agreement as an injustice, and this gave rise to a desire for revenge which would later feed into their conflicts with China and the United States.

The consequences of defeat were extremely swift and severe for Russia. However, when Mannerheim had his baptism of fire during a reconnaissance mission behind enemy lines, two days before Christmas 1904, a Russian victory still seemed entirely possible. In a letter to his brother Johan, who had by then moved to Sweden for good, Mannerheim denied that he had been scared stiff by the bullets that had whistled past him. Indeed, his fearless attitude towards the enemy's fire soon became so notorious that his fellow officers started to suspect that he was consciously seeking death. Nor would this have been so inexplicable against the backdrop of all the problems that he had left behind in St Petersburg. The fact is, however, that the constant threat of impending death, together with all the stresses and setbacks of the war, seemed instead to animate him and banish all his sorrows.

Mannerheim's dragoon regiment was placed under the 17th army corps, which in turn was part of Russia's Third Manchurian Army. The shortage of capable soldiers meant that Mannerheim was chosen as the regiment commander's assistant staff officer. On top of everything else, this entailed making valiant but largely futile attempts to keep his officer colleagues' copious drinking and low morale in check. His first taste of active service with a normal military unit soon helped him realise that the Imperial Army's officer corps was certainly not cast in one and the same mould. Nearly all classes of society were represented, starting with "the slickest officers and cavaliers of Petersburg's salons and ending with the downright wrecks in the final stage of alcoholism begging for alms to go on yet another binge", he noted, in an almost cheerful letter home to his father in Helsinki.

Around the turn of 1904–05, Mannerheim and his regiment took part in a major cavalry operation for the first time. The original aim was to sever the railway link between Port Arthur and the city of Liaoyang, which the Japanese had only recently captured. However, the manoeuvre lost most of its strategic significance when General Aleksey Kuropatkin, the Commander-in-Chief of the Russian Army, decided to dispatch his forces instead towards the port town of Yingkou. Mannerheim observed critically that the situation was not improved by the hesitation of the forces' commander General Pavel Mishchenko to undertake a sufficiently fast and strong attack against the well-prepared Japanese. This meant that the operation had to be swiftly terminated. A similarly mediocre attack was directed against the village of Sandepu straight afterwards, but this also came to nothing due to the Commander-in-Chief's contradictory orders.

Mannerheim's task during these operations was first and foremost to reconnoitre the enemies' movements and report them to the General Staff. He quickly developed a keen eye for the Japanese service branches' co-ordination, speed and precision. He most admired how the tactically adept Japanese deployed the machine gun, as well as how, unlike the Russians, they kept the positions of their artillery camouflaged, thereby causing significantly more destruction. During one of these reconnaissance missions, two of Mannerheim's squadrons unexpectedly ended up in an exchange of fire, but he reacted quickly to organise an orderly retreat, stopping the Japanese from inflicting serious damage with their machine guns. For this exploit, his regiment commander recommended that Mannerheim be promoted to colonel in April 1905. Perhaps this offered Mannerheim some consolation for the painful loss he suffered on the mission when his favourite horse, Talisman, was shot and killed. He praised the charger's qualities to the heavens in his memoirs, describing the animal as the best thoroughbred he had ever ridden in battle.

This exchange of fire took place during the three-week-long Battle of Mukden in February and March 1905, which, at the time, was one of the largest land battles in the history of mankind. Over the preceding weeks, the Russian Army had been forced north by the Japanese. With the help of the forces that had been freed up from Port Arthur, the Japanese now tried to encircle the Russian troops to the south of Mukden, which had symbolic significance as the Manchurian capital. When the vigorous Japanese incursion from the west began to yield results, the Russian military command finally gave orders to retreat a further 160 kilometres to the north, which in practice put an end to the large-scale clashes of the war. Both sides had suffered severe casualties: the number of men

Fig. 2.4: The Russian troops' chaotic retreat after the Battle of Liaoyang, 1904.

wounded or killed in action totalled 90,000 for the Russians and 75,000 for the Japanese.

Mannerheim lost many of his closest officer colleagues and men in these battles. And as the fighting reached its denouement, he bore witness to how different frontline soldiers overcame or were overcome by the enormous stress and the threat of death. Part of the regiment fought like lions until almost the last man, while others rushed to desert their comrades when the situation started to become precarious. The chaos was at its worst after the Russian Army gave the order to retreat on the evening of 9 March: the shambolic withdrawal fast degenerated into panic, which was only heightened by the infernal Japanese crossfire.

In contrast, Mannerheim's own capability under fire proved to be excellent. A number of independent witnesses certified that he remained calm and bolstered his men's *esprit de corps* with his steadfast and fearless attitude. One of these was the Doctor and Professor of Medicine Richard Faltin. In his capacity as head of a nearby Finnish Red Cross station, he saw how Mannerheim had the authority and ability to arrange for some railway carriages to be brought in order to evacuate the wounded during the chaotic retreat from Mukden. When the Russian troops retreated from the town at night, the German war journalist Richard Ullrich noted how Mannerheim assembled his horsemen at the railway station and rode at their head to the infantry's aid.

It is typical to ask at this juncture why Mannerheim was not even injured in the Battle of Mukden. This touches on a similar question confronted by everyone who returns alive from the front: why did I survive where others did not? The answer will always, to a greater or lesser extent, come down to the capricious nature of chance. Besides which, Mannerheim did not emerge from the fighting completely fit and healthy. Right at the start of the conflict he was beset by an irksome ear infection and fever. This was temporarily alleviated with strong medicine, but during the retreat it worsened to the extent that he could scarcely stay in the saddle. Eventually he was sent with other incapacitated and wounded soldiers on a goods wagon for medical treatment further from the front. During the train ride, he looked on as Russian deserters tried to break into the carriage and, when this did not work, clung instead to its roof and between the wagons. Once he reached the Finnish Red Cross station in the city of Gongzhuling, he also received treatment for a painful inflammation of the prostate.

His ear infection proved more obstinate. The aforementioned Dr Faltin, a fellow Finn, had to perforate his eardrum on two occasions, and the complaint required many weeks' recuperation, continuing at the German evangelical aid station after the Finnish Red Cross site was evacuated. Scarcely a year earlier, as the duty doctor at the Surgical Hospital in Helsinki, Dr Faltin had operated on the Governor-General of Finland, Nikolay Bobrikov, after the Russian was the victim of a political assassination attempt. Bobrikov's life could not be saved, but Mannerheim's hearing fully recovered: while less seismic at the time, this too would turn out to be of real consequence to Finland.

During his weeks of convalescence, Mannerheim had time to write several letters to his relatives, in which he not only described his dramatic experiences at the front, but also conveyed sentiments and incidents of a more civilian nature. One interesting new acquaintance he made at the Finnish aid station was Hugo Backmansson, an officer, war artist and newspaper reporter. In common with Mannerheim, he had been trained at the Finnish Cadet Corps. Already before their meeting, Backmansson had reported on Mannerheim's hardships in the Far East for *Hufvudstadsbladet*, including the incident with the yellow spats. As both began to recover and their sense of humour returned, the duo livened up the atmosphere at the aid station in a number of ways, including posing with crutches in long Chinese jackets for willing photographers. Mannerheim would later call Backmansson his "cheery comrade from Manchuria's bloody fields". Backmansson, for his part, would paint a portrait of Mannerheim in the 1920s; although not especially well known, it is one of the lightest and warmest depictions of the aristocratic officer.

Another interesting source detailing Mannerheim's experiences during the campaign in the Far East is the diary that he kept throughout most of the war. As might well be expected, his entries were extremely laconic and candid during the most frenetic periods of the conflict. But when he had more time, he put to paper vivid descriptions of the comical personalities in the ethnically diverse officer corps, of charming young nurses who appeared as if out of thin air,

MANNERHEIM, MARSHAL OF FINLAND

and of the abrupt changes in the Manchurian climate. Other recurring themes were the various conflicting rumours of Japanese advancement that circulated in the officer corps, and all the antagonisms that the setbacks in the war caused among the high command.

Mannerheim returned to his regiment in April 1905 to lead a few reconnaissance missions, including one to Manchuria's western border region with Inner Mongolia. After the naval battle at Tsushima, however, it became clear that peace was fast approaching, which plainly vexed Mannerheim. His promotion to colonel had been a long time coming, so he felt he was missing out on the opportunity to achieve more victories at the front. But long before peace was made in September 1905, the Russian Empire had been drawn into a new and far more serious crisis: namely, a wave of demonstrations, strikes and riots in different parts of the realm. During early spring 1905, these gradually forced the Emperor to agree to a series of minor social reforms.

One clear reason why protests broke out at that precise moment was that police surveillance of dissidents and revolutionaries had been weakened by the war against Japan. The disturbances had their roots in a number of deeper grievances, however. These were all, in one way or another, a consequence of the fact that Russia had rapidly begun to transform into a modern industrial nation, while remaining an autocracy stubbornly opposed to a free civil society and democratically anchored political representation. After the tumult in the summer and autumn of 1905 increasingly began to take the shape of a revolution, the Russian Government managed to convince the Emperor that reforms were necessary.

Through the imperial October Manifesto (which was called the November Manifesto in Finland on account of the country's Western calendar), nearly all the inhabitants of the empire immediately gained civil rights, specifically the freedom of speech and association. They were also granted the right to vote in elections for the State Duma, the empire's newly instated parliament. These reforms naturally affected citizens in the Grand Duchy of Finland, where demonstrations had first built up steam in autumn 1905. In contrast to other parts of the empire, in Finland these had not degenerated into acts of violence, nor were they directed against the domestic social elite. The protests targeted, above all, the Russian

52

central power and its integration efforts. These had intensified since 1899, and, understandably enough, were seen in Finnish eyes as Russification measures. They included Nicholas II's Language Manifesto of 1900, which made Russian Finland's official language of administration (although, in practice, the Senate continued to operate in Finnish and Swedish); and the 1901 conscription law, which made the Finnish Army a part of the Imperial Russian Army.

As soon as the imperial manifesto had come into effect, a wide range of Finnish voices called for the Diet of Finland to be replaced by a democratically elected unicameral parliament. A constitutionally inclined Senate took up the push for reform under the leadership of Leo Mechelin, whose extensive campaign to secure the Grand Duchy's autonomy was now starting to bear fruit. The Finnish lawyer K. J. Ståhlberg was also chosen as a senator at the young age of 39. Fifteen years later he would write independent Finland's first constitution and be elected as the republic's first president.

Mannerheim kept himself informed of these political developments in the European Russia via his relatives and various other sources. In June 1905, he was already of the opinion that there was a clear risk of civil war if the soldiers who had fought in Manchuria were demobilised too quickly. Nor did he himself look forward to returning home and, together with his fellow officers, "bearing the shame of all our defeats", when responsibility lay instead with the system and the leadership. At the same time, he realised that the Emperor's small concessions were by no means enough to calm the situation. So, when informed of the October Manifesto in far-flung Manchuria in late October 1905, he did not hesitate to pass on the message directly to his men, since it was, for Russia, a gigantic step in the direction of a functioning civil society.

At the end of November Mannerheim was ordered back to St Petersburg. He set off on a train journey through Siberia that would take more than a month and that reinforced his fears that the whole empire was about to collapse. The revolting soldiers interpreted their newly won civil liberties as a right to do whatever they wanted, including taking control of the railway line's stations and stealing locomotives from arriving trains. More order prevailed in Moscow and St Petersburg, where guards regiments had succeeded in restoring calm once the political reforms had begun to occupy the focus of the opposition forces in society. Mannerheim's faith in the future was also strengthened by his promotion to colonel, which had been confirmed on his journey home through Siberia, on 29 November 1905.

During this same trip, news also reached Mannerheim about the political changes in Finland. After being granted extended leave to treat the rheumatic pains that he had been stricken with during the war, he travelled to Finland in January 1906 to recuperate and at the same time to find out more about what was going on in his homeland. He reported to his brother Johan in Sweden that everything was changing at lightning speed: "The most persecuted yesterday are today almost the most influential men in the country." Here, Mannerheim was referring to the newly appointed Senate, which, with Leo Mechelin at its helm, was made up of those who had opposed the Russian Empire's integration measures. Now in power, they were driving through a reform of the franchise that would transform the Diet of Finland into Europe's most democratic parliament and make Finland the first country in the world to grant universal female suffrage.

As head of the baronial branch of his family, Mannerheim took part in one of the last meetings of the estate of the nobility in May 1906. It was during this that the estate unanimously decided to support the franchise reform, bringing an end to its own existence in the process. While many of Mannerheim's fellow noblemen remained sceptical of the social consequences of the development, they were almost all united behind the need to modernise and broaden the right to vote. Mechelin had long belonged to the reform-minded noblemen who would certainly have preferred to introduce a bicameral system in line with the Swedish model. But once the demands for reform had spilled over into demonstrations and riots, such a system would have been nothing like enough to appease the socialist and liberal forces in society.

A little over a decade later, in 1917–18, Mannerheim would witness the transformative unrest in Finnish society when the country was dragged into the revolutionary chaos emanating from Russia, which culminated in the Finnish Civil War. Discussing these events in his memoirs, Mannerheim would imply that the Finnish people were not yet ready for such a radical reform. However, the very fact that a single-chamber parliament had been established in 1906 proved to be of fundamental importance in 1919, for it enabled the country's political powers to finally overcome their grave differences and steer their newly independent country towards calmer waters.

3

THE OFFICER'S JOURNEY

The Spy in Central Asia

As Mannerheim sat under the decorative coats of arms in the assembly hall of the House of Nobility in Helsinki, at the end of May 1906, his mind could be forgiven for wandering from the legislative changes under discussion. The end may have been in sight for the estate of the Finnish nobility, but he was in the midst of making preparations for a new military assignment: a secret espionage

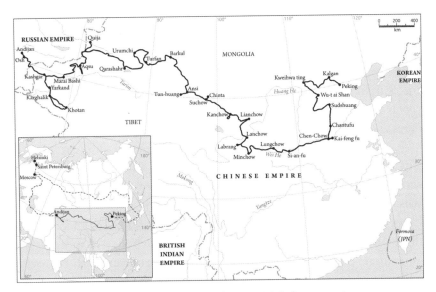

Fig. 3.1: The route of Mannerheim's 14,000-kilometre journey across Asia. Map by Hannu Linkola.

mission to Asia. This had been offered to him three months earlier when he had been summoned to the Russian General Staff; after some hesitation, he had decided to accept it.

The poorly planned and conducted war with Japan had convinced the Russian Army leadership that the empire was in a precarious position and could not afford to drift into a new conflict with the other Great Powers. It was not only their expectations of Far Eastern conquests that had been dashed. So, too, had their hopes of a decisive victory in the "Great Game" that Russia had been engaged in with Great Britain since the 1830s for control of Central Asia's interior regions. In summer 1906, the two world powers, who were being challenged on many fronts, began negotiations about where the border between their spheres of interest should go. A year later, they reached an agreement: Britain would keep control of Afghanistan, while Russia was given free rein to expand in Central Asia, that is, in Chinese territory.

Mannerheim's espionage mission was undoubtedly connected with these plans. The expedition's overall aim was to investigate how well-prepared China was for an eventual conflict with Russia in the western parts of its realm, both along the north-western border zones and in the Central Asian highlands. The instructions contained in the written order that Mannerheim received before the trip stated that he was to conduct careful reconnaissance of the Chinese border forts and road connections. He was also to investigate the attitudes of the region's inhabitants towards China, Russia and Japan. During the Russo-Japanese War, the Russian military authorities had received information that the Chinese Army had hired Japanese soldiers as advisers, which clearly was a cause for concern.

It was not particularly remarkable that Mannerheim was offered this assignment, given that he had carried out many successful scouting missions around and behind enemy lines during the Russo-Japanese War. His expeditions to the Chinese regions of Inner Mongolia during the final stage of the war were surely fresh in the memory. And once peace had been reached, it is quite probable that Mannerheim's superiors had encouraged or even exhorted him to continue such work, for he had intimated his plans to return to Mongolia to conduct new reconnaissance in letters to his relatives. In any case, he had been judged to be both sufficiently skilled and suitable for this demanding ride through the mountains and plains of Central Asia. The trip was calculated to take around two years, and it was envisaged that he would pose as a civilian member of the scientific expedition led by French researcher and Sinologist Paul Pelliot.

But why did Mannerheim agree to undertake this extremely taxing and risky mission? The most important reason was presumably that in spite of his promotion to colonel, he could not expect to become a regimental commander for some time, since many other officers had also advanced in rank during the war. While awaiting promotion, therefore, he could gain credit through military reconnaissance, in which he was demonstrably proficient. As with his decision to enlist in the Russo-Japanese War, his more personal motivation was probably to get away from his awkward existence in St Petersburg, where his social life as an officer was overshadowed by his scant means and his failed marriage. Last, but not least, Mannerheim had been fascinated by voyages of discovery since his youth, and had read all the travelogues that his paternal aunt's husband, the famous polar researcher Adolf Erik Nordenskiöld, had published over the years.

The Russian military authorities would have preferred that he travel under a French passport, but, when that proved to be out of the question, travel documents were instead ordered from Peking which stated that he was "Russian subject, Finn, Baron Mannerheim". Since the military objectives of the trip had to be camouflaged as a scientific mission, Mannerheim contacted the Finnish language researchers Otto Donner and G. J. Ramstedt during his visit to Helsinki in spring 1906. Both were well acquainted with Central Asia and advised him as to how ethnological and archaeological material should be gathered and documented. Mannerheim also had to teach himself the principles of fieldwork with the help of the available handbooks and travelogues from previous expeditions. Although he was already well versed in cartography as an officer, he did have to familiarise himself with photography as an alternative means of mapping the terrain. Mannerheim became an experienced photographer over the course of the trip, and his pictorial documentation amounted to around 1,300 nitrate negatives, which have been preserved in the Finno-Ugrian Society's archives in Helsinki.

In early July 1906, Mannerheim began his journey by train and boat from St Petersburg to Tashkent, the capital of the Russian province of Turkestan, where he met the expedition's leader, Pelliot, a little less than a month later. Their route had been plotted in consultation with the Russian General Staff, and was supposed to follow, for the most part, the ancient Silk Road between Europe and China. Almost from the outset, however, it became apparent that Mannerheim and Pelliot could not work together. Both were concerned with their own prestige, which soon led to quarrels about money and about how best to interact with the local population. More disconcerting from an espionage standpoint was the Frenchman's refusal to guarantee that Mannerheim's covert mission would not be revealed. As such, once the expedition had crossed the Russo-Chinese border and reached the town of Kashgar, Mannerheim decided to continue his reconnaissance without Pelliot. With his subordinates in tow, he made his way south towards the city of Hotan, to investigate whether there was any substance to the rumours of a Japanese presence in the area. After establishing that these rumours were false, they returned to Kashgar before setting out on an easterly path in early January 1907.

Upon first arriving in Kashgar, Mannerheim had procured another passport on the advice of the district's Russian consul-general, since the one which had been ordered from Peking had been sent to Kulja, the next major city on his route east. On the passport from Kashgar, his surname had been transformed, as was often the case in China, into something resembling its Chinese pronunciation: "Ma-da-khan". His polite Chinese sources informed him that this meant "the horse that rushes through clouds", although it should rather be interpreted as "capable horse". This new documentation worked well at first, but he later ran into difficulties when he also had to show his passport from Peking, on which his name had been spelt strictly according to how it was pronounced, "Ma-nu-ör-hei-mu". These two different names immediately awoke suspicion and led to the Chinese authorities tightening their surveillance of Mannerheim and making it periodically difficult for him to deviate from the route marked on his travel documents.

To minimise the risk of being exposed, Mannerheim sent some of his interim reports to the Russian General Staff via his relatives in

Sweden and Finland. He never betrayed his military status nor the mission's real objective to his nine-strong retinue, which consisted of two Russian Cossacks, five locally recruited men and two Chinese, of whom one functioned as his manservant and the other as his interpreter. As another precautionary measure, Mannerheim wrote both his diary and his other notes in Swedish, which had the added benefit of increasing the clarity and nuance of his observations. The journals have since been published in a variety of editions and languages, and they have been the subject of many thorough studies concerning both his scientific findings and his personal character. The researcher Harry Halén's minutely detailed version of them has, for good reason, received the most acclaim: published in 2010, it is the first complete collection of the journals in their original language. It also lays bare just how demanding Mannerheim's assignment really was.

Between early spring and summer 1907, the expedition twice rode along the treacherous passes over the Tian Shan mountain range, which cuts through Xinjiang's vast highland plateau in an east–west direction. In late July, Mannerheim and his retinue reached the city of Ürümqi, which remains one of the largest cities in north-western China to this day. From there the journey continued slowly and laboriously eastwards, along two more of Tian Shan's mountain passes. The route was dictated by the Russian General Staff's need to survey its feasibility as a means of penetrating into this Central Asian part of China. In late summer and autumn 1907, Mannerheim's hardy troop progressed in a south-easterly direction over the Gobi Desert and along the ancient caravan track following the Great Wall of China.

Straight after the new year the party reached the city of Lanzhou. From there the journey continued through increasingly densely populated regions of China to the city of Kaifeng, where Mannerheim and his entourage arrived in late May 1908. During the next two months the expedition advanced northwards, partly on horseback and partly by train, towards its final destination of Peking, which they came to on 25 July 1908. There, after a few nights in a hotel, Mannerheim was given accommodation at the Russian Embassy, where he spent the next six weeks in peace and quiet composing a nearly 150-page report on the expedition for the Russian General Staff.

Fig. 3.2: Southern Xinjiang, August 1906: Mannerheim, on the right, visiting a local celebrity, the 96-year-old Alasjka Tsaritsan. On the left is French explorer Paul Pelliot.

The trip was a total of 14,000 kilometres in length and had taken two years, as planned. In many respects, this "Ride through Asia" appears to have been a more existentially formative experience than all the wars, uprisings and political machinations that Mannerheim was involved in over his 83-year-long life. The most immediate impact of the well-executed mission was that it convinced Mannerheim's superiors of his abilities and led to his subsequent rapid rise to the higher ranks of officer. The trip was also symbolic of a turning point in his life, because it marked the end of his military service in St Petersburg. All the opulent lustre and cosmopolitanism of the imperial capital could not compensate for the personal misfortunes that had made Mannerheim's existence there increasingly difficult to endure.

As might be expected, the trip itself, with all its privations and extreme experiences, stuck with him for the rest of his days, in the form of amusing anecdotes, inspiring insights and spectacular souvenirs. Many of these adventures he depicted in some detail in his memoirs, in which fifty pages are devoted to the ride through Asia. They conclude with an ironic quote from an Englishman, stating that the longer one has resided in China, the more "one realises that one knows nothing and keeps quiet". The most genuine and personal testimony is to be found, however, in Mannerheim's handwritten journal, which, alongside fine descriptions of people and landscapes, conveys the mood during many of the trip's more existential moments.

One of these occasions took place in autumn 1906, when, south of Kashgar, Mannerheim had a return of the rheumatic troubles he had suffered during the Russo-Japanese War. For the first three weeks of November he was in such a bad way that he was unable to move at all and began to wonder if he would be forced to cancel the whole expedition. "A week or two ago I was loath to imagine the necessity of at least temporarily travelling by carriage, and now I cannot even resort to this possibility", he declared, somewhat dejectedly, on 15 November. Along with the bouts of rheumatism, another recurring problem was his Chinese interpreters, who either lacked the requisite language skills or were, in his eyes, simply indolent. Mannerheim was therefore forced to intensify his studies of different regional languages; by the time he arrived in Peking, he was already able to communicate fairly intelligibly in Mandarin Chinese.

Another extreme feature of the trip was the rapid and drastic changes in climate, which often forced the expedition to come to a halt or caused it to be led astray. In late March 1907, Mannerheim's party was hit by a heavy and prolonged snowstorm on the climb up to a pass over the Tian Shan mountain range. The snow reached "almost up to the horses' knees, and the wind whipped the white snowflakes into the face", so that they could scarcely see 50 metres in front of them. After losing their way multiple times, they eventually got back on the right track and reached the peak of the Topa Dawan pass: "The snowfall had ceased, the wind settled and a warm sun in a clear-blue sky took their place. [...] The vista [was] magnificent." On other occasions the outcome was less auspicious, and in another storm on the mountain pass one of the expedition's porters died from sheer exhaustion.

As a positive counterweight to the hardships endured over the labyrinthine mountain passes and endless open plains, Mannerheim made the acquaintance of a great variety of people and cultures. Sometimes these experiences demanded a large degree of self-control, such as in May 1907, when he listened to a choir of Kalmyks, "with widely varying [degrees of] musical talent", sing an interminably long song. This "was started without the straining of vocal powers, but the tones in the monotonous melody went ever higher, and its last quarter was performed with piercing falsetto voices". Neither was Mannerheim impressed by the battle equipment of this group of Kalmyks, nor by their cleanliness, noting that their "dirtiness is beyond what the wildest fantasy can imagine". His sanguine commentary on his encounters with local populations ultimately formed part of the anthropological surveys he carried out regularly to maintain the pretence that he was leading a scientific expedition.

Inevitably, it took some time before Mannerheim was able to suppress his Eurocentric and imperialist prejudices. But the longer the trip went on, the more deeply he understood and even admired the ancient traditions and the diverse lifestyles that he encountered. One manifestation of this was how his photographs of the local population changed across the journey, over time becoming increasingly vivid and personal. A month before his arrival in Peking, Mannerheim even requested, in vain, to photograph the Dalai Lama when the two met on Mount Wutai. Tibet's spiritual leader was staying in one of the Buddhist monasteries there as a result of the British invasion of his homeland.

In other respects, the meeting went well. Once the ceremonial aspects were done with, it became evident that the Dalai Lama's stance on the Chinese Government was not at all uncritical. Quite the reverse, he was just waiting "for an opportunity to confuse the issue for those in his company". After Mannerheim had taken receipt of a white silk cloth as a gift for Nicholas II, he strenuously affirmed that Russia's sympathies wholly lay with the Dalai Lama in the dispute with the British. At the end of the meeting, he presented his own Browning revolver as a reciprocal gift to the Dalai Lama, declaring that the holy man was obviously delighted when he demonstrated the revolver's fast loading. Mannerheim also emphasised that "besides which, the times were such that, every now and then, a revolver could do more good than the most sacred and precious object, even for a holy man like him". Mannerheim made use of the same symbolic gesture many times over. Almost exactly thirty-four years later, on 27 June 1942, he presented a Finnish sub-machine gun as a reciprocal gift to the rather less holy Adolf Hitler.

Mannerheim summarised the more formal content of his conversation with the Dalai Lama in his final report to the Russian General Staff. Having written the first version of his report in Peking, he tidied it up after returning home to St Petersburg, before it was printed in 1909 as a publication series for the General Staff's internal use. Alongside detailed reports and maps of the strategically important routes, bridges and military positions, it included informative descriptions of the native populations and the climates of the regions under reconnaissance. It concluded that the Chinese were relieved that Russia had lost the war with Japan, since it showed that Russian expansionism in Asia had slowed down, giving China more time to fortify its north-western border zones.

Mannerheim recommended that, in an eventual war, the northern city of Ürümqi should be captured, due to its factories and stockpiles of weapons. The operation should be secured by deploying a strong cavalry, flanked by light artillery and machine-gun units, to sever the connections between Xinjiang and Inner China. Xinjiang's bleak highlands were certainly not worth much in themselves, but they would serve as an excellent article of exchange in peace negotiations. There were no signs that the Chinese had had military advisers from Japan in these regions, but in the more populous parts of China the Japanese already played an active role in the economy. In summary, Mannerheim stressed that China's modernisation had for the moment advanced slowly, but that the country's vast natural resources meant that the Chinese could regain their position as a Great Power fairly quickly, especially if they should successfully establish a central power to effectively govern the economy. With the benefit of hindsight, we can confirm that this would happen seventy years later.

At the end of October 1908, Mannerheim obtained an audience with the Emperor in order to outline the results of his expedition and, at the same time, to cautiously enquire as to whether he would soon get to command his own regiment. The presentation of the trip's findings and the Dalai Lama's gift was supposed to be short, but Mannerheim's audience with the Emperor ended up lasting for an hour and a half, because the latter had such a keen interest in the topic. In Mannerheim's memoirs, he wrote that the Emperor even declared that "there were not many who were privileged to undertake such an interesting assignment as mine". Moreover, the Emperor gave Mannerheim the reassuring answer that he would doubtless soon have his own regiment. Sometime later, Mannerheim also obtained an audience with the Empress Dowager, who showed a particular interest in the photographs from the expedition.

Since Mannerheim had disguised his spy mission as a scientific expedition, he had collected over 1,200 articles of ethnographic interest during his trip, which he sent home to Finland in consignments. He donated the collection in its entirety to what was to become, a few years later, the National Museum of Finland. On top of this, he amassed a variety of objects for himself, the majority of which he sold to the Antell Delegation. This was a body responsible for acquiring cultural items with the interest from capital bequeathed to the Finnish people by the wealthy collector H. F. Antell upon his death in 1893. The delegation considered some pieces too expensive to purchase, and these Mannerheim would later donate to the Finno-Ugrian Society in Helsinki, as he did the expedition's photographs. However, individual rarities such as a quantity of Tibetan prayer mats did remain in his possession, and they can still be viewed in his former home, at what is now the Mannerheim Museum in Helsinki.

The Polish Idyll

The Emperor's vague promise that Mannerheim would get his own regiment was quickly fulfilled. While on holiday in Sweden in January 1909, Mannerheim was informed that he had been appointed Commander of the 13th Vladimir Uhlan Regiment, which was stationed 40 kilometres east of Warsaw in the small town of Mińsk Mazowiecki. Mannerheim had to give up his plans to attend his father's birthday celebration in Finland and instead make his way to Poland. Immediately after taking over command of the regiment, he instigated a thorough renewal of its training and its horse stock.

Fig. 3.3: Major-General Mannerheim in 1912, Commander of the Imperial Life Guards' Uhlan Regiment in Warsaw and General in the Imperial Retinue.

The regiment had not participated in the Russo-Japanese War, and still practised frontal attacks of the sort that had lost all effectiveness since the machine gun and an increasingly mobile artillery had become commonplace on the battlefield. Under Mannerheim's leadership, the cavalrymen instead began to be drilled to function as a kind of fast-advancing infantry. Accordingly, one part of the cavalrymen's training involved quick mobilisation on horseback, and another involved holding position in sheltered terrain on foot. These combat skills would be needed in the impending world war, which would mark the beginning of the end for the cavalry as a sepa-

67

rate service branch, as its functions were replaced, in time, by the air force and the armoured corps.

It was evident that Mannerheim, with his experience of Asia's battlefields and forbidding mountain ranges, had the credibility and the authority necessary to drive through these reforms. Despite the fact that he became renowned as a demanding commander, he gained control over his regiment so quickly that he was offered another that same year, one that was in even greater need of a shake-up. Mannerheim, however, declined this opportunity, confident that another promotion would likely soon come his way. And so it did: in early 1911, he accepted an offer to command the Imperial Life Guards' Uhlan Regiment in Warsaw, which had a reputation as one of the empire's best cavalry units.

The appointment was announced on 26 February 1911 and was perhaps the most important advancement that Mannerheim would make in his career. The commanders of guards regiments were automatically promoted to major-generals. Moreover, as head of such a military unit he had better opportunities to cultivate his contacts with the imperial family. In 1912 he received the honorary title of General in the Imperial Retinue, which made it even easier to get an audience with the Emperor and receive extra emoluments from his discretionary fund. These additions to his wages were clearly welcome: Mannerheim was constantly in debt and, true to form, he was struggling to keep his spending in check after getting involved in society life again following his move to Warsaw. Another benefit of being a major-general in the Imperial Retinue was that he could embellish his epaulettes with the Emperor's monogram; these, more than anything, were a source of admiration among those who understood their symbolic value.

Mannerheim's next promotion came just after new year in 1914, as he continued his advance up the ranks of the Imperial Life Guards in Warsaw. He was appointed Commander of the Cavalry Guards Brigade Detachment, under which was also included his old regiment. The appointment shows that his achievements as a frontline officer, intelligence officer and head of regiment were judged to be so impressive that they compensated for his lack of General Staff training. As brigadier-general he would co-ordinate and lead the operations of two regiments and a horse-drawn battery. This meant that an increasingly large portion of his service took place in General Staff offices positioned a greater distance from the units fighting at the front.

A concrete demonstration that Mannerheim was content with life in Warsaw was his rejection of an offer in autumn 1913 to take an equivalent post of brigade commander in Tsarskoye Selo, just south of St Petersburg. One reason he turned it down was, of course, that he could now afford to pick and choose between interesting posts. In the background could also be discerned an unwillingness to return to the imperial capital city, where the political quarrel between the Russian central power and Finland had again intensified. This made it all the more difficult for Finnish officers to balance their loyalty to the Emperor with their loyalty to their fatherland. For this same reason, Mannerheim had already politely declined a candidacy for the post of Minister-Secretary of State for Finland in St Petersburg. Holders of this high office had previously delivered Finnish business directly to the Emperor, but after 1907 all such matters went through the Russian Government, which surely also reduced Mannerheim's interest in the post.

Moreover, in the early 1910s there are many signs that Mannerheim was, for the first time as an adult, at peace with himself and his life. From a career perspective, his years in St Petersburg had been successful, but his private life there had been a very different story. A similar dichotomy marked his years in frontline service and on the espionage mission—they developed him as an officer and a man, but they had, at times, been so demanding that they took a grave toll on his health. In Warsaw he was able to reap the fruits of his earlier labour, even if his rheumatism demanded constant treatment. One of the advantages of his post was a spacious residence in Warsaw's modern centre, located near his own regiment's barracks. He took an active role in its interior decoration, and later, after the First World War, he was able to have a sizeable amount of the furniture shipped home to Finland. Promotions came at a fast pace, his income increased and last, but not least, he renewed his ties with his aristocratic Polish friends from his years in St Petersburg. These connections gave him excellent opportunities to pursue his favourite hobbies of equestrian sports and hunting.

Despite his position as a senior officer in the Russian Army, Mannerheim was accepted into Polish society without issue. One reason for this was that as a Finnish nobleman, he was supposed to be in solidarity with the Poles, who had lost their autonomy within the Russian Empire after uprisings in 1831 and 1863. According to Mannerheim, the Poles consequently avoided discussing politics with him, for it would inevitably have created a dangerous conflict of loyalty for his career. But obviously his Polish friends were aware of the integration measures that were intensifying in Finland at that time. Perhaps some of them had even heard that Mannerheim's brother was actively involved in the Finnish opposition against this Russian interference.

Another reason Mannerheim quickly felt at home in this company was that as a cosmopolitan, French-speaking and dandyish guards officer, he was tailor-made for this upper-class culture. In his memoirs he characterised it as being "as sparkling as it was exclusive". Among his friends numbered the brothers Maurice and Adam Zamoyski, whose aristocratic family was one of Poland's biggest landowners. So too were Prince Zdzislaw Lubomirski and his wife Marie, who made both their aristocratic network and their contacts in the Polish administration available to Mannerheim. His good relationship with the Governor-General of Poland, General Georg Scalon de Coligny, should also be mentioned. Georg was a member of the same family that had supported Mannerheim's career since the late 1880s. When the Russian gendarmerie's intelligence department in Warsaw reported that Mannerheim was socialising with his noble Polish counterparts, Scalon de Coligny saw to it that the investigation was put on ice.

Mannerheim would keep in contact with some of his Polish friends and acquaintances during and even after the First World War. Among those he maintained a close correspondence with was Princess Marie Lubomirska. These letters have been preserved, and a part of them have even been interpreted as billets-doux. In this regard, the most extreme interpretations have been made by the Finnish author Veijo Meri and the Russian writer Leonid Vlasov. Their slightly desperate attempts to find an amorous streak in Mannerheim went so far as to interpret every intimate word, every expression of friendship and even the slightest innuendo as an indication of a passionate affair. Certainly, many of their phrases were elegantly considerate and affectionate, but it should be remembered

Fig. 3.4: Mannerheim in conversation with Marquess Aleksander Wielopolski in Poland in the early 1910s.

that charming turns of phrase constituted good manners in high-class correspondence. A more credible explanation for their considerable openness with each other was, if anything, the war: this heightened the sense that life was fragile and gave all correspondence an extra emotional charge. Every letter could be the last.

During his years in Poland, Mannerheim also reconnected with his daughters Anastasia (1893–1978) and Sophy (1895–1963), who had gone with their mother to France in 1902. In their later teenage years, however, they had fallen out with her and sought contact instead with Mannerheim and his relatives. Mannerheim had already previously helped finance his daughters' upbringing, but in other respects he was unwilling to shoulder responsibility for them. He dismissed the idea that they should move to Warsaw with the excuse that the global situation was too uncertain. His daughters were instead accommodated at the home of relatives in Finland, but a short time later they both sought a return to the Continent. Anastasia converted to Catholicism and lived a part of her life as a nun, but later reverted to a secular life and died in Great Britain. The younger daughter, Sophy, returned to Paris and lived there until her death in the early 1960s, in an apartment that her father had bought for her. Neither of the daughters married or had children.

His relationship with relatives in Finland and Sweden was, in most respects, less problematic. Closest of all his siblings was, without a doubt, his big sister Sophie, with whom he corresponded diligently throughout his life and at whose home he often stayed during his holidays in Finland. He also maintained a similarly unforced relationship with his father, Carl Robert, until the latter's death in 1914, as well as with his younger brother Johan. They both appear to have accepted that Mannerheim served a regime towards which they themselves had a decidedly negative attitude. It was an entirely different story with his elder brother Carl, who remained in Sweden even after his term of exile had been revoked in 1905. He showed no indication whatsoever that he would accept Gustaf's Russian loyalties. And since he died in 1915, he did not come to see his brother's central role in the history of independent Finland.

At this point, it is important to avoid a logical error that typically occurs even in serious historical research on Mannerheim. Scholars and authors often approach his personal and social viewpoints prior to 1917 from the perspective of what would later happen in Finland and in Mannerheim's own life. When this happens it is easy to forget that for people of Mannerheim's background, the old empires and their elite cultures still appeared permanent and important at the outbreak of the First World War. As a high-ranking officer in the Russian Army, with a broad knowledge of the empire's proportions and resources, together with direct contacts in the imperial household, Mannerheim was firmly engaged in maintaining and strengthening its existence. In this he was in no way unique. To a large extent, all representatives of the Russian elite thought and acted this way, as did their counterparts in the other European empires.

It is much more important, therefore, to consider to what extent Mannerheim's outlook, choices and decisions after 1917 were guided by what he had experienced and been shaped by before these revolutionary years. The Grand Duchy of Finland's prosperity was clearly a matter very close to his heart, but the underlying frame of reference for Mannerheim's world view was nevertheless Russia and its relations with the rest of Europe. This geopolitical perspective would, in essence, guide his way of thinking about security politics for the rest of his life. But since it did not fit with the patriotic story that Finland's independence was predestined and entirely detached from whatever else was happening in the world, he gradually learnt to mediate his words. With the willing help of a nationalistic ghost-writer, he brought his language in line with this patriotic narrative in his orders of the day and later in his memoirs. But it should be underlined that this only happened gradually. In 1918 and 1919, he still conducted himself on multiple occasions in such a way that revealed that his principal goal, in reality, was to help reinstate the old regime in Russia. From a contemporary perspective, this was a far more probable scenario than the alternative: that an independent Finland, caught between belligerent Great Powers, would continue to exist.

In the years and months before the outbreak of the First World War, the European empires intensified their rearmament and their co-operation with military allies. Career officers like Mannerheim were therefore neither unprepared nor surprised when everything started to escalate after a Serbian nationalist murdered the Austrian Archduke Franz Ferdinand on 28 June 1914. All mobilisation plans were already drawn up and well rehearsed. It would have been extremely difficult and hazardous to try to halt them once the order had been given that they should be executed. When the diplomatic war of words sharpened, Mannerheim happened to be travelling in Western Europe, meeting his daughters in Great Britain and buying horses in Germany, among other things. In his memoirs he claimed that he "never for a moment doubted" that a war would break out.

After his return to Poland, he took part in a large field manoeuvre. During an attack exercise he was thrown from the saddle and sprained his ankle, but more dramatic was the order he received almost directly thereafter, which commanded him to return to Warsaw immediately with his brigade. The countdown had now begun. The following day, Mannerheim, always meticulously organised and prepared, checked that his pre-packed bags were in order. Afterwards he went to the barbers, as he always did before a long assignment.

Fig. 3.5: Mannerheim in the lead. Cross-country riding in Poland, 1914.

The World War

"A compromise has been found", declared the chairman of Mannerheim's hunting club at a gentlemen's dinner party on the evening of 29 July 1914. But just as in Jules Verne's classic tale of adventure, *Around the World in Eighty Days*, where everything has its origin in a cocksure opinion expressed in an exclusive gentlemen's club, Mannerheim would remember this totally baseless assertion as the starting shot of the First World War. For at that same moment, a club steward handed him an envelope containing an order for him to present himself at his brigade's headquarters at midnight.

Thereafter things went like clockwork. Mannerheim excused himself and hurried to the nearest telephone to summon his officers to the brigade's headquarters at the appointed time. At the head-quarters he received a telegram with the order to mobilise, and finally he opened the safe and broke the seal on the directive that stated exactly when and to what destination his brigade should depart. The first unit was expected to be onboard a train in only two hours' time, which would have been totally impossible to achieve had not a far-sighted captain begun to mobilise his men immediately after Mannerheim's telephone call. The destination was the south-ern front in Russian Poland: with Warsaw in the middle, this formed a wedge between German Prussia in the north and the Carpathian Mountains, belonging to Austro-Hungary, in the south.

In the first week of August 1914, the Allies, consisting of Russia, France and Great Britain, and the Central Powers, foremost of which were Germany and Austro-Hungary, declared war on each other. In spite of the febrile rearmament that all the Great Powers had engaged in before the outbreak of war, none of the European empires were prepared for a prolonged conflict. The Germans were counting on a similar outcome to the Franco-Prussian War of 1870–71, in which they made fast and devastating advances to settle the conflict in less than a year. The French and Russian General Staffs also had the same approximate time frame in mind, since the myriad innovations in weapons technology made any other scenario seem improbable. After the horribly bloody clashes of the first few months, in which hundreds of thousands of conscripts were killed or maimed without resolving the conflict, trench warfare increasingly came to predominate on both the Western and the Eastern Fronts. Offensives and counteroffensives were executed on nearly every part of the front, but none of them proved decisive. The battles continued in much the same vein until 1917–18, when the Americans entered the war and the Russian home front collapsed.

As has been noted, many troop units were still operating according to old tactical patterns at the start of the war. This was not least the case with the cavalry forces, which were to play their last key role at the end of August 1914, in the first big altercation between Russian and German troops at the border between Prussia and Poland. The German cavalrymen's movement and co-ordination with the other branches of their military was far better than that of the Russians, whose offensive against the German positions started the whole battle but ended catastrophically. According to many assessments, the Russian Army never properly recovered from this setback. The Germans naturally made great play of their victory and, as time went by, began to refer to the clash as the Battle of Tannenberg, which was symbolic revenge for the defeat the German Knights of the Teutonic Order had suffered against a Slavic army at the same location in 1410.

Equally bitter experiences of the cavalry's limitations in modern warfare were also evident at the more southern section of the front, where Mannerheim's brigade was pitched into battle on the morning of 17 August 1914. The attacking Austrians' fire was so frenzied that the cavalrymen's attempt, led by Mannerheim, to strike the enemy's flank was quickly stopped in its tracks. Had the infantry not come to the cavalrymen's aid, they would have ended up being encircled by the enemy. Mannerheim's riders suffered heavy losses, and although they came through this baptism of fire with their honour intact, they were forced to acknowledge something that Mannerheim had already witnessed ten years previously in the Russo-Japanese War. Mounted charges were increasingly ineffective in close combat, and the cavalry instead had to function as a fast, mobile infantry.

Mannerheim's actions during that first battle strengthened his reputation as a courageous frontline commander and resulted in him being granted the highly esteemed Sword of Saint George. A few weeks later a counteroffensive was carried out against the Austrians which achieved good results but led to large losses, particularly for Mannerheim's brigade. The operation went worst of all for a squadron of Uhlans who ended up in a fierce firefight in wooded terrain. Mannerheim was at the scene and ordered them to make a frontal assault with bayonets, which resulted in almost the entire troop being wiped out. This, unsurprisingly, cast a long shadow over Mannerheim's judgement skills among his men, and far behind the frontline it gave rise to the rumour that he had callously squandered human lives.

Mannerheim himself took the misfortune hard, even though similar losses ensued at the start of the war on all sections of the front where cavalrymen were involved, since they in particular had been trained to launch fast sallies. Subsequently, he consciously endeavoured to avoid exposing his men to overly great peril, although as a commander at the front he naturally also had to make decisions that demanded risk-taking and human sacrifice on future occasions. In autumn 1914, he was even criticised by his superiors on one occasion for not having struck with sufficient force against the enemy. However, as the war progressed and the number of fallen soldiers continued to rise, even those in the General Staffs realised that foolhardiness would do little to advance their cause.

Furthermore, Mannerheim so distinguished himself as a frontline commander during one incident in early October 1914 that to his great delight he was awarded the Cross of Saint George of the fourth class. Subsequently he always had the right to bear the little white cross, an unambiguous symbol of his military competence and character. During a retreat, his brigade had got themselves into a tight spot at a river which could have ended in panic and catastrophe, but such was Mannerheim's calmness and presence of mind that all his troops, including the artillery, crossed the waterway without losses.

Mannerheim's frontline service in the Russian Army would continue until late summer 1917. In late winter 1915, he was appointed Commander of the 12th Cavalry Division, which required him to shoulder significantly more responsibility for leadership than he had done previously. While a cavalry division (5,000–6,000 men) may have been smaller in size than an infantry division (c. 12,000–15,000 men), it was more complicated to direct and maintain. Co-ordination with other military branches was also more difficult, not least because the Russian Army had nothing like the same fluid internal understanding as the German one. His promotion clearly caused some envy, one expression of which was an acerbic comment by his colleague Serge de Witt after meeting Mannerheim for the first time at an officers' dinner: "He very rarely said 'no' or expressed disagreement, but instead turned his head slightly up and away while casting a self-possessed, sarcastic look out somewhere into the distance." One year later, de Witt had the opportunity to better acquaint himself with this superciliousness when he was designated Mannerheim's aide, and quickly became genuinely impressed by the latter's aptitude as a commander.

In autumn 1916, Mannerheim and his division were transferred to the Romanian Front, which had come into existence when Romania had sided with the Allies, in the hope that it could capture some territory from the Austro-Hungarian Empire. Mannerheim's service here would be his last active contribution as a frontline commander in the Imperial Army, which, after a period of stability, had started to lose its effectiveness and discipline in 1916 as war fatigue became more widespread. He observed that the home front was also starting to crack while on leave in Finland in February 1916, when he found out about the secret recruitment of Finns to the German Army. This had been taking place since 1915 on the initiative of the Jaeger Movement, which had the long-term aim of launching an

Fig. 3.6: Mannerheim inspects a bicycle battalion at the Transylvanian Front in Romania at the turn of 1916–17.

armed resistance to extricate Finland from Russian rule. In total, over 2,000 Finns ended up travelling to Germany for military training, forming their own unit—the 27th Jaeger Battalion—in Kaiser Wilhelm II's army.

As a loyal officer in the Imperial Army, Mannerheim naturally viewed such an operation negatively: it was clearly illegal, and a threat to the empire's unity. Reinhold Svento, who would later rise to prominence as a Social Democratic minister, described meeting Mannerheim at a dinner at the Helsinki Stock Exchange Building (*Helsingin Pörssitalo*) in February 1916. Mannerheim had complained that the Finns had no desire whatsoever to volunteer in the Russian Army, but would rather become Jaegers in the German Army, which he saw as nothing less than treason. A similarly critical attitude was fairly widespread in Finland at this time, and was shared by, among others, the politician K. J. Ståhlberg, who would go on to be chosen as the country's first president. In an attempt to counteract the imbalance, Mannerheim sought out Colonel Nikolai Mexmontan, the last commander of the Finnish Guards' Rifle Battalion, before its disbandment in 1905, and tried in vain to get him to mobilise an equivalent volunteer corps for the Russian Army.

Mannerheim never returned to this episode and firmly asserted in his memoirs that he first heard about the Jaeger Movement after he came home for good at the turn of 1917–18. It is easy to understand the reason for this active forgetfulness. Together, Mannerheim and the leading Jaeger officers would play a central role in the armed forces of independent Finland until the end of the Second World War. Neither party would have benefitted if it had been disclosed how much they had disagreed about Finland's future in 1916 and 1917. But obviously Mannerheim's point of view spread quickly at the time, and soon reached the ears of the activist groups that were behind the Jaeger Movement, not least because the self-same Colonel Mexmontan fast became one of its key figures. All this also helps explain why many former activists and Jaegers remained so sceptical of Mannerheim long after he had led the White Army to victory in the Finnish Civil War in 1918. It was difficult to dismiss the suspicion that his primary motive for participating in the war against the Finnish Red Guards had really been the restoration of the Russian Empire. Consequently, Mannerheim and many other Finns who returned from Russian service were for the rest of their lives often subjected to derisory insinuations that they continued to have the mentality of "Russian officers".

This deep rift between Mannerheim and the Jaeger officers belongs to one of the most neglected and explained-away chapters in the history of independent Finland. Their difference of opinion clearly presents a profound challenge to the patriotic narrative's interpretation of Mannerheim as the great founder of the Republic of Finland. Maybe this is the reason why so many would rather focus on his sex life or fashion sense than on how he shaped the country's future after the First World War. Either way, this taboo also hampers efforts to understand Mannerheim beyond Finland's borders. One illustrative example of this is the 2016 Mannerheim biography by the veteran Swedish diplomat Dag Sebastian Ahlander: it is an enjoyable read in many respects, but it does not discuss this fundamental schism at all.

In late winter 1917, Mannerheim was forced to witness the Russian Empire drift into such a deep crisis that almost everything he and the rest of the Russian social elite had defended and believed in quickly came to collapse. Having had responsibility for a demanding section of the Romanian Front for a little over a month, in late January Mannerheim's division was transferred to the reserve in Bessarabia in order to recover. This gave him the opportunity to take a month's leave to visit his homeland. The journey went, of course, via the recently renamed Petrograd, which allowed him, as a member of the Imperial Retinue, a short audience with Emperor Nicholas II. Detailing the encounter in his memoirs, Mannerheim makes careful noted of the ruler's apathetic bearing: "I expected that the emperor, who usually listened attentively to what one had to report, would have a particular interest in my account of the situation at the Romanian front, [as] few from there have had an audience [with him]. He was, however, noticeably absent-minded."

In contrast to the turbulent atmosphere in Petrograd, everything seemed to be running smoothly in Helsinki. Up to this time Finland had been largely unscathed by the war, partly because the Finns were exempt from national service and partly because the closest front was in the southern Baltics. Russia's warmongering had created new markets for Finnish industry and, until late autumn 1916, Finland's economy was booming. This progress could still be felt in early 1917, and stood in stark contrast to developments in Russia. Before his return journey to the front, again via Petrograd, Mannerheim heard the news about the food shortages there that had resulted in demonstrations and looting. He set off on his journey regardless, and when he awoke, on the morning of 12 March 1917, in the Hôtel d'Europe on Nevsky Prospect, the capital's main thoroughfare, the streets were teeming with flag-carrying revolutionaries clad in red armbands.

This was the outbreak of the March Revolution. After experiencing various hardships in a Petrograd terrorised by revolutionaries, Mannerheim managed to get a place on the night train to Moscow, where on 15 March he was met with the news that the Emperor had abdicated. Two days later, he travelled on towards the front and noted on his train journey how the whole of the old regime was disintegrating: strikes, demonstrations and looting were happening everywhere, as were acts of violence against officers and anyone else seen as being on the side of the collapsed empire. Increasingly chaotic conditions also prevailed at the front. Revolutionary Soviet soldiers proclaimed that the court marshal and the death penalty had been abolished, which resulted in widespread desertion and threatened to bring the whole Russian front crashing down. In the cavalry and the artillery slightly better discipline was maintained, and in the midst of the disintegration of the once proud Imperial Army, Mannerheim was promoted to lieutenant-general. As the Imperial Retinue was dissolved, its generals rose by one rank when they were brought back into the standard military order.

The promotion came in early May 1917, and, scarcely a month later, Mannerheim's fiftieth birthday was celebrated with pomp and splendour by his own division. But it was little cause for celebration that he had been made head of a corps of three cavalry divisions which, in theory, made him one of the ten highest-ranking generals of the Russian Army. In practice, his power was dwindling day by day due to the army's steadily worsening discipline. An ankle injury sustained while out riding in early September gave him the opportunity to follow events from a safer distance. He was granted sick leave to nurse his ankle in Odessa, and straight after his arrival at the beautiful port city on the Black Sea he requested leave from active service. It was approved almost immediately. On 25 September 1917, he received a telegram from the army's new commander-in-chief which announced that he was transferred to the reserves on the grounds that he was unable to comply with the current circumstances.

It was no coincidence that Mannerheim's sick leave and military discharge followed one after the other. A few weeks before Mannerheim's fall from horseback, the Commander-in-Chief of the Russian Army Lavr Kornilov had led an unsuccessful coup attempt against Russia's provisional government, with the aim of restoring order in the army and on the home front. His failure dispelled the last hopes of overcoming the growing chaos. It also meant that Mannerheim and all other generals who, in one way or another, had supported the now imprisoned Kornilov ran the risk of being held responsible for the coup attempt. In a letter to his sister Sophie, Mannerheim admitted that this threat of reprisals had contributed to his willingness to retire to Odessa to recover from his injury, which he described as "a very mild sprain". The mutual trust between Mannerheim and the provisional government had been irretrievably lost.

It was no doubt a bitter blow for Mannerheim to be forced to leave his successful officer career in Russia, especially as he could not have imagined that only four months later he would take his place at the head of a counter-revolutionary army in Finland. At this point his plan was to return to Finland, although he feared that as a 50-year-old, it would be difficult to take up something completely new. In other respects, Mannerheim was getting by without any issues in Odessa, which he had already visited on a couple of previous occasions during the war. As was his custom, he took up residence at the Hôtel de Londres on the city's fashionable beach promenade, and regularly dined at the city's best restaurants, where he gathered with fellow officers and society dames to debate and speculate about how everything would turn out. The balcony of his hotel room commanded, according to his own description, "a splendid view over the Black Sea", and thanks to the warm weather one could stroll "without an overcoat long into the night".

The return journey to Finland was delayed on account of a tailors' and shoemakers' strike that prevented Mannerheim from procuring civilian clothes. These he considered to be the most sensible choice for travelling through a Russia that was full of revolutionaries. But while he was waiting to attire himself in early November 1917, the Bolsheviks took power in Petrograd and many other northern towns. This convinced Mannerheim that he could not afford to wait any longer. On 3 December he set off in full uniform on the northbound train in a comfortably furnished Red Cross carriage, in which he had managed to get a place because of his close relationship with the organisation's British representative, Lady Muriel Paget, who was staying in the city.

Accompanying Mannerheim was his batman Ignat Karpatyov, a resourceful Ukrainian who had been an industrial worker in civilian life and who had saved Mannerheim from a tight spot on many occasions. To the annoyance of many Finns, Karpatyov, who only spoke Russian, would continue as Mannerheim's manservant during the Finnish Civil War in spring 1918. Also accompanying Mannerheim was the young Finnish officer Martin Franck, who had served as a volunteer in one of Mannerheim's cavalry regiments and whom Mannerheim encouraged to come along with him when they chanced to meet on a street in Odessa: "Martinus, we travel immediately to Finland. Report to the regiment."

4

THE CHAIN REACTION

The Counter-Revolutionary

"Restore order", said Mannerheim with exaggerated calm to Martin Franck, his temporary orderly officer, when a crowd of heavily armed Bolsheviks tried to force the Lieutenant-General from his carriage out onto the station platform during a stop on his train journey to Petrograd. Franck drew his rapier, took a few steps forward, bellowed "be gone from here" and, like a miracle, at that very moment the train set off with a jerk, causing the Bolsheviks to rush out of the carriage. This was the worst that befell them on the slowly advancing train journey to Petrograd, although they were caught up in a number of other threatening situations. At the very next station they had a reminder of how badly things could have gone, when they saw a puddle of blood at the spot where a general of the General Staff had been murdered only a short time ago.

Upon arrival at Petrograd on 11 December 1917, the resolutely status-conscious Mannerheim was appalled "to see the generals themselves lugging their bags along". And improbably enough, he succeeded, according to his own memoirs, in getting two soldiers to carry his portmanteaus to a cab that conveyed him through the city's revolution-ravaged streets to the Hôtel d'Europe. There he stayed for a week, while he tried in vain to bring about a counter-revolution led by officers loyal to the Emperor. It is notable that over a month after the Bolsheviks' coup in the city, the situation was so confused and their grip on power so weak that the old regime's elite could continue to meet fairly freely in their exclusive clubs and societies. Mannerheim mentioned in his memoirs how, at one of

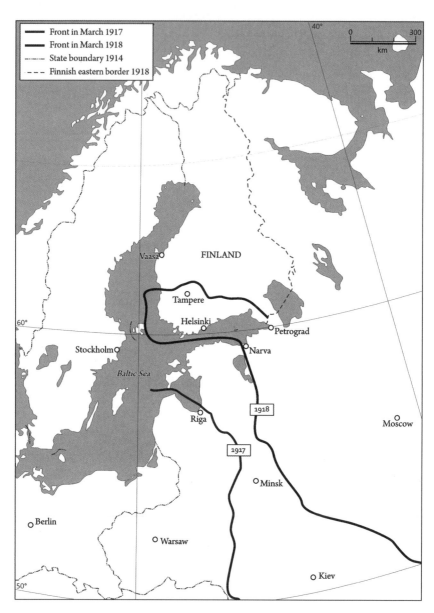

Fig. 4.1: The development of the Baltic section of the Eastern Front between March 1917 and March 1918. Map by Hannu Linkola.

these high-class club dinners, he had sat between two grand dukes who had previously been highly ranked officers in the army, but who were now so paralysed with fear that they were unable to rise up against the Bolsheviks.

A few blocks from there lay the Smolny Institute, which had been the empire's most distinguished educational establishment for the daughters of the nobility. This was where Mannerheim's younger sister, Annica, had gone to school until her death from typhoid in 1886. Now it functioned as the revolutionary headquarters of the new Bolshevik Government, the Council of People's Commissars. At the head of this was Vladimir Ilyich Ulyanov, who at that point was already far better known by his revolutionary name of Lenin. While Mannerheim had been watching events develop from Odessa, Lenin had been in hiding in Finland. A couple of weeks before the October Revolution, Lenin had taken the train from Helsinki to Petrograd, running the risk of being caught by the provisional government's militia, which had received information that his revolutionary aims were financed by Germany, and therefore had a warrant out for his arrest.

Lenin's connection to Germany has often been cited as the reason he started pushing hard for a Russian–German peace treaty once the Bolsheviks had seized power. On 15 December 1917, the countries' governments agreed to a ceasefire. A week later, peace negotiations began in Belarus, concluding after two and a half months in the Treaty of Brest-Litovsk, which was signed on 3 March 1918. With this Treaty, Russia had definitively extricated itself from the world war. This obviously benefitted the Germans, but it was also something that the Bolshevik Government had sought, since it freed up resources to subdue the counter-revolutionary forces that had started to spring up in different parts of the disintegrating empire over the winter.

On 17 December Mannerheim took the train onwards to Finland. His departure was beset with difficulties. The Bolsheviks were now monitoring all traffic out of the city, and it was by no means certain that they would allow Mannerheim to travel. However, Petrograd's Finland Station was in such a state of chaos that he managed to slip through the checkpoint with the help of the letter of assignment he had received when he was transferred over to the reserves.

Mannerheim's intention was not only to rest and ponder his own future in Helsinki, but also to investigate what preparations were in place to stop the revolution from spreading to Finland. He had tried to keep himself informed about developments there since Nicholas II's abdication in March 1917. But although he looked positively on the cessation of integration measures and the increased freedom in Finnish political life, he did not show any signs of supporting the efforts to emancipate Finland from the Russian Empire.

As such, he did not express any great enthusiasm for the declaration of independence that the Finnish Parliament first made in mid-November, and once again on 6 December 1917. In this he was far from the exception. Although the majority of Finns were critical or directly hostile towards the Russian regime, in late summer 1917 a significant proportion of them still considered that it was unrealistic, even downright dangerous, to strive for national sovereignty. The Bolsheviks' takeover of power in Russia and the concurrent disturbances that were underway in Finland contributed to a sharp upswing in support of independence among the bourgeoisie. Even so, there were many who for good reason remained sceptical that Finland would cope alone, leading to increasingly strong hopes for a military intervention by the German Army, which had advanced all the way to southern Estonia by September 1917.

Mannerheim was stridently against such a Germanophile solution. This would have completely undermined the Russian Empire's overarching strategy, the premise of which was to protect the capital city, and one integral way of doing so was to use Finland as a buffer zone in the north-west. For a military officer such as Mannerheim, German intervention in Finland was not so much about support for the country's independence as an unsettling shift of the Russo-German front closer to Petrograd. At the same time, he clearly realised that it was implausible for Finland to take on revolutionary Russia alone. Finland did not have its own army, in addition to which there were more than 80,000 Russian soldiers still stationed in the country around the turn of 1917–18.

In spite of his ghost-writers' judicious editing, Mannerheim's memoirs still indirectly show his guarded attitude towards Finnish sovereignty when he arrived in a "grey and rainy" Helsinki on 18 December 1917. Although he thought that the Finnish Senate might lack the means to suppress the increasing anarchy in the country, he became convinced of the Finns' strong will to "save their culture and their social structure". In Mannerheim's eyes, the primary question was not how to secure the country's independence, but how to prevent the revolution from spreading to Finland. It is true that the same section of his memoirs also claims that he had observed "an unbreakable will to fight for the country's liberation" among its people, and that he believed that they had a realistic chance of succeeding. However, this appears to be a conscious attempt by the ghost-writers to refashion Mannerheim, many decades later, as a zealous supporter of independence, for all available sources from the period suggest otherwise.

Over the next three or four weeks the political dispute in Finland rapidly escalated into an armed conflict between the bourgeois Senate and the increasingly revolutionary workers' movement, headed by the Social Democrats. Lenin signed the Bolshevik Government's recognition of Finland's independence a few minutes before midnight on 31 December 1917. This did nothing to temper the antagonism, even though it did cause other countries, like Sweden and Germany, to also officially acknowledge Finland's autonomy. The Bolsheviks, naturally, did not want to support the emergence of Finland as a parliamentary democracy. Their aim was, instead, to convince Finland's hesitant but nationalistic Social Democrats that the Bolsheviks had kept their promise about the right of national minorities to sovereignty. With this done, they hoped that the Social Democrats would be prepared to seize power, which would have effectively pulled the rug from under Germany's support for Finland's bourgeois government in the ongoing Russo-German peace negotiations. Of course, it would also have served Lenin's overall objective, which was still that of worldwide revolution.

Having seen the enormity of the forces that were at work in Russia, Mannerheim realised that before long Finland would become embroiled in the revolution. He celebrated the new year with family and friends in Helsinki, but then immediately travelled back to Petrograd to hand in his letter of resignation and pension application to the Russian Army's administration. His justification was that, as a citizen of the newly independent Finland, he could no longer serve in the Russian Army. His resignation was approved in February

1918 and his pension in March, but the tumultuous circumstances transpired to prevent him from ever receiving the money. Together with a supplement from the officers' superannuation fund, this would have amounted to an annual sum of 4,620 roubles.

Many have interpreted Mannerheim's letter of resignation as him definitively disassociating himself from the Russian Empire to enable him to side wholeheartedly with independent Finland. It is more plausible that he resigned so that he could take an active part in the mobilisation of a bourgeois army in Finland, free from conflicting military obligations. The intention was that this army would first quash the domestic revolution before attaching itself to the counter-revolutionary front that was being established in Russia. In fact, Mannerheim's very last visit to his old hometown, "Piter", was not solely to cut formal ties with the Russian military; in all probability, it was also to conduct negotiations with fellow officers and foreign diplomats about Finland's role in the impending counter-revolution.

One indication of this was that Mannerheim never revealed why he made the journey to Petrograd at a time when crossing the border was getting more dangerous by the day. An even clearer sign that his mission was counter-revolutionary was his discussion concerning the possibility of bringing weapons from France to Finland, via Murmansk, with a French officer in the city. The deliberations came to nothing, but they do show that he framed the approaching conflict in Finland broadly, as part of the First World War and its by-product, the Russian Revolution.

On the morning of 8 January 1918, Mannerheim returned by train to Helsinki; only a week later, he was tasked by the Senate with establishing a defence force to suppress the growing anarchy in the country. The decision had been made by a military committee appointed by the Senate, to which Mannerheim had also been assigned. At the start of January 1918, the committee was given the job of raising an army for the newly established republic. After participating in three meetings, Mannerheim had had enough of the committee's indecisiveness: he abruptly announced his intention to resign because they were wasting time on trivialities. He argued that the only functional solution was for the committee to move north to Ostrobothnia without delay, and there set up a headquarters for the proposed army. Although Mannerheim was by no means universally trusted, having previously been so loyal to the Emperor, the Senate appointed him to execute this plan on 15 January. There was no doubt that the 50-year-old General, who had just returned from the world war, was conceived of as the right man for the task. His whole being emitted the very energy and decisiveness that had been found wanting in other potential candidates.

At this point, according to Mannerheim, Senate Chairman Pehr Evind Svinhufvud gave his word that neither Sweden nor Germany would be involved either in restoring order or in disarming the Russian troops who were still in the country. Svinhufvud and his fellow senator Artur Castrén, who also took part in the talks, later asserted that the promise was only a conditional one: outside help would be requested if the situation became critical. When Mannerheim later addressed the matter, he naturally refused to concede that his demand to eschew foreign assistance must have awakened suspicions among the senators. But their overarching goal was to keep a tight hold on the country's nascent independence; if this was under threat they would, in all likelihood, have been open to any and all available help. So the fact that Mannerheim unequivocally wanted to avoid outside interference reinforced misgivings that his unspoken aim was really to restore order in the whole empire. It also probably explains why he was only later informed that the Senate had already appealed to Germany for military assistance in December 1917. The Senate did not trust Mannerheim, but it understood that his military ability was needed to keep the situation under control.

Over the next two weeks the political conflict in the country quickly escalated into open war. On 21 January, having set up his headquarters in Vaasa, Ostrobothnia, Mannerheim began a systematic mobilisation of the bourgeois defence guards that had already formed in different regions of the country. As in other parts of the splintering empire, these were called the White Guards. Alongside this mobilisation, military training was launched for other men capable of service; it was conducted by, among others, those Jaegers who had already returned from Germany. This heralded the instructional role that many from the Jaeger battalion would come to have in the army after their arrival back in Finland in February 1918. At first, Mannerheim's staff consisted principally of officers who had, like him, been in Russian military service. In February it was supplemented with voluntary officers from the Swedish Army, who lacked frontline experience but who did, at least, have a modern General Staff training.

The first armed altercation between pro-government forces and the revolutionary guard broke out on the Karelian Isthmus in eastern Finland on 24 January. Three days later, Mannerheim ordered the Ostrobothnian White Guards to disarm the Russian troops stationed in the western province's garrisons. The operation was risky insofar as these soldiers were heavily armed, but, as Mannerheim had correctly assumed, they had absolutely no motivation to fight. With the benign attitude of the troops' Russian commanders, the White Guards were able to gain control of the garrisons' weapon stores without much difficulty. This gave rise to suspicions of collaboration, which were exacerbated by the fact that Mannerheim saw to it that the surrendered Russian officers had comfortable accommodation and freedom of movement. As a consequence, rumours spread that he had been unable to shake off his Russian past.

Later that same evening, on Wednesday 27 January, a red lantern was hoisted in the tower of the Helsinki Workers' House (*Työväentalo*) as a signal that the revolution had begun. Over the course of the night, the Red Guards took control of most of the government departments and public buildings in the capital and in many other parts of southern Finland. While the beginning of the coup was almost bloodless, the decision of the Social Democrats' leadership—now reorganised as a People's Commissariat—to carry it out had irreversible consequences. In leftist quarters it was feared that the ongoing mobilisation of pro-government forces would permanently prevent the transition to a socialist society; the Red Guards, therefore, started to make similar martial preparations. Above all else, however, the decision became irrevocable because the Bolshevik Government intensified its demands for its Finnish comrades to seize power as the situation continued to escalate. If the Finns were incapable of doing this, then the Bolsheviks made it clear that they would delegate the task to the revolutionary-minded Russian soldiers and seamen, of whom there were plenty in Helsinki since a significant part of Russia's Baltic Sea fleet was located there.

In the aftermath of the conflict in Finland, the different parties involved naturally tended to stick closely to their own interpretations of its causes and consequences. As such, to this day the war in 1918 has many competing names: the Finnish Civil War, the War of Liberation, the Class War, the War of Brothers, the Revolution or the Red Rebellion. One established interpretation that most researchers do agree upon, however, is that it was a peripheral offshoot of the First World War. The Russian Revolution was an immediate consequence of the war-weariness and the shattered *esprit de corps* of the home front. After the Bolsheviks had filled the power vacuum, the disharmony in the chaotic empire intensified into a bloody civil war, which was on many levels entwined with the world war. It would continue in Eastern Europe as a number of smaller conflicts for many years after Germany's surrender, and as such it can be characterised as a forgotten extension of the Great War.

For this reason, it is hardly remarkable that the conflict in Finland largely followed the same pattern as the increasingly widespread civil war in other parts of the former empire. Only a small proportion of the population were actively engaged in it. In many parts of the empire the revolution was principally about looting, terror and local vendettas. Consistent frontlines and major clashes were to be found only in the vicinity of garrisons, densely populated areas, and strategically important railway junctions and main roads. In Finland, the revolutionaries took control of the southern population centres and gathered themselves for a northerly offensive along the railways towards Ostrobothnia and Upper Savonia. The Senate's troops marched south from the opposite direction, and slowly but surely gained the advantage in February 1918 after military conscription had been introduced and the Jaegers had returned from Germany.

Mannerheim's long experience as a frontline commander in the inadequately equipped and ethnically diverse Russian Army proved to be excellent preparation for the role of commander-in-chief of the Senate's troops. The war's harsh conditions in this snow-covered periphery of European civilisation had nothing in common with the showy uniforms, grand parades and imperial splendour that he had once known in St Petersburg. The Whites' headquarters (now at Seinäjoki) gradually started to distribute more homogeneous

*I februari Mannerheim sitt „varde"! sa — och se
ur Finlands frusna mark han stampade en vit armé.*

*Så i april kom tysken hit att slåss mot vårt patrask
och hade huvudstaden snart som i en liten ask.*

Fig. 4.2: The satirical newspaper *Kerberos*'s summary of Mannerheim's
and the Germans' role in the Finnish Civil War. The captions accompanying the strip can be translated as follows: "In February Mannerheim said
boldly 'let there be'—// and lo from Finland's frozen ground he found
a White Army. // Then in April the German came to fight against our
proles // and soon the country's capital was under his control."

uniforms and better equipment to the troops. Nevertheless, their campaign was still frequently characterised by its amateurish nature and variable discipline during the three-month-long conflict.

Mannerheim's lack of General Staff training was laid bare by his inability to make decisions through discussions with his colleagues, but his energetic leadership and fresh experience as a commander for an entire Russian Army corps compensated for this. The fact that he and nearly all the other General Staff officers at the headquarters were Swedish-speaking did cause some irritation. This inevitably led to a certain friction between the predominantly Finnish-speaking army of farmers and its emphatically aristocratic Commander-in-Chief Mannerheim, although he quickly realised that he should dress in a thick frieze uniform, and took pains to practise Finnish phrases before visiting the front or handing out medals. It would neverthe-less be misleading to characterise the language question as a big problem in the White Army, since Swedish was still, in many con-texts, the common language of the Finnish social elite.

A significantly bigger dilemma was caused by Mannerheim's Russian background and Allied sympathies, which were a matter of common knowledge, and which led to a serious crisis when the 1,400-strong Jaeger battalion returned from Germany in February. Despite Mannerheim's laudatory speech to the Jaegers at their wel-come parade in Vaasa's main square, there was a deep mistrust between the two parties at the beginning. The Jaegers saw him as a representative of the regime that they had left Finland to do battle against, and he was sometimes sarcastically referred to as "Gospodin", a Russian form of address normally used to indicate respect. The issue was not improved at all by the fact that Mannerheim had a Ukrainian batman to attend to him who spoke Russian exclusively.

Mannerheim refused to allow the battalion to continue as a sepa-rate elite force and demanded instead that the Jaegers be distributed as instructors and commanders among the contingents of conscripts that were being mobilised at the time. According to certain reports, at the time of this schism a number of Jaegers were behind an assas-sination attempt that was made on the saloon car in which Mannerheim lodged during the war. Fortunately for him, on the night in question he happened to be staying elsewhere. After pro-tracted negotiations and vague promises of establishing specific

Jaeger units at a later date, Mannerheim finally convinced them to agree to his demands.

Under German Command

However, the primary reason that the Jaegers and their head spokesman, Colonel Wilhelm Thesleff, acquiesced on the matter was because Mannerheim had just been forced to make a much larger concession of his own. In the midst of the negotiations about the Jaegers' deployment, there arrived word that Germany had decided to come to the aid of White Finland. This went totally against Mannerheim's objectives and led to him threatening to resign unless the German offer was immediately declined. But when it became clear that the Senate intended to accept their help regardless, Mannerheim quickly backed down, for he realised that he would have even less opportunity to influence the course of events if he left his post.

As Marjaliisa and Seppo Hentilä demonstrate in their excellent work, *Saksalainen Suomi 1918* (2016; German Finland, 1918), by this point neither Mannerheim's nor the Senate's outlook was of any significance to how events unfolded. Three weeks before word reached Vaasa about German help, the German military leadership had already decided to intervene in Finland. The bourgeois Senate in Helsinki had requested German help against the revolutionaries through their ambassador in Berlin, Edvard Hjelt, at the beginning of February; but this was not the reason for Germany's decision to get involved. Rather, it was because the Bolsheviks had unilaterally broken off the Russo-German peace negotiations on 10 February. The Bolsheviks, who refused to withdraw their troops from Ukraine, the Baltic states and Finland, took it for granted that the Germans were not prepared to begin a new offensive when the ceasefire came to an end. They also hoped that the chaotic situation would help spread the revolution to the German Army.

Their calculation backfired. The Germans began immediate preparations for a large-scale offensive over the Baltics to Finland with the aim of achieving two objectives. The Bolsheviks would be forced to accept peace, while by occupying the Gulf of Finland the German Army could effectively ensure that Russia would not reenter the war on the side of the Allies. To avoid accusations that they were reigniting the conflict, the Germans disguised their offensive as humanitarian aid for the countries they planned to occupy. Consequently, on 14 February, the Finnish envoy in Berlin, Edvard Hjelt, was commissioned to order a further request for German help, to justify the Army's push into Finland; since the lines of communication with Vaasa were terrible, he decided to write it himself and deliver it to the Germans on the very same day.

A week later he received a detailed account from the German army leadership of how they intended to execute their "help". First, the Germans would set up a base on the Åland Islands, and then, after the break-up of the winter ice, they would land on the west coast of Finland and advance inland along the railway lines to provide relief to Mannerheim's troops. Hjelt conveyed this plan north to the Senate in Vaasa; Mannerheim, to his indignation, did not receive any information about it in advance. The German strategy in Finland would go without a hitch, as would their offensive in the Baltics, for by the end of February they had occupied the region. With the Germans bearing down on Petrograd, the Bolshevik Government accepted a peace treaty on 3 March 1918, according to which Russia was to relinquish the Baltics and remove its troops from Finland. Two days later the Germans occupied Åland, on 3 April their Baltic Division disembarked in Hanko, and, only eleven days after that, the division's commander General-Major Rüdiger von der Goltz was inspecting his troops in a victory parade before a jubilant public in Helsinki's Senate Square.

Before the Germans had even set foot in Finland, Mannerheim had been so disconcerted by their proposed strategy that he hastened to assert his own authority. He did not want the German intervention to completely overshadow the achievements for which he and his forces were responsible. He demanded and received a promise from the Germans that their troops would be placed under his command when they arrived on Finnish territory. In reality, the promise meant nothing, since direct communications were first established at the end of April, by which time the Reds had, in practice, already been defeated. Mannerheim also gave orders to accelerate the offensive against Tampere, where a large portion of the Red forces was based, in order to have time to achieve a decisive victory without German help. The offensive was started on 15 March, and after fierce battles, in which both sides engaged all available resources and suffered high death tolls, the last remaining Red Guards surrendered in Tampere on the morning of 6 April. Similar offensives in which the Whites were victorious also occurred on the Savonian and Karelian fronts.

The conquest of Tampere took place at the same time as the German Baltic Division landed in Hanko and Loviisa. From these coastal towns they rapidly advanced on Helsinki and other population centres in southern Finland. By then Mannerheim had become involved in another foreign political imbroglio, namely an exchange of sharply worded notes with the Swedish Government, which had sent a military expedition to Åland in the middle of February without first requesting Finnish approval. The enterprise was described as a peace-keeping effort, but as the Swedes had acted without permission there were grounds to suspect that they were trying to annex the islands just when the greatest chaos reigned in Finland. After the Germans had disembarked on Åland on 5 March, the Swedish troops were quickly withdrawn. But that did little to restore Finno-Swedish relations, since at the same time the Swedish remained adamant that they could not offer bourgeois Finland any military support, citing Sweden's position of neutrality in the ongoing world war.

The Åland incident strengthened the German Baltic Division's popularity on the bourgeois side in Finland, and indirectly whittled away at the image of Mannerheim as the country's saviour. A central theme in his propaganda campaign was, therefore, to emphasise wherever possible that the armed struggle against the Reds was nothing less than independent Finland's war of liberation. By the time the last Red Guards surrendered in Kymenlaakso on 5 May 1918, Mannerheim had already sent an order to assemble troops in Helsinki for a new victory parade. His clear aim was to eclipse that of the Germans a month earlier, and it is undeniable that the arrival of the 12,000-man parade in a sunny Helsinki on 16 May 1918 was an impressive spectacle. It shone a bright spotlight on the domestic achievements of the war. Above all else, the parade marked Mannerheim's first big entrance into the capital as a public figure.

The German troops stationed in the city did not take part in the parade at all. Their commander von der Goltz and his staff officers had to make do with standing as guests of honour on the steps of Helsinki Cathedral. Alongside them also stood the German Ambassador Adolf von Brück, who was forced to admit, in his report to Berlin, that Mannerheim had been an imposing sight when he rode in at the head of his troops. It was not simply that his peerless equestrianism and elegant deportment made almost all the other central figures in this political show seem like awkward extras. He also seemed to know precisely how all the triumphant gestures, displays of courtesy and military salutes should be performed, which, the ambassador added sourly, made an almost comical impression. It was anything but a matter of luck that Mannerheim knew exactly what he should do. Never before or after would he make such use of everything he had learnt during the big parades, imperial ceremonies and assorted festivities in which he had taken part during his thirty years as a Russian guards officer.

In contrast to von Brück's cynicism, the bourgeois public's reaction to Mannerheim and his White Army was euphoric. After the march to Senate Square, Mannerheim made a speech to the Senate and the parliament. There followed a service in Helsinki Cathedral and a march-past at the statue of the poet Johan Ludvig Runeberg on the Esplanade. For many decades, 16 May 1918 would be regarded in the eyes of the bourgeoisie as the true birth date of independent Finland. The Finnish Defence Forces' Flag Day was held in Senate Square on this day until 1940. It was also commemorated through an annual wreath-laying ceremony at the monument of the fallen White soldiers, and immortalised in art and literature. Take this classic scene in Jarl Hemmer's 1931 novel *En man och hans samvete* (1935; A Fool of Faith), in which Mannerheim's first public appearance is described in messianic terms:

> Mannerheim! ... He rode as if in a snowstorm, the air flickering from flowers thrown down from windows, balconies and rooftops. Around him clamoured the street with its black banks of tightly packed humanity; it looked as though they were fighting for their lives. Their arms gesticulated, hats and handkerchiefs waved in the wind, from thousands of throats rolled an avalanche of cries and, pitched forward on this jubilant torrent, he rode slowly along the street, the army in his wake.

One of the parading soldiers was the 17-year-old grammar school student Urho Kekkonen from Kainuu, who had been promoted to unit leader of his White Guard platoon at the end of the war. That day marked his first visit to the capital city and the experience made a strong impression on him. However, he did express surprise, in the report he sent home to his local newspaper, at how slender the support for the White Guards appeared to be in southern Finland. Another unsettling detail had been the large number of red and yellow lion flags, which indicated that the blue and white one favoured by himself and others of a Finnish persuasion was not at all popular in this strongly Swedish-speaking part of the country. The defeated and imprisoned Red Guards obviously condemned the victory parade outright, not least because Mannerheim, often branded "the head butcher" in the Reds' war propaganda, was riding at the

Fig. 4.3: At the victory parade on the Senate Square in Helsinki, 16 May 1918, Mannerheim's handshake with General Rüdiger von der Goltz, commander of the German forces in Finland, was clearly reserved.

head of the White Army. Their animosity was fostered by the death penalties given to revolutionaries at the Whites' war tribunals; often based on extremely tenuous justifications, these reached their peak precisely in May 1918.

Impassioned feelings consequently bubbled to the surface across all society. The war was over, but the high death toll, the large prison camps and the ongoing food shortages combined with the muffled threat of new uprisings to reinforce the sense that quick decisions were necessary. Above all, it was imperative to establish how the country's foreign politics, military organisation and still unfinished constitution would take shape. Hence, on the day of the victory parade, Mannerheim seized the opportunity immediately after his arrival in Senate Square to go up to the Government Palace and give a speech to the Senate. In this he stressed how important it was that "the helm of the Finnish state's ship be put in a powerful hand, one that is unmoved by the party quarrels and that is not forced, through compromises, to squander the government's power".

Mannerheim's statement has sometimes been interpreted as a threatening demand to the Senate, but the fact is that the revolution in Finland had convinced many senators that the country's parliamentary democracy needed to be somehow restricted. Similar lines of thought had been publicly expressed in the bourgeois daily papers in southern Finland, once these had begun to be published again in April; many of their opinion pieces had concluded with the proposal for some sort of monarchical government. It is safe to say that the new, even more pro-German Senate under J. K. Paasikivi's leadership, was also this way inclined: in early October 1918 it elected the German Prince, Frederick Charles of Hesse, as King of Finland.

Mannerheim's relationship with the Senate had curdled directly after the victory parade, to the extent that he resigned from his position as commander-in-chief on 30 May. The reason was straightforward: he refused to be subordinate to the German command that the Senate had consciously and systematically allowed to dictate Finland's security and trade policies. Not only would the Finnish Army be organised and built up according to the German model; the Germans were also unwilling, under any circumstances, to break the Treaty of Brest-Litovsk, thinking that this would increase the risk of Russia slipping back into the Allies' camp. As such, they opposed Mannerheim's overarching plan, the premise of which was, as it always had been, to first defeat the revolution in Finland and then march to Petrograd to definitively crush the Bolshevik Empire. The Germans wanted to get rid of Mannerheim, and their wish promptly came true.

Their deep mistrust of Mannerheim and his Allied sympathies stemmed from the impression he had made on Ambassador von Brück during his first visit to the Whites' headquarters in April 1918. Von Brück described the atmosphere there as rather Russian. He opined that Mannerheim was not, in the first instance, thinking of Finland's independence, but was rather trying to make use of the German offensive on the Gulf of Finland to restore the old order in Russia, where the White commander's capitalist Finnish friends had large economic interests. That von Brück probably read the situation correctly is evident from a letter sent by Mannerheim to his brother Johan, at the end of February 1918. In it he welcomed the Germans' lightning-fast attack on the Baltics since it facilitated the Finnish Army's advance, but at the same time he was concerned "that we will not have time to get to St Petersburg before them, and that's where we ought to be going".

In the six months that followed the Whites' victory, Finland was governed as a German vassal state. This occurred without any illusions on the pro-German Senate's side, which understood that the Allies were not willing to actively support Finland's independence during the ongoing world war. The Allies needed a strong Russia as a counterweight to Germany, and this presupposed that the Russians would regain a firm grip on Finland. In a letter to a friend in late August 1918, Chairman of the Senate J. K. Paasikivi stated that the Finns' only hope under these prevailing conditions was to rely on Germany's military assistance. Paasikivi always had a cynical geopolitical outlook, and he opined that without this help, a Russian attack on Finland would be sure to happen, just as night follows day.

Finnish researchers are today largely in agreement that Mannerheim can scarcely have seen Finland's independence as real sovereignty. Rather, he considered that the country would continue to be dependent on the interests and priorities of the Great Powers in the future. In this respect, he and Paasikivi thought alike, but since Mannerheim was convinced that the Western Powers would, with the help of the United States, defeat Germany, he drew entirely different conclusions about Finland's geopolitical dependence from Paasikivi.

Certainly, Russia would undoubtedly try to reattach Finland to its empire in some way, but at that point, in Mannerheim's opinion, Germany's help could no longer be counted on. In that situation it would be unequivocally better for the Finns if the Bolshevik Government was not at the helm in Russia, but rather a bourgeois regime that had regained power in a counter-revolution in which the Finns had participated. The discussions that Mannerheim conducted with representatives of the Western Powers in 1918 and 1919 demonstrate that he explicitly adhered to this belief.

After departing his post at the end of May 1918, Mannerheim immediately took the boat over to Stockholm. There he stayed, true to form, in the city's most luxurious accommodation, the Grand Hotel, which was made possible on this occasion thanks to the generous annual pension he had been granted by the Senate. During the summer the hotel served as his base for secret negotiations with British, French and American diplomats in the city. A German spy eavesdropped from an adjoining room on at least two of Mannerheim's conversations with the British Envoy, Sir Esmé Howard. It can be inferred from the German agent's reports that Mannerheim requested that the British arrange access to a harbour in the Arctic Ocean for Finland, and that they help with food provision. In addition, he complained that the Finns had become "the Germans' slaves". Mannerheim made similar appeals to Sir Esmé's French and American colleagues, and other sources claim he also discussed how Finland and the Allied Powers could co-operate to defeat the Bolshevik Empire. However, above all else, Mannerheim wanted to establish whether Finland could support the Allied troops that were at that moment advancing from Murmansk towards Petrozavodsk in eastern Karelia.

Despite these clandestine talks, it would be wrong to claim that Mannerheim was plotting against his own nation's government. During a visit to Helsinki in July 1918, he reported on his discussions in Stockholm to the Senate. He offered to travel to London and Paris as the Senate's unofficial ambassador to encourage the Western Powers to recognise Finland's independence. His proposal was coolly declined at the time, but once Germany's fortunes in the war had irrefutably turned, the Senate contacted him again in early October. They came to an agreement that he should undertake just such a probing exercise in the capitals of the Western Powers.

Mannerheim left for London, via Bergen, in mid-October 1918. During the boat journey to Stockholm he met, to his surprise, a deputation that the Senate had sent to Germany to inform Frederick Charles of Hesse that he had been chosen to be King of Finland. When Mannerheim asked ironically whether the mission had not lost its urgency, one of the deputation replied that they intended to present this as a *fait accompli* before the world. In his memoirs, Mannerheim would add, with ill-concealed gleeful malice, that this man was to all appearances "utterly convinced that the whole world would defer to the decision made by Finland".

The Regent

Mannerheim's boat trip over the North Sea turned out to be danger-ous, if not downright life-threatening. A formidable storm broke out straight after the steamer had left the fjord of Bergen. Due to floating mines, the captain could not turn back but was forced to continue the journey all the way to the Orkney Islands off the north-east coast of Scotland. By the time Mannerheim arrived in London, on 12 November 1918, the Allies' triumph in the war was being celebrated across the city. The flush of victory must have felt bit-tersweet for Mannerheim, who, a little over four years earlier, had entered the war on the Allied side. Now it was his task to dispel the Western Powers' distrust of Finland and its German-friendly poli-tics, which he himself had consistently called into question.

Despite his perseverance during a month of negotiations in London and Paris, Mannerheim did not succeed in persuading the Western Powers' governments to recognise Finland's indepen-dence. They would only agree to do so after Finland had fulfilled a number of conditions, all of which, in one way or another, involved the country disassociating itself from its pro-German politics. Not only was Finland expected to expel the German troops from its land and to refrain from choosing a German prince as monarch; it was also required to appoint a new Western-facing government that would unambiguously distance itself from its predecessor's previous foreign policy. Finally, the Finnish parliamentary elections should be conducted as quickly as possible.

The Western Powers' attitude was even more reserved towards Mannerheim's demand that, in the event of a new confrontation with the Bolshevik Government, they pledge to support a march on Petrograd by Finland's White Army. With the dust from the Great War not yet settled, the Western Powers' attention was largely focused on solving the German question. They had reliable information that Mannerheim wanted to be seen as the saviour of bourgeois Russia, an ambition that risked complicating the whole affair. Besides which, they realised that an expedition of the sort he proposed had no prospect of success if it were not synchronised with the counter-revolutionary forces in Russia.

Fig. 4.4: The Regent gives a speech to elementary grammar schoolteachers in Helsinki, spring 1919.

In the midst of these negotiations, Mannerheim received a telegram from the Finnish Government requesting that he step into the post of temporary regent of Finland until the country had a new constitution. Mannerheim was prepared for this twist, and accepted the appointment without delay. His ready agreement cannot solely have been because, in common with the government, he supported smoothing the way for a normalisation of Finland's relationship with the Western Powers. It was also down to his continuing ambition to fight against Bolshevism, for he must have been aware that he could push this cause much more effectively as Finland's temporary head of state.

After taking up his new post, Mannerheim was able to make headway on another pressing issue in London. He persuaded the Western Powers to allow Finland to start importing grain from Western Europe once again, since the country was still suffering from a serious food shortage that stemmed from its long isolation during the war. Finland's then unofficial London ambassador, Rudolf Holsti, also took part in these negotiations, which succeeded in procuring the country's first grain shipments from the United States' food aid to Europe. By coincidence, the first cargo of grain arrived in Finland on the same day that Mannerheim came ashore in Turku, on 22 December 1918.

Mannerheim's homecoming to Finland turned into an even more personal victory parade than the one in May. In Turku harbour he was greeted by a guard of honour consisting of conscripts and White Guards, among whom was his predecessor as regent, P. E. Svinhufvud. It was a gesture that Mannerheim would still warmly recall in his memoirs. The next day he was met at Helsinki railway station by a sea of cheering people. After installing himself in the residence of the previous (Russian) governor-general on the Southern Esplanade, he issued his manifesto, in which he announced that new elections would be held, and exhorted the citizenry to practise reconciliation and to abide by the law. That same day he instructed that the parliamentary elections should be held on 1–3 March 1919.

Very conscious that his time as regent was transitory, Mannerheim threw himself into his assignment. Certainly, this was in line with his temperament, but it is also clear that he was driven by the hope that his efforts would be rewarded with victory in the presidential election that would be held after the country had secured a new constitution. At the top of his agenda was still the improvement of Finland's relationship with the West and stabilisation of the country's internal politics. But alongside this, Mannerheim continued to push forward his plans for a counter-revolutionary intervention in Russia. These would later contribute to parliament turning against him, and, ultimately, to his defeat to the young Finn K. J. Ståhlberg in the first presidential elections in July 1919.

Already in late autumn 1918, with the departure of the German troops from Finland, it had become apparent that the elected members of parliament were starting to give up on the idea of a monarchy. The Social Democratic Party had quickly shed its skin after its disappointing attempt at a revolution and had adopted an explicitly reformist party programme. When the party won eighty seats in the parliamentary elections in March 1919 upon the promise of republicanism, the matter was beyond doubt, especially as the Agrarian League, with its forty-two seats, also advocated such a policy. The solution was a form of government which defined Finland as a parliamentary, democratically governed republic, but which gave the president such great authority that even the right-wing powers could support it. On 17 July 1919, Mannerheim confirmed the government's constitution. A week later he lost the first presidential election, which, as an exception, was conducted in parliament. Ståhlberg defeated him with a large majority (143 votes to 50).

The decision to let parliament elect the president was forced through by leftist and centrist politicians who were fiercely opposed to Mannerheim. A direct election could well have gone in Mannerheim's favour, as he still enjoyed considerable support in bourgeois circles, and had achieved exactly what he had been appointed to do as regent. In mid-February 1919, he made successful state visits to Stockholm and Copenhagen which positively emphasised Finland's Nordic bonds and social system. Moreover, after the parliamentary elections brought in a more centre-oriented government, both Great Britain and the United States recognised the country's independence.

But at the same time that the Finnish Parliament was resuming its role in public life in spring 1919, Mannerheim and the political establishment started to fall out again. The Social Democrats remained categorically critical of him, not only due to his tarnished reputation as the White Commander, but also because his whole character radiated an outdated aristocratic code. Many Agrarian League members, too, were resolute in their distrust of Mannerheim. It was bad enough that he had forgotten all his Finnish during his years in Russian service. To make matters worse, in early summer 1919 the leader of the Agrarian League, Santeri Alkio, found out that Mannerheim had been in secret contact with Russian generals on the counter-revolutionary side. This gave credence to the ever-present suspicions that Mannerheim was ready to risk Finland's independence to re-establish the old rule in Russia.

It came to light that he had not informed the government about the negotiations he had undertaken with the Russian counter-revo-lutionary forces' generals Nikolai Yudenich and Alexander Kolchak. The plan was, in short, that the Finnish Army would participate in their offensives against the Bolsheviks in Petrograd. Mannerheim's unequivocal condition was, however, that this could only happen if the generals representing bourgeois Russia recognised Finland's independence. For this purpose, he demanded that Finland should be given the corridor to Petsamo on the shores of the Arctic Ocean, which Alexander II, in his time, had promised to the Finns. After the agreement had been accepted by the Finnish Parliament, the Western Powers would then be asked to support the operation. But the whole thing came to nothing when Kolchak refused to guarantee Finland's independence in late June 1919.

During the first half of July 1919, Mannerheim certainly still continued to discuss, together with a group of Finnish activists, the possibility of launching an assault on Petrograd without an agree-ment with the Russian counter-revolutionaries. The activists saw the planned assault as a way to finish the annexation of East Karelia, which they enthusiastically supported and had previously tried to accomplish without state assistance. According to this plan, which certainly bore some resemblance to a coup, Mannerheim would first dissolve parliament and then establish the government's constitu-tion. Finally, he would give orders to attack Petrograd without declaring war on the Bolshevik Government, since this, according to the new constitution, would have required that parliament accept the declaration of war. But this operation, too, ended up being shelved, since Mannerheim was not prepared to advance without the National Coalition Party's support, and its leaders, in turn, demanded that all bourgeois parties should be behind the plan.

Since a broadly synchronised counter-revolution had been an obsession for Mannerheim since autumn 1917, it was no surprise that he continued to advocate for Finland to engage in one even after his time as regent. According to him, bourgeois Russia's gratitude for Finland's support would be the best way of guaranteeing Finland's independence. The last time Mannerheim brought this up publicly was at the start of November 1919, when he had a letter published in the daily press emphasising that Finland had many reasons to attach itself to the ongoing counter-revolutionary offensive in Russia. If the Bolsheviks were crushed without Finnish support, then relations with the new bourgeois regime would be damaged for a long time to come. And if Finland's passivity resulted in the Bolsheviks remaining in power, then the whole of the civilised world would single out Finland as the most guilty party in this.

The researchers John Screen and Martti Ahti have wondered how Mannerheim could have been so credulous as to expect some gratitude from the counter-revolutionary Russians' side. But they do not take into account that Mannerheim might have expressed this hope, above all, as an incentive for his countrymen. He of course saw Finland's independence as a good thing and was prepared to fight for it, but in all likelihood he must also have been prepared for the worst, which is that Finland could be flung once more into the Russian Civil War. In order to avoid being wholly without allies in that situation, it was best to ally the country with the Russian counter-revolutionaries while there was still time.

Moreover, it is anachronistic to disregard the fact that most contemporary actors took it for granted that the Bolshevik Empire would soon either be crushed or give rise to a far more dangerous wave of revolutions across the whole of Europe. That things ultimately went so differently was a stroke of luck for Finland and all the other new states that had come into existence in these years in the space between the stunned and defeated Russian and German empires. But not many believed that this exact geopolitical balance, improbable as it was, would persist for long, let alone for another fifteen years.

During these years that were so decisive for Finland's independence, Mannerheim's strength had been his ability to see events in a wider European context. He did not predict Germany's downfall in the world war solely because he sympathised with the Allies, but also because he was an officer with a broad analytical and geopolitical outlook who had served for thirty years in one of Europe's biggest armies. But this macro-perspective would also prove to be Mannerheim's Achilles' heel. He was never able to entirely figure out how to communicate with the country's political elite. They engaged in pre-established parliamentary traditions, prioritised the national interest and upheld an ongoing dialogue with civil society, but very rarely took a serious interest in the larger driving forces that influenced Europe's development. A shining exception in this respect was the right-wing Paasikivi, but, typically enough, he was long regarded as an odd figure in the domestic politics of the inter-war years.

In wartime, however, Mannerheim and Finland's well-functioning civil society and political culture had been an unbeatable combination. His professional drive was second to none, and, with the help of broad civic engagement, he had quickly been able to mobilise an army that was ready to make large sacrifices. Of course, the German intervention had also been important to the Whites' victory in Finland. But when the Finnish counter-revolutionaries' performance is compared with that of the Russians, it is nevertheless clear that the latter's failure was above all because they could not rely on a well-organised middle-class and agrarian population.

Less significant from a realpolitik perspective, but important for the country's civil society, were Mannerheim's single-minded actions as a figurehead for the whole power of the state during his time as regent. These pointed the direction for the conduct of all his successors, beginning with Ståhlberg. In this aspect of his role, Mannerheim made good use of his extensive experience of the grand public ceremonies in Imperial Russia. He was, moreover, genuinely talented in this respect, and must also have looked on his tours of the country as a campaign for the forthcoming presidential elections. During his little more than six months as regent, the citizens got to see him meeting local decision-makers, honouring public entertainments with his presence, and inaugurating buildings and memorials of various sorts. When he had to express himself in Finnish, everything was rehearsed in advance. For that reason, he also had prompt notes with him, so that he could address "spontaneous" questions in Finnish to elementary school children and White Guards.

It should also be noted that Mannerheim initiated the creation of two state orders and their corresponding merit badges. The first was the Order of the Cross of Liberty, which was founded for military service on the suggestion of Mannerheim and confirmed by the Senate in March 1918. A little over a year later, Mannerheim, as regent, decided to replace the Cross of Liberty with the Order of the White Rose of Finland. The medals for the two orders created by Mannerheim were designed by the famous artist Akseli Gallen-Kallela, who, on the former's instruction, made their central element the symmetrical form of the Saint George's Cross. Gallen-Kallela functioned as aide to the Regent in the spring and summer of 1919. In this position he was also able to help with the design of the newly formed Defence Council's uniforms and accessories.

5

THE GENTLEMAN

A Comfortable Retirement

"But how wonderful, was it not, to enjoy this day alone with you. Every step I take reminds me of the pleasant day, or more accurately two, that we celebrated here together", wrote the 51-year-old Mannerheim in a letter to Kitty Linder, a society lady twenty years his junior, on 2 November 1918. He was then in Oslo, which at that time was still called Kristiania, and he was about to board a boat to Great Britain to occupy, once again, a key role in Finnish politics for a brief period. But just then he was thinking of his new infatuation, Kitty, whom he had got to know on an exclusive hunting trip to the Norwegian mountains. The trip had been arranged by her half-brother, the then immensely rich Hjalmar Linder, for a small circle of friends in late August and early September 1918. It had been rounded off with a couple of days in Kristiania, where the party had, just to be on the safe side, stayed in the assured luxury of the Grand Hotel.

There were many reasons why Mannerheim took a liking to Kitty Linder. The Linders had been one of the few Finnish noble families in the second half of the nineteenth century to reach, through intermarriages with Russian and Baltic high nobility, lofty positions in the court and central administration of the Russian Empire. Her father, Constantin Linder, had belonged to the same liberal circles in his youth as Mannerheim's father, Carl Robert, but he had quickly changed his tune and gone on to have a distinguished financial and administrative career in Russia. His son Hjalmar Linder had spent a brief period as an official on the

Committee for Finnish Affairs in St Petersburg and as a *valet de chambre* at the Russian court before returning to Finland, where he amassed a vast fortune as an industrialist.

It was at Hjalmar Linder's place that Mannerheim had stayed during his first few months as a Chevalier Guard in St Petersburg. A few years later, Hjalmar wed Mannerheim's elder sister Sophie, but the marriage was quickly dissolved on account of the groom's homosexuality. This minor setback in the families' relations did not obviously disturb their social interactions, which often took place on one of their relatives' estates in Länsi-Uusimaa. Mannerheim clearly felt at home in this particular niche of the Finnish social elite, and as such he could hardly help falling for the beautiful and elegant Catharina Linder, aka Kitty. It is unlikely that he met her before the First World War, since at that time she was living in Germany with her mother, who was descended from a German-Baltic noble family.

Birds of a feather flock together. Genuinely cosmopolitan ladies who met Mannerheim's aesthetic expectations were few and far between in the peripheral nation of Finland. It is quite plausible that Kitty's participation in the Norwegian hunting trip had been arranged in order to lay the ground for a homogamous marriage with Mannerheim. Put bluntly, he needed a presentable wife, since he could expect to be a public person going forward, regardless of the political situation. Besides which, his many letters to Kitty in the winter of 1918–19 are testament to the heartfelt enchantment, or even outright love, that he felt. It is also reasonable to suppose that he missed being in a settled relationship after all his years as a bachelor, although matters of the heart are notoriously difficult to explain with any certainty.

One thing is clear, however: on 12 October 1918, Mannerheim made an application to Hanko Magistrates' Court to divorce Anastasia, whom he had not seen for sixteen years since she moved to France with their daughters. At the time, it was only the Hanko and Tornio magistrates' courts that dealt with divorce cases in which one of the spouses lived abroad, and it was presumed that, as in other divorce cases, the plaintiff accused the defendant of adultery. In Mannerheim's petition, he referenced the fact that his wife had left him and travelled abroad without any intention of returning to their married life. Anastasia received a summons to appear at a hearing in Hanko at the start of March 1919. She did not show up then, nor for the rescheduled proceedings on 7 April, but on that occasion the court heard three witness testimonies and ruled that the divorce would come into effect in ten days' time. Mannerheim also stayed away from the courtroom to avoid scandalous stories in the press, and this secrecy paid off.

Unfortunately, the decision would not strengthen Kitty Linder's fragile ties of affection to Mannerheim. It is apparent from his letters to her that they often discussed the ongoing court process and that he appealed to her for patience, which hints that Mannerheim had proposed to her, or had at least expressed his willingness to do so. In any case, it seems that at some time in spring or summer 1919 Kitty came to the conclusion that she did not want to live with him, presumably both due to their large age difference and his public duties. According to Kitty's nephew Magnus Linder, she would later characterise Mannerheim as an "old bore", which perhaps best sums up why she turned him down.

This old bore was, nevertheless, doing all right by himself. At the end of May 1919, Mannerheim was awarded an honorary doctorate by the Faculty of Philosophy at the University of Helsinki for his scientific observations during his ride through Asia between 1906 and 1908. He clearly welcomed this gesture from the academic community, even if it was mainly occasioned by the fact that he was then regent. He particularly appreciated that his 24-year-old daughter, Sophy, had been chosen as the conferment ceremony's public wreath-weaver, which was an honorary task that, as a rule, went to one of the professors' daughters. Sophy had accompanied him when he returned from the Continent in December 1918, and during the spring of 1919 she had often been permitted to act as hostess at the regent's receptions and dinners. However, she did not take to her circumstances in Finland, and soon thereafter returned to Paris, where she would remain for the rest of her life.

Defeat in the presidential elections in late July 1919 was undeniably a crushing blow for Mannerheim. The victor, K. J. Ståhlberg, was prepared to make him commander-in-chief of the defence forces but did not agree to the substantial powers that Mannerheim demanded, since they would have fundamentally weakened the

President's own authority. Mannerheim, in response, politely declined the post, and quite soon after this began to be viewed as a spent force in political circles. True, he was appointed honorary chairman of the White Guards in August 1919, and he was repeatedly fêted by various right-wing organisations throughout the 1920s. But this did not dispel the other parties' distrust of Mannerheim, which stemmed from his refusal to accept that the military authorities should be subordinate to the country's democratically elected government.

In consequence, Mannerheim did not occupy any state post between 1919 and 1931. At first, he probably regarded this as a temporary climbdown, as he, in common with so many of the old social elite, remained sceptical towards parliamentary democracy's functionality. But, in time, his daily life became filled with sufficiently engaging positions of responsibility and other pleasant routines, as was still typical for well-to-do gentlemen in 1920s Europe.

As a rule, the prerequisite for such a life was that these gentlemen had a sufficiently large and well-managed fortune, which Mannerheim himself lacked. But this issue was solved for him in an auspicious fashion. Shortly after he had lost the presidential election, a petition was published in the bourgeois press which announced the collection of funds for a national gift for "the liberator of the Fatherland". This was presented to Mannerheim when he arrived back in Finland in February 1920, after a six-month sojourn on the Continent. Hundreds of thousands of Finns had taken part in the collection, the proceeds of which totalled 7,600,000 Finnish marks. Mannerheim would live the rest of his life on the generous interest income from the gift. Wisely enough, it was decided that he would not have access to the fund's capital itself and that he would be disconnected from its management. The income ensured that he henceforth led a lavish life, seldom seeing any reason to choose anything less than the highest quality or price range.

That Mannerheim was preparing himself for a comfortable retreat was also apparent when, on his return from Europe in 1920, he rented a spacious residence in the centre of Helsinki. This was at 5 Mariankatu, right opposite the House of Nobility where, fourteen years earlier, he had voted for the introduction of the democratically elected parliament, the politics of which he now found difficult to accept. He mainly decorated his home with the furniture and other personal property that he had collected in Warsaw, and which had stood undisturbed in storage throughout the entire war. Now it could all be shipped completely undamaged over the Baltic Sea back to Finland. The articles of greatest value were, naturally, the souvenirs and cult objects that Mannerheim had brought back from Asia, but he was of course also grateful for the return of his beautiful furniture and the library that he had been able to acquire over his years in Russian service.

When the three-year rental contract for the house on Mariankatu ran out in summer 1923, Mannerheim had already made up his mind to move into a wooden villa owned by his hunting companion, Karl Fazer, in eastern Kaivopuisto, a coastal park just south of central Helsinki. At that point the run-down building was divided into six small rental properties, but the intention was to convert it into a villa with all modern conveniences. This was by no means a new proposition: Fazer had previously planned to demolish it to make space for a stone house for his personal use. The residential area around Kaivopuisto had formerly been somewhat on the city's periphery, but during this period it was being transformed into Helsinki's most fashionable neighbourhood. It was not only Fazer and other rich people who were seeking to move there: many of the foreign embassies that began their operations in Helsinki in the 1920s also came to be located in this area.

In the mid-1910s, Fazer had ordered detailed designs for a stone house from the famous architect Sigurd Frosterus. Although the plans were shelved, it is evident that Fazer had them in mind when he offered to build a stone house for Mannerheim on the same site. After Mannerheim made it clear that he would prefer that the wooden villa was renovated, the architects Karl Malmström and Robert Tikkanen drew up new designs for it in June 1923. The villa was located at the very top of Kaivopuisto's steep slope down to the South Harbour, which provided a fabulous eastward view over Suomenlinna, Finland's island fortress, built in the mid-1700s by Augustin Ehrensvärd, a distant relative of Mannerheim. Accordingly, he had a portrait of Ehrensvärd's mother, Anna Margareta (née Mannerheim), hung in his dining room. The house's roof ridge was raised significantly and tiled red, while the façade was covered in simple American-style wood panelling and painted white.

The architects' interior designs called to mind Frosterus's original plan, even if many of the solutions were dictated by Mannerheim's exacting requirements. All the contemporary service operations were placed in the cellar: the kitchen, the butler's pantry, the laundry room, the boiler room, the staff quarters and garage. From the cellar there were servants' stairs and a service lift up to the other two floors; these were in a secluded section in the middle of the house, which meant that a large part of the service could be conducted invisibly and soundlessly. The home was also equipped with central heating and hot-water pipes, which were by no means the norm in new-builds of the 1920s.

The main entrance opened out onto Kalliolinnantie in the west; it was situated on the middle floor along with all the rooms intended for guests and for hosting receptions. From the entrance there was a cloakroom on the left and a spacious hall on the right, where the host greeted all guests and where, not coincidentally, all his most important honours, trophies and souvenirs were on display. After the hall came a drawing room with a grand piano and plenty of natural light. From here one could proceed to a long, narrow balcony that looked out onto the South Harbour in the east, or alternatively enter the library with its darker décor. At the other end of the floor there was an elegant dining room with space for up to forty dinner guests. On the upper floor there were three bedrooms, two bathrooms and a smaller library that also served as a study for guests.

Mannerheim carefully followed progress on the building work, and since his landlord was unusually receptive to his wishes it went mostly as he had hoped. Every skirting board, wall colour, light switch and cornice was selected and placed according to Mannerheim's instructions. In the process, he familiarised himself with interior decoration with the help of the architects and the guidebook *Hemmet som konstverk* (1923; The Home as a Work of Art), which their colleague Gustaf Strengell had published and given to him that same year. Still, it took many years before everything was in its place, that is, until Mannerheim had managed to supplement the personal property shipped from Warsaw with furniture, artworks and other decorative objects that complemented the whole. During his travels abroad, therefore, he often carried a little notebook with him containing details of the home's key measurements, so that he could more easily decide if, say, an interesting equestrian picture or Baroque chest was the right size.

The end result truly was a work of art, which today can be appreciated by everyone who visits the Mannerheim Museum now housed there. That it was designed so well, of course, was partly a consequence of Mannerheim having, for the first time in his life, both the time and his own money to realise his ideas. The art historian Bengt von Bonsdorff has observed that both the interior and exterior indicate that Mannerheim was striving for a symmetrical and beautifully coloured seventeenth-century style, of the sort that had characterised his childhood home at Louhisaari Manor. Each room had its own colour code and complementary furniture. In the middle floor's drawing and dining rooms, he had portrait copies of renowned forefathers and paintings of landscapes hung, while his articles from Asia principally decorated the table and walls in the library.

Present-day readers may well get the impression that Mannerheim's interest in interior decoration was unusual or downright bizarre. This is understandable. In the early 1920s, a large proportion of the country's populace still lived in much more humble conditions. Running water or a personal bathroom were luxuries that only the wealthiest in society could afford. It was still the case in the late 1930s that not even large working-class families could count on having more than two rooms and a kitchen, equivalent to an area of 40 to 50 square metres today. The floor space in Mannerheim's Kaivopuisto villa totalled almost 300 square metres. One caveat, however, is that people in his rarefied social stratum were expected to reserve a significant part of their home for public relations purposes, where guests were welcomed into an environment that reflected the host's social status and level of education.

These expectations meant that Mannerheim quickly had to create such a home when he returned to Finland, and, in the absence of a wife, it was also down to him to do the decorating. This was an even more daunting task because his father had misappropriated all the heirlooms around which Mannerheim would have been able to construct an elegant interior. His starting point in this respect was like that of the nouveau-riche capitalists, who valiantly tried to carve out credible upper-class homes without having their own symbolic family antiques and artefacts. That Mannerheim's reconstruction was so much more successful was due to the fact that, in contrast to the parvenus, he had spent his whole life in such environments, that is, in homes suffused with hundreds of years' worth of heirlooms.

Another structure that Mannerheim painstakingly planned was his summer villa Stormhällan in Hanko, which was built in 1922 on a small island off the east end of the town's popular bathing beach. There he found time to carry out a number of extensions to the property before he sold it in the mid-1930s. His own descriptions of his stays at the beautiful summer house indicate that he heartily enjoyed the open sea, the sunny weather and his sporadic efforts to grow flowers. "My flowers exist more in my imagination than in reality", he admitted to his younger sister Eva Sparre in the late 1920s, and in truth he rarely stayed at the villa for more than a few days at a time. Between 1927 and 1933 he also owned a summer café on the adjoining shore, which he gave a Chinese-style name: The House of the Four Winds. He gladly made a personal appearance there when the opportunity arose.

Fig. 5.1: Mannerheim (second from right) on the steps of his summer villa in Hanko with Dutch guests, 1925.

The Aristocrat's Afternoon

Stig Jägerskiöld's extensive Mannerheim biography has been denounced over the years for being in many respects uncritical or a straight-up panegyric. Nevertheless, in one respect Jägerskiöld's portrait of Mannerheim is unrivalled: he succeeded better than any other biographer in describing the aristocrat's private life and forms of sociability. This was not only due to the fact that for a long time he had sole access to Mannerheim's personal correspondence. Equally important is that Jägerskiöld had an exquisite way with words and personal experience of the epoch's upper-class culture. Latter-day historians rarely achieve such accurate descriptions, since they have a tendency to project their contemporary linguistic and class norms onto Mannerheim's time.

Over the thirty years that Mannerheim built his career in Russia, Finnish as a language gained a dominant role in Finland's public life, while the proportion of Swedish-speaking inhabitants decreased from 15 to 10 per cent. At the same time, Helsinki's population quadrupled, and the proportion of Finnish-speaking residents increased from 45 to 65 per cent. A comparable linguistic shift was also happening among the upper classes: at the outbreak of the Second World War, only a quarter of the social elite were registered as Swedish-speaking.

However, this certainly does not mean that the language used by the different social elites changed at the same pace. In the inter-war years, the Finnish-language elite spoke excellent, or at least good, Swedish, since they had been educated in it for the entirety of their schooling. Moreover, they practised it daily in the company of their countrymen, whose Finnish was, quite simply, not sufficient for a more abstract or nuanced conversation. Mannerheim, in many respects, belonged to the category of Finns who spoke stilted Finnish. It is doubtful whether his skills in this language ever reached the same level as his proficiency in Russian, which he had taken great pains to acquire. The extremely few private letters in Finnish recovered from his extensive correspondence do little to dispel this suspicion.

It is likely, therefore, that Mannerheim generally conducted unofficial conversations in Swedish when he had tête-à-têtes with

Finland's leading political and military decision-makers. By extension, this would mean that many of the decisions made about
Finland's national security between 1918 and 1946 were arrived at
in Swedish. This assumption is difficult to verify, but in both
P. E. Svinhufvud's and J. K. Paasikivi's case, it is abundantly clear
from many documents that their common language with Mannerheim
was Swedish. This was also the case, of course, for many of his closest military colleagues, such as Rudolf Walden, Hugo Österman and
Erik Heinrichs.

At the same time, it is worth keeping in mind that Mannerheim
absolutely did not self-identify with the Swedish-speaking cultural
circles in Finland. In the 1910s these had started to call themselves
"Finnish-Swedes", seeing themselves as their own nationality distinct from the Finnish-speaking majority. Mannerheim, in contrast,
consistently referred to himself as a "Finn" and never showed any
sympathies for either the pro-Swedish or the pro-Finnish nationalists in the often bitter language disputes of the interwar years. In this
sense, too, he embodied the attitude of the old upper class, for
whom it was largely immaterial which national language should be
spoken under the prevailing social conditions. This was because they
spoke their own language among themselves, in that they used
words, concepts and articulation that could only be deciphered by
those within their own circle.

Even if Swedish remained the dominant language of intercourse
in Mannerheim's private life, he regularly corresponded with his
continental friends and acquaintances in French, English and
Russian. From time to time, he also made use of these languages in
Helsinki. The diplomatic corps still used French as its common language, although English was starting to gain popularity among its
members. They gladly welcomed Mannerheim as a guest at their
receptions. In turn, they were a regular presence at his own dinner
parties. Mannerheim also used Russian fairly frequently with the
exiled Russians in Finland who, in common with himself, had
escaped Bolshevik rule in their motherland and brooded over the
idea of reinstating the old regime.

It is most likely that these Russian-language conversations typically took place in more discreet circumstances, since the long-
repressed anti-Russian feelings in Finland had quickly risen to the

surface with the onset of independence. In many cases, Mannerheim and his exiled friends could circumvent potential hostility by speaking French. It was the language they had often used together in Imperial Russia, and it was also the one that Mannerheim preferred. That said, Eleonora Joffe has shown, in her impressive overview of Mannerheim's lifelong correspondence with his Russian friends and acquaintances, that he would continue to write in Russian on occasion in the future, even if French, as might be expected, tended to predominate in this context too.

To understand how Mannerheim framed his life, it is also important to remember that he, like plenty of others in the old upper class, remained sceptical towards many of the changes that the transition to real representative democracy had wrought in independent Finland. As such, it was inevitable that he and his social class often viewed the newly elected political elite as populist and short-sighted. This was not only due to the repeated changes of government in the 1920s, but also to the fact that freedom of speech and the democratic institutions had given rise to an increasingly acrimonious public rhetoric. While class hatred, Russophobia and language persecution had been actively cultivated between 1906 and 1914, it was only after parliament had gained the political authority to drive through its demands that these wars of words took on a more serious significance.

We know today that the constitution that Mannerheim himself had ratified in 1919 would remain in force for the rest of the twentieth century. Until the mid-1930s, however, it was regarded by many on both the left and the right as a temporary and largely unstable social experiment. It was assumed that, over time, it would be replaced either by a socialist system or by a return to more authoritarian rule. It is obvious that Mannerheim numbered himself among the sceptics. Throughout the 1920s he maintained contact with various right-wing and reactionary circles, even those of far-right activists who had no confidence in the power of the democratic system to protect Finland and its independence from Bolshevik Russia. Consequently, he never explicitly disassociated himself from the far-right activists when they installed themselves at the head of the populist right-wing Lapua Movement between 1929 and 1932.

It would nevertheless be an exaggeration to characterise the Mannerheim of the 1920s as a far-right extremist. He was sooner a reactionary, in that, in common with most of his relatives and friends, he clung on tightly to the lifestyle and world view that had predominated during his upbringing in the 1870s and 1880s. He carried with him attitudes and values from the time of an estate society, regardless of the fact that civil society and democracy had broken through between 1890 and 1920. But social upheaval in no way led to the disappearance of long-established ways of thinking; rather the old and the new existed side by side. Both in the recently formed republic and in other regions of interwar Europe, a surprising number of things continued in much the same way as they had in the decades preceding 1914.

Mannerheim's private life during the interwar years is, in fact, an unusually detailed example of the continuity of the old estate culture. After moving into his spacious villa in eastern Kaivopuisto and taking on a few suitably challenging positions of responsibility, his life assumed a leisurely rhythm and regularity. His day started with a cold bath, exercises and various other morning duties that were necessary for a gentleman. At the same time, his batman put out the clothes and accessories that Mannerheim had asked for that day, while his two servants laid out a simple breakfast in the dining room below. After this he took a stroll into the city centre, or else was driven by his chauffeur either to the riding stables or out on other errands.

While his racing and show-jumping days were definitely behind him, cross-country and riding exercise remained an almost daily feature of his life until the end of the Second World War, when he was nearly 80 years old. Out in the city he usually ate lunch at one of Helsinki's most reputable restaurants, which meant that he was often seen at the Hotel Kämp, the Helsinki Bourse Club and König on the North Esplanade, and, from 1937, at the Savoy on the other side of the park. And if he did not go to a reception or dinner party in the evening, he often enjoyed going to a concert together with one of his intimate society ladies. The newspaper *Hufvudstadsbladet* served as Mannerheim's morning reading. When he retired to his library later in the day, he read personal and military histories, travel and hunting accounts and non-fiction works on hippology. Over time, his book collection came to comprise nearly 3,000 volumes.

One of Mannerheim's favourite hobbies in Helsinki was to arrange his own dinner parties. He threw himself into their planning and execution to such an extent that, over time, they became famous as one of the gastronomic and cultural high points in the city's society life. A number of books have been written about Mannerheim's talents in the culinary sphere, and how he enjoyed exchanging recipes and opinions on cooking with his younger sister Eva Sparre, now living in Sweden. It is undeniable that he knew how to put together a delicious menu with drink pairings; in part, of course, this was a consequence of his having had the benefit of being invited to countless such dinner parties. But it is clear that his gastronomic interest was just as much a reflection of a talent, and one well honed over the years: Mannerheim was a genuine gourmet, with an innate sense of which dishes would best suit a particular event. He generally favoured continental menus that borrowed elements of Russian and Polish cuisines.

The evenings were usually rounded off by a musical performance in the salon, where everyone gathered after dinner. Some of the invitation lists from these get-togethers have been preserved, and among them can even be found separate seating instructions.

Fig. 5.2: Mannerheim (second from left) as singer Aulikki Rautavaara's dining partner at the Grand Restaurant Börs in the Helsinki Stock Exchange Building, 1936.

Mannerheim paid special attention to this matter, since the dinner parties served both his social and political ends. The host would sit at the middle of the table, facing the swing doors of the kitchen staff, and directed the service with a foot-operated bell that was hidden under the rug. This he would tread on discreetly when he wanted to call staff to the room. The male guest of honour sat opposite him, while the female counterpart was naturally his dining partner. The seating arrangements for the other guests were outlined with equal care. Consideration was not only given to the guests' stations, personalities and language proficiency, but also how best to coax interesting rumours and useful information from them. Diplomats and outspoken consorts were of particular interest here.

During these dinner parties and salon discussions Mannerheim made exemplary use of his powers of conversation, which he had refined over the years and for which, moreover, he had a natural aptitude. Nonetheless, it would be misleading to describe him on these occasions as a relaxed raconteur, in the modern sense of the term. The combination of affability, tact and a suitably jocular outspokenness was a conscious role he played to perfection—and with the same aplomb that had been required of him when he obtained audiences with the Emperor, only a few years earlier in St Petersburg.

Mannerheim was also able to deploy his conversational skills with another seminal figure in geopolitical history, on those occasions when he met Winston Churchill. One such encounter took place in late January 1936, when they engaged in conversation during a dinner arranged for Mannerheim while he was visiting London as Finland's representative for the funeral of King George V. Although Churchill was a political outsider at this time, and in a very talkative mood, to boot, he still listened carefully as Mannerheim gave some critical feedback on the fourth volume of his renowned work on the First World War.

Churchill had described the victory of the Finnish Whites in the 1918 civil war as being, in essence, a consequence of the Germans' military intervention. Mannerheim, understandably, was loath to accept this interpretation, and he persuaded Churchill to revise it in a forthcoming Swedish edition of the volume. However, according to Markku Ruotsila, who has written an outstanding study on Churchill's Finnish contacts, this was more of a diplomatic gesture by the future prime minister than a sign that he had reconsidered his fundamental attitude towards the role of small nations in geopolitics.

Another of the aristocratic interests that Mannerheim regularly engaged in was hunting, which he pursued every autumn, together with his friends, both in Finland and abroad. His domestic hunting party was often invited to the grounds of Petter Forsström, an industrialist who was also a leading supporter of the far-right Lapua Movement, which were located in Bromarv, west of Hanko Peninsula. Another often obliging partner was Mannerheim's land-lord, Karl Fazer, who had long leased hunting grounds in Jokioinen. Fazer actually died there in 1932, during a particularly rough and challenging hunt. Mannerheim kept a moderate arsenal of firearms, including a British double-barrelled shotgun that was necessary for hunting small game like hares and birds. But in contrast to Fazer, who had been placed twelfth in the men's trap at the 1912 Summer Olympics in Stockholm, Mannerheim was not a particularly sure shot. What mattered, however, was not the size of the spoils, but rather the invigorating outdoor life and the evening get-togethers that the hunt host usually put on.

One almost annual destination for Mannerheim's hunting expe-ditions during the interwar years was the Austrian Alps. There he rented grounds for his real passion, big-game hunting, which prin-cipally involved stalking chamois at dawn high in the Tyrol moun-tains. As a rule, the trips were combined with promenades and drives through the cultured Austrian landscape. He made the last of these hunting trips in the summer of 1939, when the Great Powers were already conducting secret negotiations on the adjust-ment of Europe's political map which would soon have negative consequences for Finland. But Mannerheim had an unusual ability to enjoy the moment and make the most of every opportunity that came his way. Or, as his close military colleague Erik Heinrichs would later put it: "the extraction of the utmost possible from what life had to offer, such was the slogan he never uttered, but always followed".

During this period, Mannerheim also embarked on two trips to British India, where he collected numerous hunting trophies and exotic anecdotes, which he would later enthusiastically transcribe in his memoirs. Without a doubt, his most renowned trophy was the tiger-skin rug, replete with snarling head, that he had acquired during a hunt led by the King of Nepal in January 1937. Measuring over 3.2 metres in length, it furnished the floor of his salon. Each trip was arranged in co-operation with British servicemen whom he had got to know during their stays in Finland, and who were, at those moments, stationed in India. Mannerheim also had political motives for carrying out these expeditions. He saw his first trip, in spring 1928, as an opportunity to avoid the ten-year anniversary of the 1918 victory parade, for he was largely dissatisfied with the direction the country's defence had taken since then. A little over eight years later, at the turn of 1936, he was happy to stay away from Finland to avoid getting mixed up in the political battle that was underway in advance of the presidential elections in February.

As fate's whim would have it, both these trips coincided with a death that affected him deeply. In spring 1928 his elder sister Sophie passed away, and in 1936 so, too, did his former wife Anastasia; these were the two women who presumably knew him best. Sophie's death struck him particularly hard, and after his younger brother Johan also died, in 1934, he carried on his most intimate correspondence with his younger sister, Eva Sparre, and with Rudolf Walden. In a letter to Eva, Mannerheim described the industrialist and Russia connoisseur Walden as "my best friend after my brother [Johan]". Mannerheim has often been characterised as a lonely person who stood high on a pedestal, but perhaps someone who had been so psychologically scarred was no longer capable or even interested in close interpersonal relationships. Each person in his vicinity performed a special function in his commitments and pastimes, but beyond this they were expected to slip discreetly out of the spotlight, like extras in a play.

Anastasia died in Paris on 31 December 1936. Her unobtrusive existence had, over the years, become less and less glamorous, despite the fact that Mannerheim had paid her a small allowance since the 1920s and had otherwise tried to support her. In the 1930s she started to have serious health problems, and in autumn 1936, just before her death, the former couple met in a spirit of reconciliation for one last time in Paris, after a 34-year interval. Mannerheim was in India when he received the sorrowful news of her passing in a telegram from his daughter Sophy. At the same time, he also received a last letter from Anastasia, in which she had dictated her gratitude for their reconciliation. "I am unutterably thankful to Providence that so many bitter moments and memories could be erased", wrote Mannerheim, who, at the age of 69, had by that time already started to make preparations for his own departure.

However, that would not befall him for another fifteen years. Despite his occasional bouts of melancholy, Mannerheim was a decidedly sanguine person, who continued to enjoy the company of stylish, high-class ladies throughout his life. In the first half of the 1920s, he periodically consorted with the beautiful French countess, Jeanne de Salverte, and later in the decade he was enchanted by the French competitive yachtswoman Virginie Hériot. Even in the 1930s, he delighted in dining with society beauties and other celebrated women in Helsinki. It is impossible to say to what extent the elegantly framed courtship gave rise to an active sex life. Perhaps Mannerheim had realised his limits in that department when he turned 60 in the late 1920s. Or perhaps it was simply the case that he was able to appreciate the benefits of enjoying food, wine, trips and the right environment in the most pleasant company possible.

Grey Eminence

As has been noted, the further the 1920s progressed, the less likely it became that Mannerheim would ever return to public office. For want of another occupation, he therefore took his place at the head of a number of organisations and institutions, which could, in different ways, benefit from his leadership skills, reputation and contacts. In autumn 1920, a humanitarian organisation was founded to support the wellbeing of vulnerable children and youths, partly on the initiative of Mannerheim's sister Sophie. It was christened General Mannerheim's League for Child Welfare, and its namesake was appointed as its honorary chairman. At the beginning he engaged with the association in a variety of ways, giving it a considerable sum of money (75,000 marks) and allowing for the use of a room as its office at his apartment on Mariankatu. The league's awareness-raising activities soon became nationwide, but, until the 1930s, it was met with opposition within both the labour movement and the Agrarian League on account of its connection to Mannerheim.

Fig. 5.3: The inauguration of the new Lastenlinna Children's Hospital in Helsinki, October 1921. From left: Bishop Jaakko Gummerus, Head Nurse Sophie Mannerheim, Gustaf Mannerheim, Head Nurse Toini Leikola and Professor Arvo Ylppö.

In February 1922 Mannerheim was appointed chairman of the Finnish Red Cross on the suggestion of his old schoolmate, senior physician Richard Faltin. The doctor realised that Mannerheim would be the best person to make the organisation more efficient, and sure enough the Red Cross developed into a central actor in the country's medical care during his nearly 30-year stewardship. At the start, it was a matter of procuring better office space, stockpiling supplies for emergency aid, erecting field hospitals for crisis situations and establishing connections with other national healthcare organisations. In the late 1920s, under Mannerheim's leadership, a fund-raising subscription was launched for the organisation's own hospital, and in 1932 the Red Cross Hospital, built in a functionalist style, was opened in Helsinki. Alongside the usual medical care, the hospital also offered further education in war surgery, which would soon need to be put into practice.

In autumn 1920 Mannerheim was appointed chairman of the Union Bank's supervisory board. He continued to hold the honorary position until 1936, even after its merger with another bank

(Helsingin Osakepankki) in the early 1930s. Among Mannerheim's other civilian positions of responsibility were his honorary chairmanship of Finland's Boy Scout Association, the activities of which broadly corresponded with his own outdoor interests and Anglo-Saxon sympathies. Moreover, it is evident that he saw the Scouts as a suitable nursery for the bourgeois White Guards, who played such an important role in interwar society that they in many instances dictated the limits of what was politically possible in Finland.

Certainly, Mannerheim's relationship with the White Guards organisation was somewhat complicated, even if he was appointed its honorary commander right after losing the 1919 presidential elections. In summer 1921 a serious schism emerged between the government and the White Guards' leadership. It had its origins in a faction of Germanophile White Guard activists who were strongly critical of the government's current border-state policy. After two swift changes in the White Guards' leadership, the government ultimately agreed that their commander-in-chief could report directly to the President.

During this upheaval, Mannerheim was nominated to the post, but President Ståhlberg rejected this out of hand. Ståhlberg had reason to suspect that the intention was to transform the White Guards into a militia faithful to Mannerheim; if that were to happen, they could not be counted on to remain loyal to the state's leadership. The position went instead to Lieutenant-Colonel Lauri Malmberg, who, in his capacity as a Finnish-speaking Jaeger officer, was judged to be more loyal to the government than Mannerheim. He was also seen as more dependable than other older servicemen with an imperial career behind them, who, like Mannerheim, had been widely branded "Russo-Swedish" officers since 1918.

Malmberg would remain in this post right up to the disbandment of the White Guards in autumn 1944, and under his leadership their paramilitary activities were gradually developed as a complement to the country's conscription army. At the same time, their original role as a domestic military police force was downplayed. Nevertheless, this did not significantly allay the labour movement's distrust of the organisation, since throughout the interwar years the White Guards and their veteran groups ardently reinforced the Whites' self-glorifying interpretation of the 1918 civil war.

Mannerheim was obviously not pleased at having been sidelined. Furthermore, he was among those who thought that the White Guards ought also to remain a defence against domestic enemies, that is, revolutionary socialists. The situation did not improve in the mid-1920s, when the government replaced Chief of General Staff Oscar Enckell and the commander-in-chief of the armed forces, Karl Wilkama, with two significantly younger Jaeger officers. Both Enckell and Wilkama had risen high in the ranks during their military careers in Russia, and both were forced out of their positions in the Finnish Army by the vitriolic campaign of former Jaegers. On this occasion, Mannerheim again appeared as a candidate for commander-in-chief of the armed forces and for other key positions in defence. But, just as before, it all came to nothing because his distinctly elitist profile awoke suspicion among both Agrarian League members and liberal progressives, for whom his clash with President Ståhlberg lay fresh in the memory.

This is also why his supporters were unsuccessful in driving through Mannerheim's promotion to field marshal before the ten-year anniversary of the White Army's victory parade in spring 1928. The loss of prestige was also an essential reason why Mannerheim decided to avoid the anniversary parade by setting out on his first trip to India. But his close friends made an urgent appeal to him, declaring that his protest had occasioned great disappointment among the thousands of veterans who were set to take part in the parade. And so, Mannerheim swallowed his annoyance and returned home in time to put on a brave face and take a visible role in the celebrations. Behind the scenes, however, he continued to make cutting remarks about the incessant party conflicts and the short-sighted decisions of the country's parliamentary democracy.

As has been noted, Mannerheim's underlying mentality was reactionary. But it is important to stress that his sullen attitude towards parliamentary democracy was nevertheless not particularly unusual in interwar Europe. On the contrary, this system of governance was proving to be a disappointment for most European countries experiencing it for the first time. The sudden multiplicity of opinions and needs made the processes of parliamentary decision-making considerably slower, while exposing more clearly than ever the class conflicts, and other social ones, that had earlier been kept hidden. On the political right there were many, in common with Mannerheim, who were dissatisfied with how their social status and real power had declined. As long as the economic forecasts were good, the middle class had a decidedly more positive attitude towards democracy. When, however, the whole capitalist world was dragged into a deep economic crisis in 1929, they too became more receptive to anti-democratic or outright fascist ideas. Within the labour movement, many were again tempted by the prospect of communist rule directed from afar by Moscow, as the Social Democrats' reformist socialism had failed to produce the desired result.

As a consequence, the majority of European countries had abolished their parliamentary democracies by the late 1930s, having instead introduced different forms of authoritarian or downright dictatorial rule, such as in Italy, Germany and Spain. Finland managed to escape this fate, even though the rise of the far-right Lapua Movement, in autumn 1929, followed a pattern that resulted in autocratic rule in every other newly formed state in Eastern Europe. Just as in these countries, Finland had gained its independence through an intense conflict with Bolshevik Russia, which meant that, in bourgeois quarters, there was widespread unease about the ever-present threat of a Soviet invasion. At the outset, therefore, many were sympathetic towards the Lapua Movement because of its radically anti-communist aims. In summer 1930 the movement forced a change of government, and in the autumn the new government pushed through a prohibition on all communist activities in Finland. However, at this time a broad parliamentary front took a stand against the movement, following the kidnapping and murder of Social Democrat councillor Onni Happonen in September, and the kidnapping of former President K. J. Ståhlberg and his wife a month later. It was ultimately disbanded after an ignominious coup attempt—the Mäntsälä Rebellion—in March 1932.

There is no doubt that Mannerheim sympathised with the Lapua Movement and kept himself well-informed of its objectives through his friends, who were initially part of its unofficial leadership. Many prominent figures in the country's export industry belonged to this clique, such as Mannerheim's confidant Rudolf Walden and relative Jacob von Julin. The latter financed a large portion of the movement's public activities, and also saw its anti-communist ambitions as a way to take the wind out of the labour movement's strike actions. Mannerheim, however, was careful not to actively involve himself in the movement, as doing so could have damaged his reputation and hindered his own objectives, namely, to regain a position at the forefront of the country's national defence. At the same time, it was worth his while to tactfully support the anti-communist movement's overall aim. Consequently, he stood together with the President and the Prime Minister as guests of honour at the Peasant March in Senate Square, in the centre of Helsinki, on 7 July 1930. Three months later, in advance of the parliamentary elections, he gave a public statement in which he supported the candidates who, in the spirit of the Lapua Movement, promised to vote for a prohibition of all communist activities in the country.

Fig. 5.4: Field Marshal Mannerheim on a ride in Helsinki's Central Park, 1936.

This time Mannerheim managed, by and large, to get the balance right. After parliament had accepted the anti-communist laws in October 1930, the domestic political debate continued to be heated until the presidential elections in February 1931. In these, the Conservative Svinhufvud triumphed over K. J. Ståhlberg, the anti-Lapua figurehead, by the narrowest possible margin in the electoral college vote (151 to 149). Svinhufvud's victory ensured Mannerheim's return as a central actor in the country's defence and security policy. The idea that Mannerheim could be appointed chairman of the government's consultative Defence Council had already been posited within the Lapua Movement in 1930. The proposal was in line with the movement's other demands, and also received the support of the government of the time. Mannerheim signalled his interest in the role, but only gave a definite answer after it became clear that Ståhlberg—his political antagonist since 1919—had lost the presidential elections.

The formal appointment of Mannerheim as Chairman of the Defence Council came three weeks after Svinhufvud had taken office, on 20 March 1931. While its consultative function persisted, upon Mannerheim's request it was also given a far more active role in the preparation and planning of the defence budget and in the development of national defence as a whole. The council could now make proposals directly to the President, thereby clearly disengaging itself from government oversight. The Defence Minister, who had previously functioned as the chairman, was not even allowed to continue as an ordinary member, although he still had the right to attend the council's meetings.

As Kari Selén has established in his extensive study of the Defence Council, this meant that its parliamentary ties were severed and it was converted into a distinct military organ, since all its members, with the exception of Mannerheim, were officers in active service. Mannerheim's unusual position in the restructured council was also down to the fact that he was already 63 years old at the time of his appointment, three years over the pensionable age for a general. Moreover, he had come to an unofficial agreement with President Svinhufvud, that, upon a possible outbreak of a war, he would be appointed as commander of the defence forces. This was something that the council's other members got wind of, as did others with key roles in security politics.

While the hushed prospect of him once again assuming the role of commander-in-chief certainly increased Mannerheim's prestige and his opportunities for influence, we should consider whether it was seen as particularly likely to happen at that moment in time. In spring 1931 there were no obvious signs that Europe was drifting towards another war between the Great Powers. It is true that Finland's chilly eastern relations reached their freezing point in 1930 and 1931, due to the campaign of terror pursued by the Lapua Movement against the Finnish Communists, as well as the Finnish nationalists' criticisms of the Soviets' forced collectivisation of Ingria region's Finnish-speaking farmers. But the tension was quickly alleviated when Finland and the Baltic states entered into a non-aggression pact with the Soviet Union in 1932. Furthermore, it was no secret at the time that the Soviet Union was still badly drained by the civil war and the Bolsheviks' dictatorship.

The appointment of Mannerheim as the Defence Council's chairman was probably, first and foremost, a way to quieten the right-wing Lapua sympathisers in the military, and to mitigate the White Guards' irritation that a democratically elected parliament still had the last word in the country's domestic politics. Even though Mannerheim was in fine fettle and was not shy about his desire to direct the country's defence policy, the majority of his peers must have assumed that the sexagenarian would fairly soon be forced to step down from the post, or, failing that, die with his boots on. This calculation presumably also lay behind the broad support that Mannerheim's comeback received from high-ranking Jaeger officers, all of whom were in their forties. He was, quite simply, no longer seen as an obstacle, but rather as a means of increasing the army's prestige and its independence from parliament.

It is more difficult to evaluate how Mannerheim himself regarded the future. An educated guess is that he wanted to make rapid headway in improving the country's defences. He regarded doing so as a necessity, since he was convinced that sooner or later Finland would be drawn into an armed conflict with the Soviet Union. As John Screen has pointed out in his superb Mannerheim biography, the fight against the Bolshevik Empire in Russia would continue to be the guiding star for all Mannerheim's activities throughout the rest of his life. Nonetheless, no one at the time could have imagined that this would entail him acting as commander-in-chief in two further wars against the Soviet Union.

The influential right-wing extremists in the Lapua Movement had wanted Mannerheim to put himself at the head of their anti-democratic demands and to acquire similar authoritarian powers to those of Józef Piłsudski in Poland or Kemal Atatürk in Turkey. Mannerheim, however, had grown wise as a result of his previous missteps in the power play of domestic politics, and was no longer willing to risk his reputation by openly challenging the country's

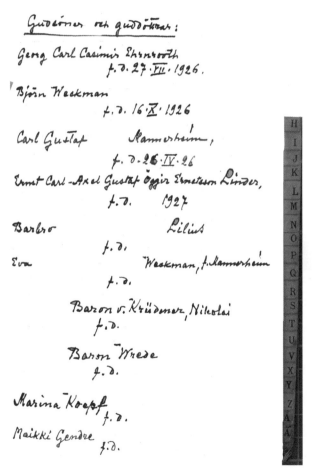

Fig. 5.5: A page from Mannerheim's hand-written telephone directory, listing his godchildren, late 1920s. Among the list is his older brother's grandson and namesake, Count Carl Gustaf.

democratic institutions. He chose, therefore, to pursue his aims as a grey eminence through his informal channels to President Svinhufvud and others in central positions of power in the country. This happened, for example, in relation to the Lapua Movement's attempted coup in Mäntsälä in 1932. Mannerheim strongly urged Svinhufvud to agree to a change of government and to appoint his friend Rudolf Walden as the new prime minister, but when this was unsuccessful Mannerheim retreated surreptitiously into the exclusive club of extra-parliamentary influencers.

6

STORM WARNING

Hitler's Bombshells

"If they don't come from some other country, Hitler will make sure that the bombshells follow each other in quick succession", wrote Mannerheim, somewhat light-heartedly, about the global situation on 21 March 1933. He was corresponding with his younger kinsman G. A. Gripenberg, who had been appointed the Finnish Envoy in London earlier that spring. Mannerheim was quite correct: three days later, Hitler, Germany's newly appointed Chancellor, pushed through the Enabling Act, which strangled the

Fig. 6.1: Mannerheim with his aide-de-camp in front of his private residence in the mid-1930s.

Reichstag's real influence; and in July of that year the Nazi Party became the only permitted political party in the country. In August, Mannerheim sent his brother Johan a short review of *Mein Kampf* from *The Times*, describing its careful characterisation of the book as a "well-made analysis". In December 1933, he wrote to Johan's wife, Palaemona Mannerheim, that the consequences of Hitler's use of power undeniably raised questions, "but I think that they will clear the air and that the situation out in the world, which is now crystallising, will have gained a great deal of clarity".

In other words, Mannerheim's reaction to Hitler's seizure of power was initially one of vague curiosity and, in certain respects, open admiration. He had not previously paid much attention to the 44-year-old Nazi leader, whose strident demagogy and surprising electoral successes had received many column inches in the Finnish press. Until this time, however, the media had treated Hitler as a passing political fancy, but now such dismissive attitudes were vanishing fast. In late autumn 1934, Mannerheim shared his impressions with his sister Eva after a private trip to Germany, revealing that he had realised the price the Germans had paid for the Nazi regime's unquestionably rapid advances: "The methods are often closely related to Moscow's, but it all happens at such a pace, that sometimes it seems utterly terrifying."

At this point in time, no one could have known what Hitler's rule would result in. In the first half of the 1930s, North America and Europe's capitalist economies were ravaged by the Great Depression, which had far-reaching consequences for social development and political culture in most countries. It was not only in Germany that the economic troubles and political conflicts led to an ultra-nationalistic and anti-democratic regime, comparable to Mussolini's fascist leadership, which had snatched power in Italy back in the 1920s. Most of the new states that had come into existence in Eastern and Central Europe after the First World War also developed along similar lines. Their representative democracies proved to be far too fragile to successfully provide welfare and social stability.

Even in those countries that held on to their parliamentary democracies, the economic crisis pushed to the fore a more far-sighted and state-led form of interventionist politics. In the United

States the big social project was named the New Deal. In Sweden, the Social Democrats carried out similar social and economic reforms with the vision of "The People's Home" (*Folkhemmet*; the Swedish welfare state model) in mind. Equivalent initiatives were concurrently launched in the other Nordic countries too. At the same time, this meant that nation states turned increasingly towards protectionism and corporatism, which brought an end to the free trade that had driven the global economy since the 1890s. A decisive shift in the direction of closed economies came when Britain abolished its gold standard and its policy of free trade in September 1931. In just a few weeks, the Nordic countries' central banks announced that they, too, were giving up the gold standard.

All these changes in Europe's political and economic landscapes resulted in an increasingly strong allegiance to the nation state. It was by no means only fascists and ultra-nationalists who, inspired by Hitler's rhetoric, demanded that their countrymen should subordinate themselves to the nation and to the *Volksgemeinschaft*, the German concept of the "people's community" adopted by the Nazis. Also on the Social Democratic side, the reformist labour movement's patriotic and nationalistic aims were emphasised increasingly systematically, paving the way for governments that crossed the left-right divide in all Nordic countries during the 1930s. The fraught great power politics obviously also strengthened aspirations for national unity, resulting in an emphasis on anything that was seen as an expression of cultural homogeneity.

These political shifts in Europe were an important reason why Mannerheim's return to Finnish foreign and security politics was more permanent on this occasion. There were other contributing factors too: Mannerheim had grown wise after previous failures and now avoided collisions with the country's political elite; moreover, he was no longer so burdened by his former reputation as a Russian officer whose patriotism could not be fully relied upon. Hitler's power grab occurred at roughly the same moment as Russia's nascent revival as a great military power in its Soviet guise under Stalin. This inevitably heightened the risk of a conflict between these two dictators into which Finland could get drawn, which in turn increased the need for geopolitically minded strategists like Mannerheim to steer the country's foreign and defence policies.

Until the outbreak of war, Mannerheim's official platform for this strategic planning remained the Defence Council's chairmanship. In late summer 1933, Mannerheim was authorised by the President to supervise and, if necessary, direct the commander of the armed forces and his General Staff in operational planning and in the preparations of the country's defence for a possible state of war. In principle, this was a clear downgrade of the commander's authority, but in practice most things continued as before, since Mannerheim rarely interfered in the General Staff's work and, to all intents and purposes, supported its proposals. One of the most important reforms was the introduction of a territorial defence system in 1934, which made the mobilisation of wartime forces significantly faster and gave the regional military districts a key practical role in its implementation.

A symbolic indication of Mannerheim's new status was his promotion to field marshal on 19 May 1933. He sincerely appreciated this designation, and, in a letter to his brother Johan, he interpreted it as recognition for the work he had done to prevent the spread of Bolshevism across Europe. Naturally this was, strictly speaking, just an honorary title, as there was no rank of field marshal in the Finnish Army's hierarchical structure. Mannerheim himself even had to pay stamp duty so that he could take receipt of the impressive title. But, of course, the new status and the ornate marshal's staff increased the aura around him and meant that he was even more rarely subjected to open criticism from the political left. In addition, he took the liberty of endowing the sleeves of his London-bought Burberry trench coat with marshal insignia, for there were no stipulations about how a Finnish field marshal should be dressed.

Mannerheim was immediately confronted by the government's tight purse strings when he began to call for an increase in the annual defence budget. But when Finland's economy had recovered, there followed a significant increase in defence resources between 1934 and 1939, which markedly improved the material readiness of the armed forces. Nevertheless, these improved resources did not satisfy Mannerheim and the military elite, and, as ever, the debate became whether the state should prioritise an increase in welfare or the strengthening of external security. To this day there remains a persistent idea that the politicians' parsimonious approach to the development of the defence forces led to the Finnish Army being ill equipped when the Winter War broke out in 1939. The symbol of this alleged military neglect became the so-called "Model Cajander", the conscript soldier clad in civilian clothes, marching out to defend the country with an old rifle and a blue and white cockade on his fur cap. The fact is, however, that the Finnish state's investment in defence was clearly at a higher level than the European average during the entirety of the interwar years. During National Progressive Party representative A. K. Cajander's three-year period as prime minister between 1937 and 1939, defence funds were raised further, and in the 1938 annual budget over 28 per cent of all expenditure went on defence.

The clear problem was that the Soviet Union—recognised, just like before, as the only conceivable enemy—had a very different level of resources at its disposal. Keeping pace with the acceleration of the other Great Powers' rearmament in the late 1930s, the Soviet Union had built up a military capacity that was on a completely different scale from that of Finland. As such, right from the start in his role as Chairman of the Defence Council, Mannerheim chose to consciously emphasise this difference, and, as long as it was reasonably possible, to accentuate the Red Army's superiority in order to extract more resources for Finland's armed forces.

Some researchers have claimed that Mannerheim's pessimistic statements stemmed from the fact he was not sufficiently familiar with the army's readiness at the time. But it would be a logical error to see the Finnish Army's relative success in the Winter War as proof that its military capacity was nearly at the same level as that of the Red Army. Certainly, the Finnish resistance was heroic and well organised, but, as is common knowledge, the war's end result was also, to a large degree, the consequence of a number of fortuitous circumstances for Finland. These could not have been counted upon when the country's military readiness was being discussed and developed in the 1930s.

Another reason for Mannerheim's gloomy statements was that his analysis of developments from a geopolitical perspective convinced him at an early stage after Hitler's entry into great power politics that a German-Soviet showdown was imminent. His Finnish officer colleagues were inclined to draw the same conclusion, but thanks to his political and diplomatic network, Mannerheim was clearly better informed than they were about the political games of the Great Powers. These were driving the hostility forward and, in a worst-case scenario, could decide Finland's destiny completely regardless of the country's military preparedness. Mannerheim's Russian past helped shape his perspective, of course, and made him prone to viewing the Baltic Sea region as the perennial site of a Russo-German struggle for supremacy.

Nonetheless, the most important people in Mannerheim's network proved to be a domestic circle of powerfully positioned conservative politicians, who, in consultation with Mannerheim, supported tying Finland's foreign and security policies more closely to those of the other Nordic countries. Belonging to this unofficial clique, alongside President Svinhufvud and Mannerheim, were also the then Prime Minister K. M. Kivimäki, Foreign Minister Antti Hackzell and J. K. Paasikivi, chairman of the right-wing National Coalition Party (1934–36) and future president. The latter's geopolitical convictions had been diametrically opposed to those of Mannerheim fifteen years previously, but now the two men saw things more or less eye to eye.

Their intention was, by any means necessary, to avoid Finland ending up in a tight corner when the two dictators came to blows, or, alternatively, when they united to draw up a new dividing line for their spheres of influence through the Eastern European border states. The League of Nations had already shown signs of its inability to stop Hitler's expansionist desires. In a private letter to Paasikivi in 1934, Mannerheim therefore outlined a secret three-step programme, the idea of which was to first proclaim Finland's Nordic orientation, then fortify the Åland Islands in collaboration with Sweden, and, finally, make a Finno-Swedish defensive alliance.

An early indication of these endeavours came in autumn 1933, when Finland joined a customs agreement that the other Nordic countries had entered into with the small Benelux countries (Belgium, the Netherlands and Luxembourg) a few years earlier. The programme's first objective was achieved in December 1935, when Foreign Minister Hackzell announced to parliament that the government proposed to strengthen Finland's co-operation with the other Nordic countries and adopt their mutual policy of neutrality.

Behind the scenes, Mannerheim was talking about "pushing through the Swedish orientation", but in public he stuck to Hackzell's vague Nordic framing and stressed that, at a time of crisis, Finland could make great use of the fact that it could import necessities from and through the Nordic countries.

Another part of this effort to bind Finland more closely to the Nordic bloc was the government's attempt to subdue the language dispute that had regularly flared up since the 1870s. After Finland gained independence and became a parliamentary democracy, the language question had given rise to increasingly incendiary criticism from the nationalistic "real Finn" (*aitosuomalaiset*) movement against the country's bilingual public identity. Such censure had also spilled over into diatribes against Sweden. In the 1930s, the schism was, above all, centred on the "real Finn" student movement's demand that all teaching at the University of Helsinki should be carried out in Finnish. A compromise was finally reached in conjunction with a change of government in spring 1937, the gist of which was that Swedish-language teaching at the university could continue, but in a more scaled-back form.

Fig. 6.2: Mannerheim as a guest of the British General Staff, September 1936. Second on the left is General Sir Walter Kirke.

Mannerheim's attitude towards the language dispute had always been measured, since he felt it to be blown out of all proportion and a risk to the country's national unity and capacity for defence. One of the most heated debates about the university's future took place in parliament in early 1935, after which he stated, in a letter to his relative G. A. Gripenberg, that he had had enough of all the unproductive discussions and debates. "Well, God bless everything to do with democracy and parliamentarianism", he declared, "I am too old to seriously appreciate it."

On the same day he wrote these words, on 6 February 1935, he also had an appeal published in the daily press. Together with his friends Rudolf Walden and Hannes Ignatius, he urged all parties to work towards language reconciliation, underlining that it would be necessary when the country's very existence was at stake. When such calls for unity failed to have a noticeable effect, he no longer took a position on the issue. Three months later he advised his Swedish friends against engaging in the debate, since a defence of the Swedish-speaking Finns' interests could become a source of irritation in Finno-Swedish relations. "I don't believe in direct interference from the Swedish side in this sensitive question, but a closer association between the nations will surely prove indirectly effective", he wrote to his old friend Ernst Linder, Swedish general and cousin to Hjalmar and Kitty, in April 1935.

The change of government in 1937 also smoothed the way in another respect for the Sweden-orientated security policy that Mannerheim was advocating. Tradition dictated that the government should step down after a presidential election. In February 1937, the experienced Agrarian League politician Kyösti Kallio was chosen as the republic's president, with the Social Democrats' backing. Kallio's predecessor, Svinhufvud, had refused to give the Social Democrats an opportunity to form a government, in spite of their significant successes in the two previous parliamentary elections. As a consequence, the Agrarian League and the Social Democrats saw to it that Kallio replaced him as president, before forming a majority coalition like those which had recently come into being in the other Nordic countries. At the same time, closer connections were established between the countries' governments since their Social Democrat ministers were well known to each other. Indeed, from the early 1930s, they had, in consultation, supported raising their parties' profiles as nationally unified forces.

The foremost of these strategists on the Finnish side was the Chairman of the Social Democrats, Väinö Tanner, who had directed the party along a reformist path since the 1920s. As Minister of Finance in the new government, Tanner kept in regular contact with Mannerheim and broadly supported his efforts in security policy. It is true that he remained suspicious of Mannerheim's alarmist demands for increased defence budgets, and gradually came to think that talented younger officers could take the chairman's mantle in the Defence Council. But this on no account meant that he actively opposed Mannerheim, whose regular appeals for national reconciliation were also valued among the Social Democrats. Early in the summer of 1938, Tanner stated as much in a speech, noting that "the labour movement is no longer bitter towards Mannerheim". This, above all, testified to the change in attitude that had occurred in the Social Democrats' leadership since 1920.

Nevertheless, Tanner was guilty of a clear embellishment when he spoke in so conciliatory a fashion on behalf of the whole labour movement. At the end of the 1930s, a significant portion of the working class still had personal memories of Mannerheim's central role in quelling the Red uprising in 1918. The conflict had claimed the lives of over 35,000 Red Guards, including many who had been unlawfully executed by firing squad both during and after the war. Such experiences could by no means be erased from the collective memory in just a decade or two. Nonetheless, in tandem with the rise in working-class living standards and the spread of knowledge about the brutality of Stalin's Soviet regime, the labour movement had gradually come to accept the market economy, while the left's co-operation across party lines had begun even earlier, on a local level, since the 1920s. This willingness to compromise also made it easier for the labour movement to tolerate White Finland's veneration of its living folk hero, Mannerheim.

The Åland Question

The second phase of Mannerheim's discreetly orchestrated effort to establish a Finno-Swedish Defence Council was, as has been noted, the fortification of the Åland Islands in collaboration with Sweden. The archipelago's great strategic significance had been evident already during Swedish rule, when Russian troops occupied Åland on two occasions and were close to advancing from there further towards Stockholm. When Finland, inclusive of Åland, became a Grand Duchy of Russia in 1809, the threat to Sweden increased further, but after the Crimean War Russia was forced to agree to the demilitarisation of the island group in the 1856 Treaty of Paris. This status was renewed in the Åland Convention in autumn 1921, which was established under the guidance of the League of Nations after the Finno-Swedish dispute over the islands had been settled in Finland's favour. Finland was forbidden from fortifying the island group or stationing troops there, but was bound at the same time to defend its neutrality in the event of a war. The convention was signed solely by the then members of the League of Nations, but not by the Soviet Union, which would later prove to be a decisive obstacle to Finno-Swedish co-operation in defence of the archipelago.

The agreement was welcomed by the Ålanders, whose heritage and mother tongue was Swedish rather than Finnish. They saw the convention, in combination with Finland's obligation to uphold their linguistic and cultural identity, as a guarantee that the islands would not have the Finnish language imposed upon them. It did not, however, convince the Swedish and Finnish officer corps, for whom all the military activities on the islands during the revolutionary winter of 1917–18 remained fresh in the memory. During the 1920s, the countries' General Staffs began discussions, the aim of which was to co-ordinate their defences, including working together to protect the Åland Islands in the event of a military threat from the Soviet Union. But these plans went nowhere until Hitler's power grab forced the countries' governments to take action. In autumn 1933, the Swedish Government made a secret proposal to its Finnish counterpart that they should begin negotiations to jointly strengthen the Åland Islands' neutrality and defence.

Mannerheim and the Defence Council recommended that negotiations should initially take place between the countries' General Staffs. These began in early spring 1934, in parallel with the Finnish Government consciously adopting Nordic orientation as an integral part of the country's foreign policy. Although an announcement of this new direction was given in the Finnish Parliament in late autumn 1935, and although it was also welcomed by the Swedish Government, there remained a number of obstacles to an agreement on the Åland question. The Swedish Government and its foreign minister, Rickard Sandler, wanted to minimise the risk of military conflict on Åland by inviting the Soviet Union to become one of the Åland Convention's signatories. This proposal was, however, categorically rejected by the Finnish side, since in the worst-case scenario this could lead to the League of Nations deciding to permit Soviet occupation of the islands to protect their neutrality.

Behind this divergence of opinion, which was obviously not debated in public, lay the countries' different geopolitical situations, which, unsurprisingly, also resulted in the two nations' leaders drawing contrasting conclusions from Hitler's seizure of power. Both realised that the risk of a German-Soviet conflict in the Baltic Sea region had increased. But while Finnish strategists feared that such a struggle would increase the risk of a Soviet attack on Finland, their Swedish counterparts began to be concerned that it could also lead to a German assault on Sweden from the south. As a result, negotiations between the governments did not noticeably advance before spring 1938, when alarm about an impending war made both sides more prepared to make concessions.

Mannerheim had no official role in the discussions at a governmental level. His possibilities for influence were further limited by the fact that he had long been on bad terms with Foreign Minister Rudolf Holsti, who had taken office in 1936. The two had been involved in a confrontation back in late summer 1919, when Holsti, who had then just been appointed to his first term as foreign minister, contributed to the scuppering of Mannerheim's plans for a Finnish intervention in the Russian Civil War. Holsti had also been an ardent advocate of the collective sanctions system that the League of Nations' entire credibility had been built on since its foundation in 1919, which Mannerheim and other like-minded strategists did not hold in high regard.

After Hitler's Germany had withdrawn from the League of Nations and begun a systematic dismantling of the terms of the Treaty of Versailles, the whole sanctions system started to crack. In early summer 1936, Finland, along with the other Nordic countries and three other non-aligned states, backed a declaration protesting the League of Nations' ineffective sanctions against Italy's invasion of Abyssinia. In March 1938, Germany annexed Austria without intervention from the Western Powers, which led to Finland, Sweden and Norway announcing, two months later, that they reserved the right in future to decide when they would participate in the League of Nations' sanctions. The system had gone from being seen as a defence against aggressive neighbouring states to being a danger for smaller states, who could be drawn into a war between the Great Powers against their will. Finland's Nordic orientation was an attempt to avoid this fate.

When these announcements were made, the Swedish and Finnish governments had already been negotiating the co-ordination of Åland's defence for a month. The Swedish Government's newly awakened interest in the matter stemmed from suspicions that Finland would, in any case, fortify the islands in collaboration with Germany. This was because a delegation of Finnish and German officers had carried out a covert tour of inspection on the islands at the turn of 1937, only for their mission to be exposed by the local press, feeding rumours that remilitarisation was imminent. A little over a week after Austria's *Anschluss* in March 1938, General Hugo Österman, the Commander of the Finnish Defence Forces, visited Berlin; this, too, increased the Swedish Government's concern that Finland was slipping into Germany's grip, just as in 1918.

There followed an intense negotiation process both at government level and between the countries' General Staffs. Mannerheim was indirectly involved via the Defence Council, and, thanks to his close contacts in the Swedish General Staff, he made a large contribution to guiding the negotiations to a successful resolution. In January 1939, the countries' governments signed the so-called Stockholm Plan, the premise of which was that the Åland Convention should be adjusted to allow a Finnish force of 1,000 men to be stationed on the main island, and on two coastal forts located on rocky islets in the southern part of the island group. While Sweden would supervise the remilitarisation, it did not in any way commit to defending Åland, even though the plan gave the country the right to station forces on the western Åland islands in peacetime.

The plan fell far short of what Mannerheim had hoped for, but since it ultimately improved Finland's ability to defend the islands, he lent it his support. He also, of course, saw the agreement as a means of paving the way for a Finno-Swedish Defence Council. But the Swedish Government had no intention of tying its destiny to Finland. Its purpose with the Stockholm Plan was to prevent Finno-German co-operation, and to dissuade the Soviet Union from trying to take control of the islands for as long as possible. As such, the plan stipulated that it would only come into effect after the signatories of the Åland Convention, the Soviet Union, the countries' parliaments and Åland's regional council had all accepted the arrangement. All the signatories initially indicated that they were prepared to agree to the plan, but in May 1939 the Soviet Government issued a communique taking strong exception to it. This caused both the League of Nations and the Swedish Government to give up on the whole idea.

This was a fairly sudden U-turn, for the Soviet Union had signalled on multiple occasions over the previous six months that it was ready to accept the Stockholm Plan. The first sign came in August 1938, when Foreign Minister Holsti was contacted by Boris Yartsev, an official from the Soviet legation stationed in Helsinki. Yartsev let it be known that Moscow could agree to the fortification of Åland, provided that the Soviet Union got to supervise the work and that it was given the right to fortify Hogland, the large island that lay in the eastern part of the Gulf of Finland. The initiative perplexed the Finnish Government, as it did not come through official channels, and so did not result in any action being taken. But according to J. K. Paasikivi, who was then the Finnish Envoy to Stockholm, Mannerheim immediately took the proposal seriously, commenting: "This is our first warning."

During winter 1938–39, the Finnish Envoy to Moscow Aarno Yrjö-Koskinen and Soviet Foreign Minister Maksim Litvinov continued to sound each other out. But when these efforts did not bear fruit, Stalin sent Boris Shtein, the Soviet Ambassador to Rome, to Helsinki to investigate the Finnish Government's view on this acute national security issue in the Baltic Sea region. Shtein's opposite number was the new Finnish Foreign Minister Eljas Erkko, the energetic newspaper magnate who had replaced the increasingly unstable Rudolf Holsti in late autumn 1938. According to Shtein, Moscow was prepared to support the Stockholm Plan and the fortification of

Fig. 6.3: Finnish Envoy to Stockholm (and future President of Finland) J. K. Paasikivi at Helsinki Central Station, November 1938.

Åland, if, in return, Finland agreed to exchange a number of islands at the eastern end of the Gulf of Finland for a 200-square-kilometre area in Soviet North Karelia. Erkko, however, stuck fast to the Finnish Government's strict line, with the concern that such a territorial concession could lead to a similar demand from Germany. Shtein's ominous closing remark was that the Soviet Government would not relinquish its demands. When not even that could persuade the Finnish Government to change its mind, Moscow announced in May 1939 that the Soviet Union would not accept the Stockholm Plan.

It is important to note that before he turned down Moscow's proposal, Erkko had conducted a number of discussions with Shtein. At the same time, the question was debated in detail within the government, and both former President K. J. Ståhlberg and Mannerheim were also consulted. On this occasion, as so often before, the two gentlemen's standpoints starkly diverged from each other. Prime Minister Cajander's considerable respect for Ståhlberg proved decisive, however, and the latter's legalistic and negative attitude to territorial concessions came to dictate the government's line. Mannerheim's persistent attempts to convince the government to agree to the Soviet demands were, accordingly, unsuccessful. Since this was to have long-term consequences for Finland, it was something that Mannerheim would later go on to discuss at length in his memoirs.

He had tried to convince Erkko that Finland did not have any military use for these islands in the Gulf of Finland, while they were, on the contrary, extremely important for the Soviet Union because they lay alongside the Soviets' Kronstadt naval base and their coastal fortifications in Luga Bay. Through a tactical climb-down of this sort, Mannerheim thought that they would not only improve relations with Moscow, but also get the Soviets to endorse the fortification of Åland. In addition, it would buy valuable time to improve defences before the war between the Great Powers, that was, by his own pessimistic calculations, fast approaching. When his attempts at persuasion came to nothing, he turned to President Kallio and Prime Minister Cajander, who rejected his demands on the basis that the concessions would have immediately toppled the government. For this reason, they were not mollified by Mannerheim's suggestion that he himself would publicly defend a transfer of the islands.

In his broad study of 1930s Finnish security policy, Timo Soikkanen has described the approach advocated by Mannerheim as a "policy of strengthening appeasement". This is a pertinent characterisation, especially in the light of Mannerheim's overarching intention with the concessions, which was to use them to help secure the fortification of Åland and to move a step closer towards a Finno-Swedish defence alliance. On this occasion, as so many times before, Mannerheim saw Finland's national security situation and the Great Powers' intentions in a far wider European context than the country's politicians, who at this time were mainly concerned with the foreign policy's repercussions for their success in the parliamentary elections of summer 1939. Or, as Paasikivi sarcastically noted in his diary in November 1938, the Finnish state was directed "as if it were a municipal matter or some association in Peräseinäjoki [a small municipality in western Finland]".

After the Soviet demands had been rejected and the Stockholm Plan ran aground, Mannerheim considered that there was now an even more acute risk that Finland, in one way or another, would be seriously affected by a Russo-German conflict. It was not much help that Finland, in common with Sweden and Norway, declined a German proposal for a non-aggression pact in May 1939. The Soviet intelligence service was well informed about the Finnish General Staff's close ties with Germany. As such, when a German officers' delegation participated in the big jubilee parade on 16 May 1938, to commemorate the White Army's victory twenty years earlier, the Soviets saw it as a sure sign that Finland was yet again on the verge of slipping into an alliance with Germany.

Finland's precarious geopolitical position was behind Mannerheim's emphatic reaction in late May 1939, when he felt that the Defence Council's viewpoints were being disregarded by Defence Minister Juho Niukkanen in the government. In a letter to President Kallio, Mannerheim declared that this should not happen under any circumstances, and demanded that going forward, the government should always be informed of the Defence Council's point of view if it differed from the Defence Minister's proposals. President Kallio's failing health meant that Prime Minister Cajander, as his deputy, was designated the task of trying to solve this schism. But when he was not prepared to meet Mannerheim's demands, which undeniably conflicted with the constitution, the 72-year-old Field Marshal tendered his resignation as Chairman of the Defence Council in the middle of June. His explanation was that he did not want to contribute to the preservation of a baseless sense of security in society.

The schism gained instant publicity and threatened the sitting government's credibility before the parliamentary elections in early July 1939. It made President Kallio react, too: he forced the government to agree to Mannerheim's demands, which persuaded the Field Marshal to rescind his resignation. Mannerheim's triumph in this power struggle obviously strengthened his authority in relation to the political establishment. The reaction of the politicians was sullen. Prime Minister Cajander had been prepared to let the impatient Field Marshal go. Tanner, the Minister of Finance, considered that Mannerheim's moment had passed, noting that the Field Marshal had acted erratically and was forever being drawn into new schemes. At the end of July 1939, Tanner informed the President that he was inclined to share the view of his colleague Risto Ryti, Governor of the Bank of Finland, that Mannerheim "was an old Russian general [who] had copied his methods from that time and covered his back against possible future losses by providing himself with scapegoats in advance".

A few days later, Tanner also wrote to his old friend Paasikivi in Stockholm, asserting that Mannerheim had lost his nerve because he kept warning about the threat of war. Paasikivi replied sharply that Tanner evidently did not appreciate the situation's seriousness at all. He provided a wordy defence of the Field Marshal, with whom he had discussed the global situation during Mannerheim's visit to the Swedish capital in early July 1939: "One does not need to discuss long with Mannerheim to realise how intelligent and experienced he is. Which other officers do we have? In practice no one who would be capable of such great duties."

History's Revenge

It is worth noting that Mannerheim opined, during one of these discussions with Paasikivi, that the impending war between the Great Powers would once more end in defeat for Germany. Nonetheless, at this stage it was no longer evident that the conflict that he predicted would be fought only, or even initially, between Germany and the Soviet Union. After Hitler had ordered the *Wehrmacht* to occupy the rest of Czechoslovakia in March 1939, Great Britain and France realised that the promises of peace that Germany had made in the Munich Agreement the previous autumn had been a bluff. As a countermove, they immediately gave Poland guarantees of security and began negotiations with the Soviet Union about an alliance against the expansionist Germany. But these talks soon ended in deadlock, since the Western Powers were not prepared to let the Red Army march through the border states if war broke out against Germany. This lent further support to Stalin's deep-rooted suspicion that the Western Powers were not sincerely interested in stopping Hitler, but rather actually hoped to crush the Soviet Union.

A telling expression of Stalin's mistrust was a criticism that, on his suggestion, was written in a short version of the Soviet Communist Party's history, which was published just before the Munich Agreement in 1938. According to this, the capitalist democracies accepted the expansionist wars of fascist states in different parts of the world because they were more afraid of their own labour movements than they were of the fascists. This short-sightedness would, however, come at a high price, and, in all probability, "history's revenge will strike even England's ruling circles and their friends in France together with the United States". In accordance with this judgement, in spring 1939 Stalin started to prepare his party members for the possibility that they might reach an agreement with Germany instead. Covert discussions along these lines were initiated at the same time as negotiations with the Western Powers were still ongoing; when the latter did not make any progress, a Russo-German dialogue at a governmental level followed in late June.

A month later, the negotiations resulted in a draft of the non-aggression pact, which the Soviet Union's Minister of Foreign Affairs Vyacheslav Molotov and his German counterpart, Joachim von Ribbentrop, signed in Moscow on the night between 23 and 24 August. In a secret additional protocol to the agreement, both parties were in accord that Finland, the Baltics, eastern Poland and Bessarabia should belong to the Soviet sphere of interest, going forward, while western Poland would fall in the German sphere. It is hard to say exactly when Mannerheim realised that Finland, too, would be affected by this redrawn political map of Europe. The risk of such a turn had already been discussed in national security circles, where he and Paasikivi, together with a few others, had aired their pessimistic prognoses for Europe's future. In any case, in mid-September he mentioned the German-Soviet division of Poland in a letter to his younger sister Eva Sparre, wondering "whose turn it will be next, when the appetite of these gentlemen has had time to grow".

By this stage, the Baltic countries' governments had already received strong signals from different parts of Europe that the Molotov-Ribbentrop Pact was likely to include an agreement about spheres of interest, and that the Baltic states and Finland fell within the Soviet Union's buffer zone. One of the sources was Finland's Envoy in London, G. A. Gripenberg, who had already given his Estonian colleague this information on 26 August. In early September, Gripenberg also informed Foreign Minister Erkko that the Foreign Office had let it be known that Moscow, during the summer's negotiations with the Western Powers, had demanded that the Soviet Union be permitted to establish military bases in both the Baltics and Finland. On this occasion, Gripenberg probably did not pass the news on to Mannerheim due to the risk of leaks.

But even if Mannerheim had known the details, the Finnish Government simultaneously received entirely contradictory information from its Envoy in Moscow, Yrjö-Koskinen, who had just conducted a friendly conversation with Molotov. Nothing, apparently, pointed to Finland being in jeopardy. On the contrary, Yrjö-Koskinen drew the conclusion that "the opportunities to develop Finland and the Soviet Union's intimate and, for both parties, favourable relationship have been significantly improved". This optimism lasted for a few more weeks. Then, on 17 September, the Soviet Union entered eastern Poland, and at the turn of September the Baltic states were forced to enter an agreement with Moscow, allowing it to establish Soviet bases on their territory. By then, the Finnish Government had realised that Finland would soon be next and had already appointed Paasikivi as chairman of the delegation that would travel to Moscow for negotiations.

On the evening of 5 October 1939, the Finnish Government was invited to Moscow to negotiate "concrete political questions" concerning the pressing situation in Europe. Mannerheim had kept himself well informed of all the developments and undertook two long discussions with Paasikivi before the latter left for the Soviet Union. Mannerheim now advocated, with even greater urgency than in spring 1939, a solution that also paid heed to the Soviet Union's security interests. The islands in the Bay of Finland filled no essential function in Finland's defence, and could, therefore, be given up in return for some form of compensation. Mannerheim stressed that the main thing was for the negotiations to reach a compromise, advice that he also passed on to President Kallio. But when Paasikivi travelled to Moscow on 9 October, he had the government's significantly more rigid instructions in his briefcase. The drift of them was that the islands in question could only be given up in exchange for something that the wider world would construe as reasonable compensation.

The upshot was that the negotiations in Moscow reached an immediate deadlock, as such a solution would have required equally strong bargaining positions. Paasikivi's delegation returned to Helsinki on two occasions to get further instructions from the government, whose stubborn line was dictated by Foreign Minister Erkko, playing the part of self-assured statesman. Before the third trip to Moscow, Erkko gave Paasikivi defiant advice: "Forget that Russia is a great power." Erkko was convinced that Stalin, who was taking part in the negotiations himself, was bluffing when the Soviet leader explained, in increasingly blunt terms, why the Soviet Union demanded, alongside the disputed islands, a military base on the Hanko Peninsula and border adjustments on the Karelian Isthmus. When the Finnish negotiators assured him that Finland would parry all attacks directed against its territory, Stalin pointed at Hanko Peninsula on a map of the Bay of Finland and declared that "a great power will land here and continue its advancement regardless of resistance".

Erkko's optimism did not solely stem from the fact that as a successful newspaper magnate he had an unusually large ego. He was confident that the support of the Western Powers would bring about a successful resolution to the negotiations in Moscow. In fact he was so certain of this that he had not mentioned to his government colleagues that he had been informed by the Swedish Government in mid-October that it could not provide military support if Finland was attacked by the Red Army. Erkko was proved wrong, however, for on 9 November the third round of negotiations was terminated in Moscow without a resolution. This evidently surprised Stalin, who had presumed that the Finns would agree to his demands after having first demonstrated their uncompromising nature for the sake of their domestic political reputation.

Fig. 6.4: The "Insurance" Man. The Soviet bear knocking on the door of the small Baltic states. A satirical cartoon in *The New York Times*, autumn 1939.

Part of his assumption was based on intelligence acquired in late September, when Soviet agents at the Foreign Office in London had intercepted correspondence from Mannerheim to the British Government. According to this, Finland would be forced to accept the transfer of bases and airfields out on the Bay of Finland, for the Finnish Army was quite simply not in fighting shape. This prediction reached Stalin on 5 October, that is, the same day that the Finnish Government received an invitation to negotiations in Moscow. The summons to Moscow would have been issued irrespective of what Mannerheim had conveyed to the British, since Stalin's autumn agenda had been fixed by the additional secret protocol of the Molotov-Ribbentrop Pact. But Stalin had assumed that it was Mannerheim who was really guiding the Finnish Government's line, hence he drew the incorrect conclusion that Finland would give in to the Soviet demands.

Consequently, due to this leak, Mannerheim was also indirectly culpable for the breakdown of the Moscow negotiations in autumn 1939, and for the Soviet Union launching an armed attack on Finland early in the morning of 30 November. Not that he saw it like that: in his mind, it was clear that the blame lay with Erkko, although Mannerheim's memoirs are careful to avoid offloading responsibility onto the Foreign Minister. Until autumn 1939, the two self-confident gentlemen had been relatively civil towards each other, even if Erkko was quick to backbite "the old Russian officer" and Mannerheim was clearly less than impressed with the conceited newspaper magnate. In late October, however, things came to a head at a meeting of the Foreign Affairs Committee, when Erkko brusquely waved away Mannerheim's words of warning that the army was not prepared for war. His optimistic dismissal of Mannerheim's concerns had been supported by Defence Minister Niukkanen. Thereafter, Mannerheim flatly refused to communicate with Erkko. Despite the collapsed Moscow negotiations, the government continued to hold fast to the belief that no war would come, and proposed that the army's raised state of alert should be downgraded. Defence Minister Niukkanen managed to prevent this, but the unconcerned attitude otherwise persisted, causing Mannerheim to again begin making threats to resign. If this had happened, the Commander of the Finnish Defence Forces, Lieutenant-General Hugo Österman, would most likely have taken over as the army's commander-in-chief at the outbreak of war.

All this meant that, in autumn 1939, the Finnish Government's capacity for internal communication was in a sorry state and it was hopelessly unprepared for a crisis. The burden of responsibility for this clearly fell on President Kallio and Prime Minister Cajander. Government protocol dictated that they should steer the ship, but since they had shown themselves utterly incapable of doing so, power had slipped into Erkko's hands. He was not receptive to Mannerheim's points of view, and all the while Moscow and London thought that the Field Marshal's opinions carried the most weight. But as has been noted, Mannerheim was also to blame for the stumbling blocks in the country's national security and foreign policies.

He and Erkko supplied such different messages to the Western Powers that the other Great Powers also became conscious of the Finnish state leadership's de facto uncertainty in the face of the Soviet demands.

Moreover, the conclusion of the Winter War in March 1940 showed that Mannerheim had been wrong when he supposed that the Finnish Army could not repel a Soviet invasion. Most historians therefore consider that the concessions recommended by Mannerheim and Paasikivi towards the Soviet Union would have been catastrophic in the long run. In the short term they might have avoided a war, but already in the summer of 1940 the Soviet Union would, in all likelihood, have replicated its actions in the Baltics and tried to occupy Finland via its bases in the country. Finland's capacity and willingness to oppose such an invasion would then have been decidedly worse than in 1939. National unity would probably already have started to rupture by then, while all prospects of foreign help, which had bolstered the Finns' fighting spirit during the Winter War, would have disappeared.

Should one conclude from this that Mannerheim, quite simply, did not understand how mentally and materially well-equipped the Finnish populace really were for a defensive war? True, Finland fought and survived, but, as ever, the outcome not only depended on how well prepared both sides were for the conflict. To a large extent, it was also the consequence of a range of other, sometimes random, factors, which could not have been anticipated and which might very well have ended in a military catastrophe. Furthermore, if one shifts one's gaze from the prevailing balance of power at the Finno-Soviet border in autumn 1939, and instead scrutinises Finland's geopolitical situation from a wider perspective, it is clear that Mannerheim's judgement was correct, and would, in practice, come to be the guiding light of post-war national security policy. If Finland wanted to survive as a nation, its state leaders had to take into consideration the Soviet Union's so-called legitimate security interests in some way, which boiled down to its need to protect Leningrad (the name given to Petrograd in 1924 after Lenin's death).

It was inevitable that this Soviet perspective did not generate much enthusiasm among those in positions of power in late 1930s

Finland. They belonged to a generation whose outlook on the world had been shaped by the idea that Finland's relatively recently won independence had been a historical necessity. It was not just Risto Ryti, Eljas Erkko and Väinö Tanner who continued to talk about Mannerheim as the old Russian officer behind the scenes. A similarly scornful attitude also persisted among Mannerheim's younger officer colleagues, who, due to their participation in the Jaeger Movement, had advanced quickly through the ranks without ever having to concern themselves with geopolitics and international diplomacy. Mannerheim, of course, also noted these shortcomings, and probably expressed unflattering judgements along such lines to those in his inner circle. Three days before the outbreak of the Winter War, Paasikivi stressed to Erkko that the reason Mannerheim was irreplaceable lay precisely in the lack of "sophisticated understanding" among the rest of the general corps.

This mutual prejudice, however, had to be set aside in early October 1939, when the Finnish Defence Forces received permission to mobilise the whole field army. The mobilisation was a response to the Moscow negotiations, but it was camouflaged as extra reserve exercises, which meant that every serviceman got a call-up through the mail. While the troops were receiving the order to take their posts, a voluntary evacuation of population centres was begun, for it was not inconceivable that the Red Army would bomb civilian targets. Nearly 300,000 servicemen were quickly called up; since the war only broke out a month and a half later, there was plenty of opportunity for further training and reviews of kit. The lack of regulation equipment was, of course, a cause for concern. Significantly more serious, however, was the acute shortage of ammunition and air power, which there had been no opportunity to rectify despite extensive increases in the defence budget during the second half of the 1930s.

Another sign that the military machinery was starting to crank into gear was Mannerheim's appointment, in connection with the covert mobilisation of the field army, as Commander of the Defence Forces. A decree had to be issued especially for this purpose: Mannerheim had exceeded the statutory age for active officer service back in 1927, and as the country was not yet in a state of war, the President could not designate him commander-in-chief. On

18 November 1939 the General Staff and a number of personnel from the Ministry of Defence assembled at their headquarters. During the first days of the war these were based at the Hotel Helsinki at the north end of Kluuvikatu, in the centre of the capital. However, they were promptly relocated to Mikkeli in south-eastern Finland, from where Mannerheim would direct Finland's defence during both the Winter and the Continuation Wars.

On 26 November Moscow staged a Finnish provocation in the village of Mainila on the Soviet side of the Karelian Isthmus. This false flag attack gave Stalin an excuse to terminate the 1932 non-aggression pact between the two countries and to begin regrouping the Red Army for an offensive. The next day, Mannerheim sent yet another resignation request to the President. On this occasion, it included a verbose critique of the government, which had not been prepared to invest in sufficient rearmament of the country's armed forces. This has typically been interpreted as Mannerheim, at the age of 72, simply no longer having the bottle to cope with the demanding situation.

It is clear that Mannerheim's frustration over the conduct of the negotiations with the Soviet Union had reached its peak during these days and weeks. There is, however, a more plausible explanation for his resignation attempt than a loss of nerve, which is that it was another effort to induce the Finnish Government to accept the concessions to Moscow that he had recommended. If Mannerheim had really intended to resign, he would in all likelihood have done so immediately after the Moscow negotiations had broken down in early November. That the move was a feint on his part is also borne out by the fact that the President had no trouble persuading Mannerheim to withdraw his request straight after war had broken out.

7

THE WINTER WAR

The Commander-in-Chief

On the day before the outbreak of the Winter War, the Soviet Ambassador to London, Ivan Maisky, wrote irritably in his diary about the Western Powers' attempts to meddle in the escalating Finno-Soviet crisis: "Still ... do the Finns not understand that if they meet with difficulties, they cannot count on anyone coming to help them? The Swedes? The Brits? The Americans? No, like hell they will!" Maisky was writing from an informed position; the Soviet intelligence service had already got confirmation from many sources in October 1939 that the Swedish did not intend to make a military intervention if Finland were to be attacked. Maisky had also received corresponding information in Great Britain. The Finns would undoubtedly have strong moral support in the Western press, but troops and artillery weaponry were not a serious prospect. Over the autumn, information came from Washington, DC, that the

Fig. 7.1: Molotov cocktail. Photo from the Finnish Front during the Winter War, early 1940.

only concern of the United States Government was that the Soviet Union's impending invasion of Finland would harm American economic interests.

During the first days of the war, as the Red Army's forces began to pour in over the Finnish border and the Soviet bombers carried out air attacks against Finnish population centres, a change of government was being hurriedly forced through in Helsinki. Just as Maisky had predicted, the Western media's banner headlines about the Soviet attack did not, in fact, influence the Western Powers' governments. The United States described the massive attack as a "military incident", but quickly gave up on the idea of taking decisive action after a clumsy attempt to intervene in the conflict. And when the Foreign Affairs Committee in Finland's new coalition government, led by the Governor of the Bank of Finland, Risto Ryti, convened for its first meeting on 2 December 1939, it was struck a body blow: namely, an announcement by the Swedish Government that the country was not prepared to participate in the defence of the Åland Islands.

By then, Erkko had already been dismissed as foreign minister, and his assertion that the Soviet threats were a bluff and that Western democracies would stand up for Finland was proved to be a monumental error of judgement. The often sharp-tongued Paasikivi would later refer to the conflict as "Erkko's war", and everything pointed to the like-minded Mannerheim sharing this opinion. But it was no longer any use the pair fretting over all the missed opportunities now that the war they had predicted had finally broken out, especially as both immediately had to take key political roles in it. While the leader of the Social Democrats, Väinö Tanner, was appointed foreign minister, Paasikivi was designated his closest colleague, whose future task as a minister without portfolio was to try to re-establish a negotiating contact in Moscow by any means necessary. And as Mannerheim was moving with his headquarters to Mikkeli, his trusted friend, the industrialist Rudolf Walden, was appointed as his spokesman in the government.

Mannerheim's opportunities to influence the government's line were also significantly strengthened following a decree at the start of December 1939 which gave him far greater authority than a commander-in-chief would usually have. He was placed directly under the president, which meant that he was released from the government's supervision, and he was given the right to present to the government foreign and domestic political measures which he saw as necessary for the country's defence. By these means, Mannerheim was able to shape the delineation of government policy throughout the years of conflict, even though his influence was later downplayed when the question of responsibility for the wartime decisions became pertinent.

Innumerable works and studies have been published on the military history of the Winter War. In one way or another they all deal with the reasons why Finland was able to fend off the Soviet invasion attempt so successfully that the conflict concluded in a peace treaty on 13 March 1940. It is true that this forced Finland to cede nearly a tenth of its territory to the Soviet Union, but the outcome was still a relative triumph from the Finnish perspective. After a fast retreat on many sections of the front during the opening days of the conflict, the Finnish forces rallied to put up an increasingly stubborn resistance. This put a stop to the Soviet advance on the Karelian Isthmus and meant that many of their divisions could be surrounded north of Lake Ladoga, where they suffered large losses.

The most successful of all these encirclement battles was fought in Suomussalmi and Raate up in Kainuu, where the enemy's death toll was so devastating that Stalin had many of the frontline commanders who were responsible executed by firing squad. In February 1940, however, the Red Army began a big offensive on the Karelian Isthmus, and the front was pushed ever closer to Vyborg. In early March, a Soviet division marched over the unusually thick ice in Vyborg Bay and created a bridgehead to the mainland, 20 kilometres south-west of the city. By that time, the vastly unequal strengths of the warring armies had become so obvious that the Finnish Government, on Mannerheim's recommendation, accepted Moscow's harsh conditions for peace.

From an objective perspective, it is a small miracle that things did not go worse for Finland. The Swedish Government, for obvious reasons, was not prepared to allow Sweden to get mixed up in the war, but it gave Finland extensive material support in the form of both weapons and necessities. Moreover, Sweden admitted almost 10,000 evacuated Finnish children. In late February 1940, a more than 8,000-strong Swedish volunteer force, together with just over 700 Norwegians, assumed responsibility for the Salla Front up in Lapland. Finland could also hurriedly buy fighter planes and weapons from the Western Powers. Nevertheless, no other European country stood up for Finland anywhere near as much as Sweden, a fact that was often disregarded both during and straight after the war, due to resentment over the fact that the Swedish Army did not come to help.

Despite its acute shortage of weapons, the Finnish Army had three aces up its sleeve in the winter of 1939–40: a strong *esprit de corps*, a fairly impenetrable terrain and exceptionally cold weather. In addition, the Red Army's fighting capability was clearly weaker than expected, because of Stalin's bloody purges in his highest officers' corps and the Soviets' presumptuous attitude towards the Finnish Army's ability. Relevant too is the fact that the Finns had a home-field advantage, to borrow a sports analogy, in that they knew far better than the enemy how to exploit the terrain that the latter sought to capture. The war therefore became a significantly more equal confrontation than it ought to have been.

The Finnish frontline soldiers had grown up in the newly formed republic in a social climate which saw the Soviet Union as Finland's only conceivable foe. The Finnish Communists were the only exception, but their political activity had been criminalised in 1930, and many of those who subsequently sought shelter in the Soviet Union had ended up victims of Stalin's Terror. Otherwise, the population was fairly certain that a Soviet invasion would mean the end of Finland's independence and its Western civilisation. This was an established outlook even in the social democratic labour movement, and it was only reinforced by the Red Army's attack, which was a grotesque contravention of Moscow's assurances of peace and friendship.

For Mannerheim, the outbreak of war signified both a bitter disappointment and a confirmation of what he had been anticipating for the last twenty years. The government's uncompromising line meant that the country had been drawn into a military struggle against the Soviet Union for which, in his view, it had not been sufficiently prepared. When the war became a reality, however, he quickly changed his tune and had an order of the day published on

1 December 1939 to the country's soldiers, in which he emphasised that the erupting conflict was nothing other than "the continuation and final act of the War of Liberation [the war of 1918]". It was rather ill-considered to use the loaded term "War of Liberation", with its strongly bourgeois connotations, at the very moment when it was necessary to strengthen national unity and encourage citizens to defend their country. But the choice is emblematic of how Mannerheim and his ghost-writer viewed the war and the communist regime in Russia. Ever since his return to Finland in late autumn 1917, he had regarded it as the greatest threat not just to his home country, but to European civilisation as a whole.

"You know me, and I know You and know that every man in the ranks is ready to fulfil his duty to the death", stated Mannerheim in the same order of the day, which brought to the fore another of his guiding principles. He had not led an army into battle for twenty-one years, but he took a firm grip of its command the instant he was back in charge. This quickly resulted in friction between Mannerheim and some of the strong-willed officers in the General Staff and among the frontline commanders. Mannerheim expected absolute obedience from them, while these younger officers, with better formal training, had difficulty accepting Mannerheim's sometimes impulsive decisions and impatient leadership style.

The first and perhaps most well-known of these power battles happened in the first week of the Winter War. When the Red Army began its assault on the Karelian Isthmus in early December 1939, Mannerheim demanded that the protection squadrons, which had been established earlier in the autumn to shield the formation of the wartime field army, should be strengthened, and should hold their positions at the border for as long as possible. His demand ran against the plans that had been outlined by the General Staff well before the outbreak of war, that took into consideration the fact that the protection squadrons' fighting capacity was deficient, since the men were largely old and poorly equipped reservists.

When Mannerheim's command was not executed as he wished, and the protection squadrons instead retreated to the already fortified Mannerheim line, Mannerheim transferred one of the front commanders responsible to other assignments. This commander was thereby made a scapegoat for a strategy drawn up by Lieutenant-

General Hugo Österman, who, as Commander of the Army of the Isthmus, had also allowed it to be carried into effect. In the long run, this crisis of confidence would lead to Österman being replaced too. In February 1940, when the Red Army engaged in its next big offensive on the Karelian Isthmus, he became so dissatisfied with Mannerheim's defence strategy that he requested a transfer. Mannerheim assigned the command of the Army of the Isthmus to Lieutenant-General Erik Heinrichs, while Österman was subsequently appointed to administrative or diplomatic duties only.

It was only when the conflict transformed from threat to reality that Mannerheim began to use the leadership methods he had developed in the three previous wars in which he had fought. As an experienced officer, Mannerheim did not hesitate to discipline his subordinates with abrupt reassignments and sarcastic comments, which soon put the generals in their place and efficiently took the wind out of their willingness to challenge his viewpoints and conclusions. These interactions were also informed by a generational rift. At the outbreak of war Mannerheim was 72 years old, while most of his generals had not yet turned 50—in other words, they could have been his sons. He was certainly still full of life, and, as Chairman of the Defence Council, he had tried to keep up to date with the development of new weapon technologies. It was nevertheless another matter entirely to be able to make fast but considered decisions around the clock, as the head of the whole field army.

Mannerheim's lack of a General Staff education had not been a particular handicap for him during the First World War. During the Second World War, however, it resulted in the decision-making process in the headquarters in Mikkeli being markedly different from the regulations in which the other officers had been trained. Consequently, Mannerheim's resolutions and orders did not come from collegial discussions. These would typically entail the Chief of General Staff presenting alternative solutions to the situation or operation at hand before the General Staff discussed the question together; only after this would the Commander-in-Chief form his decision. Instead, the Chief of General Staff had to content himself with both colleagues at headquarters and the front commanders reporting directly to Mannerheim. This made internal communication more difficult and often made the issuing of orders unpredictable.

Fig. 7.2: Mannerheim at his desk at Headquarters in Mikkeli, January 1940.

This top-down control certainly also had some advantages. It gave Mannerheim a better insight into such questions that would otherwise have been only dealt with by lower authorities. At the same time he also had more direct contact with the front commanders and with the prevailing morale in the lower ranks of the army. On the other hand, it also resulted in many thinking that he favoured certain officers or condemned others as too passive or timid. In his extensive study of Mannerheim's leadership style, the historian Lasse Laaksonen has therefore concluded that it was built more on his absolute authority and personal relationships than on the army's military hierarchies and formal decision-making processes.

At the same time, Laaksonen calls attention to the fact that the war inevitably gave rise to heightened conflicts and clashes of opinion among the general corps. Just as with the frontline soldiers, it was only in an actual war that the generals' readiness was revealed. Therefore there is nothing that unequivocally points to the idea that interpersonal relations would have been better in the headquarters if Hugo Österman, or another Jaeger general of the same age, had functioned as commander-in-chief instead. The General Staff's decision-making should obviously have been more professional, but on the other hand, the Commander-in-Chief's authority, both among his officer colleagues and throughout the army as a whole, would presumably have been more fragile. In the worst-case scenario, the competition between the former Jaeger officers could have degenerated into a destructive power battle, which not only would have made communication with the Finnish Government more difficult, but would also, perhaps, have been exploited by foreign powers. How would, for example, a commander-in-chief with a Jaeger background have managed to maintain distance from Germany in 1944, and ultimately guide the country out of the war with its independence intact?

Counterfactual discussions of this sort have their weaknesses, of course. But it is difficult to envisage that another officer would have been able to accrue as much reputation and influence in such a short time as Mannerheim had obtained in 1939. Finnish military historians usually avoid comparing "our" war with the situation in other parts of Europe during the Second World War. But the fact is that no other war-waging country had a commander-in-chief with such a large political influence in tandem with such a high level of public support as Mannerheim. In Hungary, Romania and Vichy France, the commanders-in-chief were also heads of state, but their power was dictatorial and consequently independent of the will of the people. In Great Britain, Germany, the Soviet Union and Italy it was the opposite. Their political leaders interfered with the military debates to such an extent that it often led to short-sighted decisions with fatal consequences. In Finland, however, Mannerheim efficiently ensured that the political leaders did not meddle in the practicalities of war and that the military accepted the decisions of the democratically established government.

The Northern Pawn

For the balance of power between the political and military leadership to function, it required that both Mannerheim and the government were willing to co-operate. Moreover, both parties engaged in a variety of negotiations during the whole Winter War about military help and the prospect of peace talks, which suggested that Mannerheim was in constant and close communication with the leading governmental ministries. In the first days of the war, Ryti's government tried in vain to make contact with Moscow through the United States and Sweden, with the aim of starting new negotiations. However, the Soviet leadership announced that they had already signed a "peace-keeping" friendship and mutual assistance treaty with the so-called Terijoki Government. This had been formed by Moscow as a Finnish puppet government just before the outbreak of war to support the Soviets' planned invasion of Finland. Germany also flatly rejected all Finnish requests for help and for it to make peace enquiries on the Finns' behalf, which confirmed suspicions that Berlin had agreed in the Molotov-Ribbentrop Pact that Finland came under the Soviet sphere of interest.

The American Government's indifferent attitude stemmed from the fact that they were not particularly interested in what was going on in the distant hinterlands of north-eastern Europe. This attitude was also in line with President Roosevelt's priorities, since he was targeting re-election and wanted to steer well clear of initiatives that went against the isolationist foreign policy supported by his voters. Besides which, the American administration had been infiltrated by people who were spying on the Soviet Union's behalf, and who saw to it that, at first at least, the Winter War was characterised in Washington, DC, as a similar "incident" to the invasion of Poland. But as it became clear that Finland was not a mere morsel for the Soviet Union to swallow, attitudes started to change. Herbert Hoover, a potential rival to Roosevelt in the presidential elections, was happy to portray himself as a humane statesman by putting himself at the head of the nationwide Finnish Relief Fund. This organised a number of attention-grabbing shows of sympathy for war-torn Finland.

These created a lot of good will towards Finland and contributed to the American Government's decision to sell 44 fighter planes to the country in February 1940. While only eight of them made it to the country before the Winter War was over, the decision was, nonetheless, a sign of a shift in the American position. Encouraged by this, Mannerheim sent a personal telegram to Roosevelt in early March 1940, requesting that the United States either donate or sell 160 fighter planes to Finland. Roosevelt now also saw the chance to portray himself as a great benefactor and ordered his officers to take care of the matter. But when it became clear that the only way to quickly deliver these planes to Finland was to take them from a quota that had already been promised to France, the French Government intervened.

The Swedish Government's statement at the start of the Winter War that they could not take Finland's side did not come as a surprise to Mannerheim in the slightest. Throughout the war he stuck loyally to his government's efforts to get Sweden to change its position. All the while, however, he was also using his Swedish contacts to secure and expedite the transportation of the considerable quantity of weapons and ammunition that the country had agreed to deliver to Finland. Besides which, Sweden was undoubtedly the most important middleman for weapons that were purchased from or donated by Western Powers. Mannerheim, therefore, was very expectant when in January 1940, he received signals from the Western Powers that they were planning a large military operation in northern Fennoscandia, the area comprising the Nordic countries and the Russian regions of Karelia and Kola. His desire to secure weapon deliveries via Sweden continued to be central to his plans even after he heard that the Western Powers had decided, on 5 February 1940, to carry out the military intervention via the Norwegian coast to the ore fields in northern Sweden, since part of the forces could be sent on to provide some relief to Finland. Mannerheim understood, however, that the real aim of the manoeuvre was to stop the Swedish export of iron ore to Germany, which, in all likelihood, would have resulted in German countermeasures and the cessation of the weapon deliveries from Sweden.

Stalin, through his diplomats and spies in London and Paris, had also garnered knowledge of the intervention plans in mid-January 1940. The mission caused him a great deal of anxiety, since it was also revealed that the Western Powers planned to simultaneously attack the Soviet oil fields in the Caucasus. Oil deliveries from there were vital to the German war machine, and an attack must, therefore, be warded off by any means necessary. Not only could it cause the Soviet Union to end up in a war with the Western Powers, but in the worst-case scenario it could also result in Germany switching sides and allying itself with them against the Soviet Union.

At the end of January, Stalin sent word to the Finnish Government, through Stockholm, that the Soviet Union was prepared to open the door for peace talks with Finland. At the same time, he gave orders to begin a big offensive on the Karelian Isthmus to improve the Red Army's tarnished reputation and force the Finns to agree to harsher peace conditions. On 7 February 1940, the Finnish Government's trio of leaders, Ryti, Tanner and Paasikivi, met to debate how to react to Moscow's peace advances and the Western Powers' intervention plan. The next day, the Field Marshal's spokesman, Rudolf Walden, was involved in the discussion and, on 10 February, Ryti and Tanner travelled to Mikkeli, where, together with Mannerheim, they outlined a joint negotiation strategy. They decided to first aim for peace negotiations with the Soviet Union and continue to request military assistance from Sweden, but to only request military support from the Western Powers as a last resort. This final option was not regarded as at all desirable, in respect of the consequences for Sweden, but it was seen, soberly enough, as a way of getting the Soviet Union to accept a reasonable peace. At the same time, Ryti, Tanner and Mannerheim agreed that Finland ought to be prepared to cede Jussaari, an island east of Hanko, as a military base for the Soviet Union, and the next day they were able to persuade President Kallio to get behind the strategy.

Mannerheim's demand that they ought to begin peace negotiations as quickly as possible was not only borne out of his scepticism regarding the prospect of military help from Sweden or the Western Powers. While he delineated the survival strategy with Ryti and Tanner, the Red Army was steamrollering its way through the Finnish positions on the Karelian Isthmus. At this point, the Soviet war machine was starting to reach the capacity that Mannerheim had presumed it to have in autumn 1939. This made him press for a quick peace all the more urgently.

At the same time, it was still important to maintain the Western Powers' interest in a military intervention in northern Sweden and Finland, for the Soviet Union's sudden interest in peace negotiations was obviously a reaction to the planned operation. Mannerheim's opponent in this game of chess, in which Finland was a northern pawn, was no less than Stalin himself, whose information sources in London and Paris continued to convey highly alarming reports to the Kremlin in February. According to these, the United States and the Western Powers were on the verge of sending several hundred fighter planes and three well-armed squadrons to Finland's aid. In reality, none of this held water, although it was the case that in the final weeks of the war, France made big promises of military help to Finland in order to try and prevent a Finno-Soviet peace agreement. Stalin, however, took the reports seriously and struck a swift deal with Finland. The terms of the peace treaty were, of course, extremely harsh from a Finnish perspective, but they did not correspond at all to what Stalin had expected to gain from the Winter War.

The groundwork for the peace negotiations in Moscow had, in the main, been laid through Stockholm and the Swedish Government, which obviously also had a vested interest in bringing the war to a swift conclusion. As such, the Swedish Government categorically rejected all Finnish requests for military help, and in mid-February it even made a public rebuttal to expedite the peace process. The statement, without a doubt, worsened Finland's negotiating position in relation to the Soviet Union. But an extension of the Winter War would have increased the risk that the Western Powers might intervene and Sweden be drawn into the conflict, which the Swedish Government, in the increasingly squeezed conditions in northern Europe, was forced to guard itself against. In return, Finland received strong diplomatic support from Sweden during the whole peace process.

Behind the scenes, the Western Powers' intervention plans also pushed the German Government to encourage Finland to make a quick peace. At the end of February 1940, the Finnish Envoy to Berlin, T. M. Kivimäki, conveyed Reich Marshal Hermann Göring's demand in this vein, together with a vague intimation that Finland would get its transferred territories back when the war was finally over. His promise had a certain significance, since many of the Finnish Government's ministers still nurtured hopes of help from the Western Powers, and so took a negative stance towards

Moscow's demands for peace. Prime Minister Ryti therefore placed emphasis on Göring's message to encourage them to change their minds. Both this and Mannerheim's increasingly alarming reports from the front led to a clear majority of the government ultimately agreeing to peace.

The historian Heikki Ylikangas has interpreted Ryti's invocation of Göring's message as the state leadership's first conscious step on the road to a Finno-German military alliance. But it was naturally in Ryti's interest to make use of all arguments that could convince his reluctant government colleagues of the advantages of peace— even those that he himself did not find persuasive. It seems highly unlikely that Ryti and Mannerheim should have counted on the German Government's promise when there was good reason to suspect that Germany had accepted the Soviet occupation of Finland only half a year earlier. In early spring 1940, no one could have foreseen when and how the German-Soviet alliance would break up. Some assumed, quite correctly, that the Western Powers at that point were contemplating the possibility of making peace with Germany, but it was impossible to predict to what extent this would have improved the situation of the border states in Eastern Europe. It was just as likely that this would have restored the order that had prevailed in Europe before 1914.

Moreover, there is plenty to indicate that Ryti assumed, just as Mannerheim had in early spring 1940, that the ongoing conflict between the Great Powers would, in the long run, result in victory for the West. Ryti was an ardent Anglophile and a liberal banker with close contacts to London's financial circles, which is why he was appointed prime minister when the Winter War broke out. In Mannerheim's case, the calculation reflected his geopolitical outlook; that is to say, he took into consideration the vast resources and territories that the Anglo-American power bloc had at its disposal across the world. His viewpoint was clearly also reinforced by his experiences from the First World War. Besides which, Germany's rapid territorial conquests on the Western Front and in western Scandinavia had not yet happened, and therefore did not cloud Mannerheim's confidence in the Western Powers' military capacity.

The Moscow Peace Treaty came into force at 11am Finnish time on 13 March 1940. Wartime censorship and the media's exaggerated optimism in its reports from the front led to a great deal of consternation in Finland when the harsh conditions of the peace were announced. Alongside the forfeiture of Karelia, Finland undertook to lease the Hanko Peninsula as a military base for the Red Army for thirty years. The government had clearly prepared itself for an even stronger reaction, and immediately published a number of statements as to why it had been forced to accept the Moscow Peace Treaty. Since Prime Minister Ryti was on his journey home from Moscow, it fell to Foreign Minister Tanner to announce the news on the radio and try to convince the nation that there was no better alternative available.

It was not Finland's fault that "the democratic states either did not want or were unable to help us in this unequal conflict", Tanner stressed, pointing out that Sweden and Norway were also culpable for Finland being left to fight against the Soviet invasion alone. The same bitter message was also encapsulated in Mannerheim's order of the day, which was published the following morning. He thanked the Western Powers and Sweden for their extensive help with weapons and equipment, but added in the very next sentence that the country had unfortunately been unable to receive "the grand promises of help", because "our neighbours, out of concern for their own houses" did not allow shipments through their territories to Finland.

This was, at the very best, an edited version of the truth. Mannerheim had been critical of the Western Powers' intervention from the very start, since the motive had not, of course, been to help Finland, but to occupy the Swedish ore fields to force Germany to take action. If Finland had really wanted to call on the Western Powers for help, then it could have done so regardless of the prevailing opinion in Stockholm or Oslo. This did not happen, however, since the state leadership realised, from Mannerheim's criticisms, that the help would nevertheless have been all too insufficient to alter the balance of power at the front. Besides which, Finland would have damaged its relationship with Sweden, which was the last thing in the world that it wanted to do, when it had no other friends to rely on.

Why, then, did Mannerheim make this slight against Sweden? One obvious reason is that he was conscious of the collective frustration felt by the Finns that the Swedish Army had not stepped up to defend Finland. This feeling had to be verbalised in some way so that the Commander-in-Chief's order of the day could both connect to the nation and express its sentiments. At the same time, the caustic words also reflected his own disappointment that the Nordic orientation that he had championed had accomplished so little. Mannerheim would return to this dissatisfaction again in his memoirs, where he concluded that he was "inclined to believe" that the Winter War could have been avoided "if a Nordic defence alliance, even merely a Finno-Swedish one, had existed".

Mannerheim's order of the day referencing the conclusion of peace was also charged with other phrases that would become legendary. He directed his most majestic words of thanks, brought deep from the heart, to the country's conscript army: "Soldiers! I have fought on many battlefields, but I have never seen warriors the like of You. I am proud of You as if You were my own children." With these words, along with the whole spirit of sincere national reconciliation that the order of the day emanated, Mannerheim managed to shake off much of the aversion that many in the labour movement had felt towards him in the interwar period. He no longer let out a word about the War of Liberation or the events of 1918. Instead, he took pains to make every part of the order of the day appeal to all social classes and emphasise their common destiny.

Mannerheim continued to produce carefully composed daily orders of a similar style until late autumn 1944. As a member of the armed forces, he was not expected to make speeches on the radio or to give other public addresses in the name of the nation; this task was reserved for the country's democratically elected state leaders and parliament. As such, the orders of the day became his most important channel of communication with his army and the country's citizens. It was actually just as well that it played out this way: Mannerheim, with his halting Finnish and unabashedly aristocratic bearing, would not have had a hope of appealing to the masses as a modern people's tribune.

In this respect, Mannerheim differed from Churchill and Hitler, whose leadership and collective influence was essentially built on their oratory and their ability to perform effectively in front of large crowds. Churchill, like his fellow nobleman, Mannerheim, certainly had a predilection for diction and metaphors that had started to come across as long-winded and bombastic even before the First World War. This did not diminish his reputation as a great orator, but it did result in members of parliament in the House of Commons struggling to take his words of warning about Hitler seriously, since his phrasing had such a theatrical elegance that the actual content ended up being of secondary importance. But after the war had broken out and everything had gone precisely as Churchill had warned, his rhetoric proved to be enormously effective, and resulted in him being appointed prime minister in May 1940. When the bombs started to fall and the human cost of the war increased, the nation needed just this sort of strong and sentimental language to get through each day and keep itself together.

It was precisely the same with Mannerheim's rhetoric. It was seen as thoroughly passé in the late 1930s, when Finland's economy was growing astronomically and the majority of the nation wanted to forget the old grudges from 1918. The outdated impression was clearly not helped by the fact that Mannerheim continually took part in parades in his old cavalry uniform, which was inevitably associated with the nineteenth-century estate society and the class differences that had contributed to the revolution in 1917 and 1918. But when the Winter War wrenched the entire nation out of its pleasant torpor and Mannerheim learnt to avoid wording that reopened old wounds, his orders of the day gained a whole other momentum to his previous public statements. It also helped that, from this point on, he left the cavalryman's skeleton uniform (so-called because the stripes on the jacket resembled rib bones) hanging in the wardrobe.

Another concrete expression of Mannerheim's efforts to tone down his White heritage was his decision in spring 1940 to discontinue the celebration of the Finnish Defence Forces' Flag Day on the anniversary of the Whites' victory parade in 1918. Mannerheim had good reason for organising an alternative military tribute at this time, since the country was mourning the loss of almost 24,000 soldiers who had been killed in battle. As such, he gave the order that henceforth the fallen soldiers would be commemorated on the third Sunday in May. In so doing he announced that the day would also honour the memory of those who had died for their convictions during the civil war in 1918, regardless of which side they were on.

The memorial day was first held on 19 May 1940, and included a parade in memory of the fallen in Senate Square.

Another oft-analysed sentence in Mannerheim's order of the day at the end of the Winter War is its conclusion. He stated that the Finnish people were proud of their historic mission to protect "Western civilisation, which has been our inheritance for centuries, but we also know that we have paid every last penny of the debt that we owed the West". The "every last penny" was, without a doubt, a reference to Zacharias Topelius's poem "Originala skuldsedeln" (The Original Promissory Note) from 1872, in which the renowned poet defended the notion that Finland owed a debt of gratitude to Sweden. This had been called into question by the Fennoman movement of the period. Topelius responded in his poem that of course the promissory note could be ripped up, but then Finland should also relinquish all the Western cultural heritage that it had acquired during centuries of Swedish rule.

It is hard to say how many readers understood that Mannerheim, in his order of the day, was implying that Finland, through its own fight for survival, had paid off the debt of gratitude which the country

Fig. 7.3: The first Commemoration Day of Fallen Soldiers at the war memorial in Joensuu, 19 May 1940.

had felt towards Sweden and the rest of Western civilisation. The source of inspiration for this literary flourish in the order of the day could well have been a lecture that the Swedish-Finnish academic Henning Söderhjelm had given in Sweden just before the Winter War. Söderhjelm, with reference to Topelius's poem, had reminded his audience that the debt of gratitude was reciprocal, since Finland had always functioned as Sweden's defensive wall in the east when war had broken out in the Baltic Sea region. The real intimation of Mannerheim's closing words was, therefore, that it was now Sweden that was in Finland's debt.

Lessons and Consequences

Nonetheless, as noted above, it is unlikely that many people read so carefully between the lines that they grasped this subtext. Moreover, it was certainly not in Finland's interest that its relationship with Sweden should worsen, which was why the Finnish state leadership addressed Sweden in very conciliatory and grateful tones in March 1940. The country also continued to support Finland on a broad range of fronts after peace was declared. The foreign power towards which the Finns felt by far the most rancour at that moment was, unsurprisingly, the Soviet Union, which had started the war under false pretences but, as was typical of a Great Power, only admitted this a long time later.

However, censorship and the justified fear of a new war effectively quelled all the anti-Russian propaganda that, until this point, had been allowed to flourish fairly freely in the young republic. For the older generation, this meant a return of sorts to the public discourse that had prevailed during most of the country's time as a Grand Duchy, when it had been both dangerous and futile to criticise Russia too openly for its lack of justice or morals. For the younger generation, such compliance was a greater affront to their honour, but as the Soviet Union began tightening its grip on the Baltics, even the most outspoken Russophobes learnt to bite their tongues.

The Finnish Government's most important and longest-lasting lesson of the Winter War was that no Western Power was prepared to bleed for Finland if the conflict was about something as insignificant as the Finns' independence and continued national existence.

Consequently, the country's national security policy has ever since been guided by a level-headed aim to ally itself or at least keep on good terms with the Great Powers of the Baltic Sea region that have an interest in protecting Finland's independence and maintaining stability around the Gulf of Finland.

This understanding meant that Ryti's government, on Mannerheim's advice, decided not to call for the Western Powers' help but instead to quickly make peace with the Soviet Union. Ryti's scepticism towards Mannerheim had considerably softened, and since both remained in their posts their co-operation to a large extent came to shape the course of the country's national security policy until the Continuation War broke out in summer 1941. Neither of them counted on the peace with the Soviet Union proving permanent. Their suspicions were heightened already at the end of March 1940, when Moscow issued a strong protest at the fact that Finland had begun negotiations about a defensive alliance with the other Nordic countries. According to the Soviet Minister of Foreign Affairs Molotov, this contravened the third article in the peace treaty, in which the countries pledged not to enter into alliances that were directed against the other party. Thereafter, there was no doubt that Moscow regarded Finland as being in its sphere of influence.

Another indication that the Finnish state leadership only saw the Moscow Peace Treaty as a temporary ceasefire was Mannerheim's continuation as commander-in-chief. This was contrary to the government's constitution, which directed that the commander-in-chief's authority should be returned to the president upon a declaration of peace. But since the national security situation in northern Europe intensified again straight after the treaty had been signed, the government elected to remain in the state of war that had been declared when the Winter War broke out. In early April 1940, Germany occupied both Denmark and Norway to protect itself against the Western Powers' military plans and their future attempts to interrupt Sweden's iron ore exports to the German war industry. In May, the Germans began their large western offensive, which resulted in a considerable part of the Central European continent being under German control in late summer 1940. This also gave the Soviet Union greater scope to carry into effect the Molotov–Ribbentrop Pact's division of Eastern Europe into German and

Russian spheres of influence. In summer 1940 the Baltic countries were occupied and incorporated into the Soviet Union through a simple manoeuvre. Moscow concurrently also cranked up the pressure on Finland, whose last remaining hopes of support from the Western Powers had gone up in smoke after France's collapse.

In practice, there were now only two alternatives remaining. Either Finland would succeed in keeping itself out of the ever-expanding war in Europe by allying itself more and more closely with Sweden, or else it would sooner or later slide into conflict with the Soviet Union once again. In this situation, Prime Minister Ryti took an increasingly large share of responsibility for the country's national security, since President Kallio's already limited capacity as head of state had declined further due to his increasingly fragile health. When the government was restructured after the Winter War, Ryti's closest colleagues were Foreign Minister Rolf Witting and Rudolf Walden, whose opportunities to champion Mannerheim's cause were bolstered by his new role as defence minister and acting prime minister. The outgoing foreign minister, Väinö Tanner, had become persona non grata in Moscow due to his brazen outspokenness.

The appointment of the Germanophile Professor Witting as foreign minister has been interpreted as a conscious attempt to strengthen relations with Germany. Ryti and Mannerheim would certainly much rather have seen the Anglophile diplomat G. A. Gripenberg in the post. However, the German historian Michael Jonas has shown that Witting had been on good terms with Germany's influential Ambassador to Helsinki, Wipert von Blücher, since the mid-1930s. As such, it is entirely possible that von Blücher had, in some discreet way, lobbied for Witting's candidature and that this was obliged, since the appointment of the Germans' favourite would not, in all likelihood, irritate the Soviet Union. The two Great Powers were still allies, after all. As such, although Ryti and Mannerheim still hoped to install a pro-Western politician in the role in late March, they were quickly forced to think again. And since relations with Germany were constantly becoming more important, Witting soon acquired a key role in the close-knit circle of ministers which, together with Mannerheim, directed the country's foreign and national security policies until the summer of 1941.

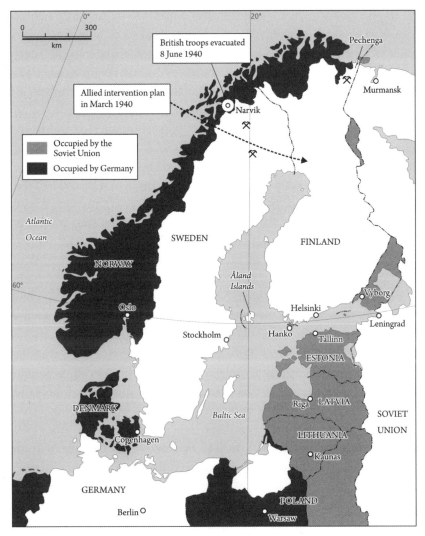

Fig. 7.4: The transformation of the political map of Northern Europe in 1940. Map by Hannu Linkola.

There is no question that Mannerheim, during the fifteen months between the Winter and the Continuation War, had more power and prestige than he had ever had before—or would ever have again—in his life. In contrast to his periods as regent and later as president, the Field Marshal enjoyed broad support among all political parties at this time, which allowed him to drive through his own agenda in government, even on the few occasions when Ryti tried to dig his heels in. It helped that the country's democratic institutions, in this pressing situation, were prepared to transfer part of their power to Mannerheim, and that he also wielded it as discreetly as possible. That this state of affairs suited Mannerheim to a tee was noted by those around him. In late April 1940, Mannerheim invited a delegation of Swedish officers to a lavish lunch at the Savoy restaurant, during which one of the guests was astonished at the host's energy and engagement: "Mannerheim looked like a 60-year-old, fit and magnificent. He was also fully lucid and up on all the details."

Mannerheim's assurance was further strengthened by the fact that such a large portion of the population and the state's resources were mobilised to improve the country's defence capabilities. Concern about a new Soviet attack meant that the headquarters kept many of the conscripts on active duty and extended the period of service from one to two years. At the same time, the state continued to make significant acquisitions of weapons and ammunition, which, in combination with the work to construct a new large-scale defensive line close to the new border, contributed to improving both national harmony and the citizens' faith in Mannerheim. This faith was also on display during his public appearances, which showed, beyond a shadow of a doubt, that it was Mannerheim and not President Kallio who was recognised as the nation's figurehead.

The significant turning point for the country came in July 1940. Finland and the Soviet Union had concluded an extensive trade agreement at the end of June, which would have alleviated Finland's worsening grain and fuel shortages. At the same time, however, Moscow escalated its other demands, which meant that the implementation of the agreement was postponed. Finland immediately acquiesced to the demand to tear down the fortifications that had been erected on the Åland Islands during the Winter War, but when the Soviet Union further insisted that it be permitted to transfer troops to its new military base on the Hanko Peninsula along Finnish railways, negotiations ground to a halt. Things were not improved when Moscow also demanded a concession to the nickel mines in Petsamo, in which Germany, too, had shown an interest. To top it off, in July the Society for Peace and Friendship with the Soviet Union, founded by the Finnish Communists and supported by Moscow, arranged a number of large demonstrations in Finland against the government's unwillingness to comply with the Soviet demands. The demonstrations were, in substance, reminiscent of those that were being staged in the Baltics around this time, which resulted in the countries' forced Sovietisation.

The outlook was undeniably gloomy, but in these same weeks the Finnish Government's inner circle received the first signals from Berlin that there was an interest in developing relations between the two lands. At the end of June, the two countries signed a trade agreement that would raise the proportion of German imports to Finland from 16 per cent in 1939 to a little over 50 per cent in 1940. At this stage Berlin stressed, via various diplomatic channels, that Germany was not prepared "in the immediate future" to upset its alliance with the Soviet Union. Embedded in the wording was, however, the inference that the situation could change, and at the end of July both Ryti and Mannerheim were called on by Hitler's secret emissary Ludwig Weissauer, who had been sent to Helsinki to investigate Finland's defensive capacity and its willingness to fight. Both men communicated an unambiguous message to Hitler. If Finland was forced once again to fight alone in a war against the Soviet Union, it would be able to hold out for a maximum of three months. This was, of course, a cause for concern, but more important was the information that Finland would not capitulate to the Soviet Union under any circumstances. Hitler could draw the conclusion from this that German weaponry supplied to Finland would not go to waste.

A few days later, Hitler gave his military leadership the task of planning a massive attack on the Soviet Union. In the plan they would count on flank support from Finland and Romania, both of which had been forced to cede territory to the Soviet Union and were therefore presumed to be harbouring thoughts of revenge. On 10 August Hitler gave the order to sell weapons to Finland in exchange for Germany being allowed to transport troops through Finnish territory. Eight days later the inner circle of the Finnish Government received this offer; they responded in the affirmative without delay. Mannerheim had already received information about the German message before Hitler's envoy, Lieutenant-Colonel Josef Veltjens, arrived in Helsinki. Before the Field Marshal gave his answer to Veltjens, he had consulted with Ryti, Witting, Walden and Paasikivi during a late dinner at the Seurahuone Hotel in the centre of the capital. Yet curiously, when Ryti was asked about this dinner by the prosecution during the war-guilt trials in the winter of 1945–46, he had absolutely no memory of it. The supper would remain a secret up until the 1980s, when Paasikivi's diaries were made available to researchers for the first time.

The reason for Ryti's selective memory was that the positive response to Veltjens was the first step in a gradually deepening co-operation between the countries' military leaders, which resulted in their joint attack on the Soviet Union in June 1941. Had Ryti admitted how that decision had really been reached, it would have cast a long shadow over Mannerheim and Paasikivi as well. In 1944, they would rise to the posts of president and prime minister respectively, and therefore they had to be protected. Accordingly, it was in all the decision-makers' best interests to stick tightly to the official version of events, which was, more or less, that Finland had been forced into conflict in 1941 against its will and had fought a "separate war" until a ceasefire was agreed in 1944. Now, however, there is a broad consensus among researchers that the Finno-German preparations for war in 1940–41 resulted in an outright military alliance, even though Finland carefully avoided making a formal agreement with Germany. At this point, it is worth emphasising the three stages in these preparations that illustrate Mannerheim's central role in the whole process.

The first took place in late autumn 1940, when the Germans had already been transporting troops through Finland for many months and the Finnish Army had started to fill its depots with German weapons. Until this point, the Germans had been very reticent to say how long they were prepared to work with Finland, as the German-Soviet pact was still in force. In mid-December, Mannerheim's secret messenger Major-General Paavo Talvela travelled to Berlin to probe whether Germany could support a new proposal for a Finno-Swedish defensive alliance. Talvela was also charged with co-ordinating their General Staff plans, with one eye on going to war with the Soviet Union.

It was obvious that Mannerheim took the initiative to dispatch Talvela after hearing that Hitler, during Molotov's visit to Berlin in November 1940, had refused to agree to the Soviet Union's planned invasion of Finland. Germany was at war, and so it could not forgo the Finns' nickel and timber. On 18 December 1940, Talvela met Reich Marshal Göring, who made it clear that Germany did not support a Finno-Swedish alliance. Instead, Germany wanted Finland to participate in the impending war with the Soviet Union; the code name Operation Barbarossa was coined that same day. However, Finland was instructed to keep a low profile until the operation was set in motion, and to hold out against the Soviet demands in the dispute over the concession to Petsamo's nickel mines. This information was also immediately supplied to Ryti, who had just been elected as the new president. After this point, and with Mannerheim's backing, he took an increasingly hard stance against the Soviet Union.

The second concrete step in the preparations was taken in late January 1941, when Mannerheim sent his Chief of General Staff,

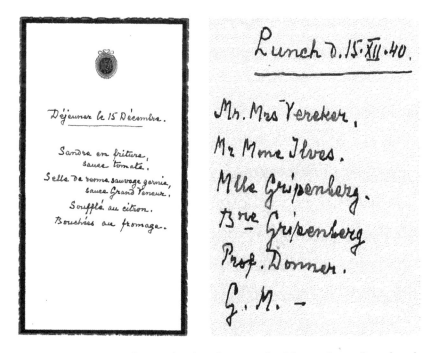

Fig. 7.5: A menu and guest list handwritten by Mannerheim for a lunch put on for the British Minister-Plenipotentiary to Helsinki, Sir Gordon Vereker, on 15 December 1940. At this lunch Mannerheim revealed to Vereker that Prime Minister Risto Ryti would four days later be elected president.

Erik Heinrichs, to Berlin for the purpose of secretly outlining the broad plans for the joint war. In summer 1940, Hitler had given his generals the task of preparing an attack on the city of Moscow, but after deciding in December 1940 to instead direct the first strike against St Petersburg, the German military leadership became interested in the active flank support of the Finnish Army from the northwest. Heinrichs stated that Finland was prepared to take part in the operation, but initially through an offensive on the north and east sides of Lake Lagoda. At the same time, he called attention to Finland's food shortage and stressed that the brotherhood-in-arms would be awkward, since Finland could not enter into a military pact that destroyed the country's relations with the United States and Great Britain. The Germans were accommodating in all these matters and promised to take charge of the defence of the northern half of Finland.

Once Hitler had been informed of Heinrichs's positive answer, he immediately gave his generals free rein to draw up a more detailed plan for the brotherhood-in-arms. A similar order came from Mannerheim's General Staff while they were waiting to receive information about an exact date for the attack. At the end of May 1941, Heinrichs travelled with a delegation of officers to Salzburg to finalise various details of the joint offensive, after which the Finnish General Staff, in all secrecy, set the military machine in motion. Mobilisation orders were posted to all reserve officers and the General Staff awaited the Germans' final confirmation that the attack would take place, as planned, on 22 June. Meanwhile, six German divisions took up their positions in the northern part of Finland, in preparation for an attack on Murmansk.

So came the third and final phase of the preparations for war. On the evening of 16 June, the newly appointed German liaison officer in Helsinki, General Waldemar Erfurth, sent word to Berlin that the Chief of the Finnish General Staff, Heinrichs, had informed him that Mannerheim wished to delay the Finnish offensive by two or three days "in order to convey a political impression to the nation and parliament that circumstances had forced them to take action". This did not interfere with the Germans' plans, and the next day they sent word to Finland that they would launch the offensive on the pre-arranged date. With this confirmed, on

18 June the Finnish military authorities began dispatching mobilisation orders to all conscripts.

By this stage an increasingly large number of Finns already sensed what was in the works. On 10 June, the President had informed the whole government and the chairmen of the parliamentary parties that a war between Germany and the Soviet Union was an imminent possibility, which could require a full mobilisation since it could not be discounted that the Red Army might also attack Finland. This explanation in no way convinced those politicians who had been kept in the dark about the preparations for war, but despite this it did not result in a government crisis. The critics realised that the President had been forced to act in secret due to the fraught global conditions, and that a government crisis would only have plunged Finland into an even deeper quagmire.

In his memoirs, Mannerheim, of course, denied that he had been intimately involved in the Finno-German war preparations, nor did he accept that the decision to take part in Operation Barbarossa had stemmed from an expectation that Germany would crush the Soviet Union. But this had really been his dream for over two decades, and when he touched on the topic in a private conversation with Paasikivi, in autumn 1944, he openly admitted that in 1941 he had believed that Germany was capable of beating "Russia". He also added, of course, that he had been fully conscious that "by joining the war everything was staked on one card, namely Germany's victory".

We do not know how else Mannerheim evaluated this gamble. Against the background of his experiences in the Winter War and all the other brutal attacks in the previous world war, it is plausible that by summer 1940 Mannerheim had given up hope that Finland could survive between the two dictators without allying itself with Germany. Certainly, the Finnish state leadership could have chosen for the country to remain neutral, but the consequence would most likely have been its occupation by the Soviet Union, or, as with Poland, that it would have been divided up between Stalin and Hitler. Who imagines that Mannerheim's countrymen would have thanked him if one of these scenarios had transpired?

8

BROTHERS-IN-ARMS

The Finnish Front

At 5.30am on Sunday, 22 June 1941, Germany's Minister of Propaganda Joseph Goebbels read out a long speech by Hitler on the radio. He accused the Soviet Union of treachery and provocations that Germany could no longer tolerate, and therefore declared war on "the Jewish Bolshevik leaders" in Moscow. To emphasise the extent of the Soviet treachery, Hitler revealed that in November 1940, Molotov had demanded that they get to take control of Romania, Finland and Bulgaria. This was the last straw, proclaimed the German Chancellor's spokesman, adding that they now stood before the biggest battle for Europe's freedom in world history. Romania and Finland were to fight on Germany's side to save the whole of Europe, he continued, announcing that "the German divisions under the command of Norway's conqueror, together with

Fig. 8.1: Finnish postage stamp depicting Field Marshal Mannerheim, 1941.

the Finnish champions of liberty with their Field Marshal at the helm, will protect the Finnish land".

In reality, the intimate brothers-in-arms had already started to lay out significantly more offensive plans. Germany would crush the Soviet Union and then transform European Russia into a German protectorate. In May 1941, Berlin requested that the Finnish Government deliver a proposal outlining where the boundaries of the future Greater Finland should be drawn. President Ryti gave the researchers Väinö Auer and Eino Jutikkala the task of investigating the question, and in autumn 1941 they produced the report *Finnlands Lebensraum*. In this they used both geographical and historical arguments to assert that Finland's borders ought to be drawn from the White Sea down to Lake Onega, and from there westwards along the Svir and Neva rivers to the Gulf of Finland.

But, as noted, despite the fact that everything was synchronised for a joint attack, the Finnish state leadership was very keen that it should appear as if the Soviet Union had forced Finland into a defensive fight. Hitler's speech was altogether too revealing in this respect. In response, the Finnish Government published, on two successive days, a communiqué about Finland's neutrality in the erupting conflict. However, since the Germans immediately began making use of airfields and harbours in southern Finland, Moscow was not at all convinced by these assurances, and over the next three days the Red Army's air force directed a number of bombing raids against Finland. All went just as the Finnish Government had wished. On the evening of 25 June, the Finnish Parliament stood in support of Prime Minister J. W. Rangell's statement that Finland was again at war with the Soviet Union.

The following day, President Ryti's radio speech finished laying the foundations for Finland's "second defensive fight". He blamed the Soviet Union as solely responsible for the conflict, referencing the Winter War and Moscow's continued extortion. Ryti's triumphant and vengeful tone was, however, inescapable. In contrast to the Winter War, Finland's chances of survival were markedly improved, since "Greater Germany" was on its side: "Now the Soviet Union has entered into war with an equally strong enemy and in this conflict the successful outcome of our own war of defence is assured." In the process, Finland would, once and for all, free itself of the eternal threat from the east and "secure a prosperous and peaceful future for generations to come".

It certainly demanded rhetorical dexterity to describe, in that moment, the conflict between the Great Powers, in which Finland was actively engaging, as "our own war of defence". Nonetheless, it was a description that Hitler had tacitly accepted, and Ryti could, as such, adhere to it during the forthcoming three years of war, especially in communication with the United States and Great Britain, whose diplomatic ties with Finland remained intact up until autumn 1941. One reason for the Western Powers' waiting game was that their embassies in Helsinki were excellent bases from which to conduct espionage on Germany. That aside, in the early days of the conflict both London and Washington, DC, displayed an understanding of Finland's decision to enter into it. In early July 1941, the American Ambassador to Helsinki, Arthur Schoenfeld, reported that Ryti had stressed to him that Finland intended to wage its own defensive war until it was able to extricate itself from the conflict with the Soviet Union. According to Schoenfeld, the Finnish state leadership had an overarching purpose with the war, namely to once and for all rid itself of the Soviet Union's political and military threat, "which according to Finland had become unendurable".

The interpretation espoused by Ryti, that the Continuation War was a "separate war" for Finland and not part of the Second World War, also came to play an important role in his domestic political rhetoric. Not only did it serve to maintain the image of Finland as a democratic and independent country in Scandinavia and among the Western Powers. Just as vital was that it helped appease all Ryti's pro-Western and liberal-minded countrymen, for whom collaboration with Germany could be nothing other than a distressing necessity. This conscious neglect of Finland's strong connection with Germany became, therefore, a means of preserving national unity. For the same reason, it would long remain one of the linchpins of the patriotic narrative of Finland.

Tellingly enough, there is no evidence that Mannerheim would have uttered the term "separate war" since it so plainly contradicted the facts of the conflict. When the war broke out in June 1941, the Finnish field army was better equipped than ever before thanks to the large-scale purchase of weapons and equipment, above all from

Germany. Its firepower had been doubled and its mobility had significantly increased. Nearly half a million men stood at arms; in a country of just 3.7 million people, this meant that a considerable part of the male population was mobilised. It was, in fact, a greater proportion than in any other nation at war, and it was therefore taken for granted that women assumed a significant responsibility for keeping both the army and civil society functioning. As the Germans took charge of the defence of the whole northern half of the country, this also increased the Finnish Army's fighting capacity on its section of the common Eastern Front.

Of course, for as long as possible Mannerheim also avoided openly acknowledging the obvious advantages that came from the Germans' strong flank support to the north and south of the Finnish part of the front. On 28 June 1941, Mannerheim issued a plan of attack that in essence followed the broad outline that had been determined in consultation with the German military leadership in early spring that year. The Karelian Isthmus would be recaptured, but otherwise the main focus of the offensive would be on the northern and eastern sides of Lake Ladoga, since Finland was happy to leave the capture of Leningrad to the Germans. This gave Mannerheim good reason to describe the planned attack, in his order of the day, as a last and decisive crusade, in the wake of which "Karelia's population will again stand up and the dawn of Finland's new day will rise before us."

Anyone who was still uncertain about how far east Mannerheim wanted to see this dawn appear could find the answer in his subsequent order of the day on 10 July. This was issued on the same day that the Finnish Army began its large offensive against Ladoga and East Karelia, and its openly expansionistic and nationalistic turns of phrase caused astonishment in many quarters. In this so-called "Sword Scabbard Declaration", Mannerheim gave assurances that he now intended to accomplish what he had promised to do back in 1918, namely that he "would not sheathe his sword until Finland and East Karelia were liberated". In this cavalcade of Finnish nationalist slogans, however, it was the messianic concluding paragraph that went the furthest: "Soldiers! The ground on which you tread is holy ground, steeped in the blood and suffering of your kin. Your victories will grant Karelia its freedom, your deeds will create a great and auspicious future for Finland."

Censorship prevented open criticism, but from the cool comments expressed by the spokesmen of the Social Democrats and the Swedish-speaking liberals, it was plainly evident that they were not at all fond of Mannerheim's Greater-Finnish rhetoric. When the Western Powers requested clarification, the government implied that the order of the day had been published without its knowledge, which was not the case, as both Defence Minister Walden and President Ryti had been informed of it in advance. Mannerheim did not actually write the order himself: Erik Heinrichs suggests in his Mannerheim biography that it was, as usual, penned by Major-General Heikki Kekoni. Whoever the ghost-writer was, it is clear that they were well-versed in the nationalist romanticism that had run rampant in Finland ever since the country gained independence. But obviously Mannerheim was responsible for its contents, and when he later commented on the incident to Heinrichs, he characterised it as an expression of *licentia poetica*—that is, of the poet's right to exaggerate in order to achieve a desired emotional effect.

When Heinrichs addresses the order of the day in his biography, he writes: "at any rate, Mannerheim did not seek East Karelia's incorporation into Finland". But this is nothing more than a demonstration of Heinrichs's systematic efforts to save Mannerheim's reputation and depict the Continuation War as a separate war. Heinrichs, as much as anyone, had been involved in the preparations before the war and thus knew about the grand plans for Finland's future eastern border. Indeed, Ryti presumably did not offer any objections to the Greater-Finnish turns of phrase in the order of the day, precisely because they reflected Finland's goal at that time. Moreover, they largely corresponded with the concrete plan of attack to which Mannerheim and Heinrichs had agreed with the German liaison officer, General Erfurth.

The military historian Martti Turtola characterises Mannerheim's decision to occupy East Karelia as both remarkable and short-sighted. But, as he himself adds, the plan was built on the assumption that Germany would crush the Soviet Union before the end of the year, which was a very reasonable calculation in the eyes of contemporary military strategists. Moreover, the East Karelian military campaign was an operation that had been planned in close consultation with the German military leadership, and therefore ought to be understood as part of the common plan of the brothers-in-arms to capture Leningrad. The idea was that the city should be surrounded by both Finnish and German troops, who would advance from their respective positions on the Aunus peninsular, between Ladoga and Onega, before finally meeting with "a hand-shake at the River Svir".

One proof of this systematic synchronisation is that the German military leadership dictated the date when the Finnish attack on East Karelia should begin. At the end of May, the parties had come to an agreement that the Finnish offensive north of Ladoga would start at the same time as the Germans approached Leningrad. On the morn-ing of 9 July, General Erfurth informed Mannerheim that the German forces would continue their march towards Leningrad the next day from the city of Pskov at the southern end of Lake Peipus. Later that same day, Mannerheim gave the order that the attack on East Karelia would commence at 3pm on 10 July.

It was no coincidence that the Finno-German brotherhood-in-arms functioned with great precision. Not only were most of the Finnish generals former Jaeger officers, who, owing to their service history, felt a strong solidarity with their German counterparts. On the eve of the Continuation War in 1941, 1,400 Finnish volunteers enlisted to be German SS troops: they would participate in the German offensive all the way to the Caucasus, and only return home two years later. Even though this was a German initiative, and the recruitment was conducted by independent civic organisations, the whole thing was sanctioned by the Finnish Defence Forces. Finally, it should also be mentioned that a German division took part in the offensive on the Finnish section of the front and that, in turn, Finnish forces aided the Germans on their section of the front in the north-ern part of Finland.

Another early preparation for the approaching war was the intro-duction of two new classes in the Order of the Cross of Liberty, the prestigious mark of distinction for valour in war which had been created in 1918 and reintroduced during the Winter War. Accord-ing to the new statutes that Prime Minister Ryti, in his capacity as President Kallio's deputy, accepted in late autumn 1940, a soldier in the Finnish Defence Forces who achieved important results in conflict or led an operation with merit, "irrespective of his rank shall

Fig. 8.2: Finnish infantry crossing the 1940 border (defined by the Moscow Peace Treaty), July 1941.

be named Knight of the Mannerheim Cross of the Order of the Cross of Liberty's 1st or 2nd class". Each one of the 191 people who were appointed knights of the Mannerheim Cross went through a thorough review before they received the mark of honour from the Field Marshal personally. In some cases, soldiers who were killed in action were posthumously awarded the honour. In autumn 1941, Mannerheim agreed to receive both classes of the mark of honour himself, and in so doing help further inflate their status.

The military leadership had good reason to be optimistic when the offensive began in July 1941. The Finnish field army had stood armed and ready for over a week, highly motivated to begin its war of revenge against the Red Army. And since the Germans were concurrently engaged in their large offensive south of the Gulf of Finland, the enemy was now at a substantial disadvantage. This enabled the Finnish Army north of Ladoga, with its four-fold numerical superiority, to quickly advance eastwards. By mid-August 1941, it had recaptured the whole of Lake Ladoga's northern shore. With the completion of a similar offensive over the Karelian Isthmus in early September, the Finnish forces arrived at the limits of the 1939 border and began to await the Germans' seizure of Leningrad.

A month later, the Finns had reached the River Svir and taken Povenets on the northern shore of Lake Onega. Here their offensive came to a definitive halt, which the Finnish military leadership justified to the Germans by stating that they had arrived at the positions they had promised. Moreover, the war had taken a grave toll on the Finnish Army and the country's economy. Over 25,000 men had been killed and 75,000 injured in the five-month-long assault. At the outset of the conflict, the Finnish soldiers had referred to it as a summer war, but such optimism was now in short supply.

The extensive mobilisation of servicemen had also resulted in a serious deficit of manpower on the home front, leading to an acute food shortage in the winter of 1941–42 which hit the Soviet prisoners of war and the most vulnerable people in society worst of all. Consequently, a new mass evacuation of children to Sweden began. This would go on for the next three years, reaching its culmination in the spring and summer of 1944, when nearly 30,000 Finnish children were taken in by the Swedes. Due to the large-scale importation of grain from German-occupied Europe until summer 1944, the availability of food, despite everything, gradually began to improve.

This assistance came at a cost, since the Germans exploited it to keep Finland in the war. When the Finnish food shortage became acute in October 1941 and the government requested a significant delivery of grain from Germany, Hitler saw to it that this was quickly organised. In order to secure the arrangement, however, Finland was forced to enter into the Anti-Comintern Pact that had been established by the Germans. The country would continue to have a sizeable trade deficit with Germany over the coming years, which meant that it was the only one of Germany's allies whose war was subsidised by the Germans.

Despite this aid, the food shortage still lasted long enough to affect many in Finland, not least the more than 67,000 Soviet prisoners of war who were interned in prison camps across the country between 1941 and 1944. Almost 22,000 of them died from malnutrition, neglect and, above all, forced labour. This was a horrifically high proportion, even compared to the death tolls of the German prison camps in northern Finland (20 per cent), and a significant number of the total deaths occurred in 1942, when the food shortage was at its most severe and Finland's readiness for a long drawn-out positional war was at its very worst.

The historian Mirkka Danielsbacka has shown that Mannerheim was informed about the high mortality rate in the prison camps, but that he did not agree to raise the food rations since other population groups were also suffering from malnutrition. When the extent of the catastrophe became common knowledge and received international attention, however, the authorities made sure that the prisoners' food rations were increased and that their work duties were reduced. The prisoners also began to be sent to the countryside as manpower, and little by little the situation improved. These measures also received Mannerheim's approval, which demonstrates, according to Danielsbacka, that the mistreatment of prisoners of war did not stem from a desire for ethnic cleansing of the sort that the Germans were pursuing.

The reality was that the short summer war had begun to transform into a positional war as early as August or September 1941, one that would ultimately last for over three years. This was the point when it became apparent that the Germans were not at all capable of taking Leningrad. Through General Erfurth, they started to make appeals to Mannerheim for the Finns to take a more active role in the siege of the city from the Karelian Isthmus. Mannerheim, however, parried these recurrent requests with the excuse that he did not have sufficient tanks, dive bombers or heavy artillery at his disposal to break through the Soviet front. And to lend weight to his words, he referenced the heavy losses on the East Karelian Front and the President's dismissive attitude.

Based on this, some have argued that Mannerheim and Ryti saw to it that Finland did not really participate in the siege of Leningrad. The Finns' passive war on the Karelian Isthmus and at the River Svir undoubtedly made it easier for the Soviets to maintain their defence of the city, for they could continue to go over Lake Ladoga and along the north side of the River Neva throughout the whole siege. But as the Leningrad region was also under intensive attack from the German side of the front, the slowly advancing Finnish positions nevertheless made the defence of the city more difficult, with between 1.5 and 2 million Soviet soldiers and civilians losing their lives over the course of the siege.

Geopolitics and Grievances

In order to understand the complexities of Finland's role in the fighting on the Eastern Front, it is important to examine the Finnish war in a wider context. Since autumn 1939, the war in northern Europe had been primarily about two things: Leningrad's security and the control of the Swedish ore fields. The Winter War was a consequence of the first question and the occupation of Denmark and Norway a consequence of the second. From the Great Powers' perspective, then, this barren and sparsely populated part of Europe was chiefly of interest in respect of their own national security and their need for raw materials for the war.

This also explains why Hitler accepted the Finns' refusal to enter into a formal alliance when he was making plans for the Finno-German brotherhood-in-arms. In that situation, it was more than enough that the Finns, with their sixteen efficient fighting divisions, should participate in driving the Red Army from the Baltic Sea, thereby securing the Germans' extensive iron imports from the Swedish ore fields. At the same time, the Finnish section of the front significantly tied up Soviet forces that would otherwise have been directed against the Germans. It was also true that Hitler understood the advantage of being able to point to the democratic and Nordic social conditions of the Finnish brothers-in-arms in Germany's European war propaganda.

One fair and oft-cited argument against the claim that the Finno-German co-operation should be seen as a military alliance is that the Finnish populace did not feel any strong attraction towards the Nazi ideology and the racial hatred it propagated. Although this is true, the fact remains that for over three years the fundamental theme of this brotherhood-in-arms was a pronounced anti-communism that was supported by both countries' state leaderships and a significant portion of their populations. This shared opinion was more than enough to bridge various ideological disagreements, in a situation where the overarching objective was to eradicate Bolshevik rule in Russia once and for all. In an analogous way, Great Britain and the Soviet Union were also united, in spite of their vast ideological differences, by their collective desire to crush Hitler's Germany.

It is clear that the anti-communist fervour made it much easier for the old Anglophiles Mannerheim and Ryti to co-operate with

Hitler's Germany. Mannerheim readily admitted to his friends and acquaintances that he went to war with the express purpose of bringing down the Soviet Union's communist social system, not its people or culture. In summer 1942, in a letter to an old officer colleague from his Russian days, he stressed that many did not understand that he was drawing his sword against Russia because it was "the last opportunity to get even with Bolshevism, this scourge on humanity". In Ryti's case, it does not appear that he had any particular consideration for the Russian people. Rather, he coldly calculated that a conflict between the two dictators could be to the benefit of Finland.

In autumn 1941 it became increasingly difficult for the Allies to accept the claim that Finland was waging a separate war, especially as the Finnish offensive continued far into East Karelia. Since August, Stalin had called for Great Britain to declare war on Finland, and in early November he intensified these demands when the Finnish army corps drew near to Murmansk's railway line. As a result, the British heightened their diplomatic efforts to convince the Finnish Government to bring the assault to a halt. At the end of November,

Fig. 8.3: Mannerheim gazes eastwards over the Karelian Isthmus from Mainila hill, September 1941.

the Finnish Government received an ultimatum from Britain: if it did not send word that the offensive had been called off by 3 December, at the latest, then Britain would declare war on Finland.

In parallel with this, Churchill sent a personal letter to Mannerheim, in which he stressed that if the offensive was simply brought to an end there would be no need for Britain to declare war. The Finnish Government replied that it was not far from achieving its objectives in the conflict, while Mannerheim, in his response, stated that unfortunately he could not put a stop to the offensive before the army had reached positions that guaranteed Finland's safety. These evasive answers were not, however, enough, and on 6 December 1941 the British declaration of war came, meaning that Finland was now formally in conflict with the two biggest empires in the world. The Western Powers had unofficially been informed that the offensive would be over in a matter of days, but this did not make any difference, since the British intended to comply with Stalin's demand for a declaration of war regardless.

In his posthumously published memoirs, Ryti asserted that he had tried to get Mannerheim to tell Churchill that the offensive would be over in a few days, but that the Field Marshal had felt it unnecessary because it was already evident from the letter. When the question came up in the war-guilt process in autumn 1945, Mannerheim denied that Ryti had suggested he change the wording, which meant that it was the latter alone who got the blame for failing to persuade the British to take another course of action. But as Ryti himself conceded in his memoirs, Great Britain was so dependent on the Soviet's flank support in late autumn 1941 that "in the long term it nevertheless could not have opposed the Soviet Union's demands to declare war on Finland".

Since August 1941, Stalin had also called for the United States to put pressure on Finland. After some attempts to sound out peace, Washington's tone sharpened at the end of October, at which point the Finnish Government received a note from the American foreign minister, Cordell Hull. This urged Finland to end its war with the Soviet Union and withdraw back to its 1939 borders, so as not to spoil its good relations with the United States. If the American aid convoy to Murmansk was threatened from Finnish territory in Petsamo, then this would lead to an acute crisis in the relations between the two countries.

President Ryti responded to the note with a long explanation, in which he emphasised, once again, the separate nature of the Finnish war, and reminded the Foreign Minister that the Western Powers had done nothing to safeguard Finland's independence. As such, it was "almost incomprehensible" that America, as a large democracy, could demand that a small country that was fighting for its existence should voluntarily retreat to wait for a new attack from an enemy fifty times its size. His answer must have made an impression on the Americans, since they never declared war on Finland, even after the United States was drawn into the fight against Germany following Japan's attack on Pearl Harbor. Of course, in contrast to the British, the Americans did not have an urgent need to keep Stalin on side, and this no doubt contributed to the greater tolerance they displayed towards Finland. That said, the United States did deliver great quantities of war materiel and other necessities to the Red Army throughout the whole war.

Japan's decision to attack the United States instead of the Soviet Union was significant—perhaps even decisive—in its impact on how the situation on Europe's Eastern Front developed. In November 1941, the Soviet Union received information about Japan's plans to attack the United States, and immediately began to transport twenty divisions from Asia to Europe. In early December, the Red Army started its first counter-attack against the Germans, and in January 1942 it also increased the pressure on the Finnish section of the front. The development troubled Mannerheim, who had begun to look even more pessimistically on the Germans' chances of victory after America's entry into the war. Therefore he was increasingly explicit when he warded off the Germans' renewed demands for Finland to take an active part in the siege of Leningrad and begin a new assault against the Murmansk railway line. "I will not attack any longer", Mannerheim informed the German liaison officer Erfurth in mid-February 1942.

All Mannerheim's answers were given with Ryti's endorsement, and the two of them, together with the government's inner circle, concluded that it was advisable to wait and see how the situation developed between the warring Great Powers. Finland's military and economic dependency on Germany was far too great at this stage for the country to attempt to extricate itself from the war, or to risk irritating the Germans in other ways. At the same time, it was essential to avoid participating in further offensives against the Soviet Union so that Moscow was not given cause to strengthen its demands that the United States should also declare war on Finland. Here, as on so many other occasions during the Second World War, Mannerheim's final position was shaped not by narrow military motives but by cold geopolitical considerations. In these, there was little room for moral principles and scant expectation that justice would prevail.

This arduous balancing act would continue for the next two years, but the Finnish leadership duo were confronted with a particularly precarious situation in June 1942. On the evening before Mannerheim's 75th birthday, they received word that Hitler wished to make a brief visit to Finland to congratulate Mannerheim. Later, it became apparent that the initiative for this had come from Prime Minister Rangell and Foreign Minister Witting. In conversation with the German Colonel-General Dietl, they had suggested that Hitler should make a trip to Finland when a fitting occasion arose, naively assuming that a high-level meeting would be beneficial for the country. It would, however, have been extremely undiplomatic to call off Hitler's visit at that late stage, and so the dictator's private plane was directed to Immola's airfield in south-western Finland, from where he was transported onwards to a nearby railway line by a beautiful bay on the shore of Lake Saimaa. Both Mannerheim's and the Nazi Government's private carriages were already stationed here, ready for a fairly modest birthday lunch with about fifty guests of honour.

And so, Mannerheim's birthday celebration suddenly acquired a whole new order of magnitude. Everyone's attention was naturally focused on how the meeting between Hitler and Mannerheim would go. President Ryti welcomed the Führer and his seven-man retinue at the airfield, and upon arrival at the temporary site of the festivities they were met by Mannerheim, who was always suitably disarming in such situations. The meeting was captured both on film and by a crowd of German and Finnish war photographers, with the result that it quickly became a political sensation, and not only in Finland. Nazi propaganda also efficiently used the meeting for its own ends, showing it in cinemas in different parts of German-occupied Europe.

Mannerheim's elegance and restrained body language did not signal any hint of subservience. On the contrary, the general impression emerged that he and Hitler were two statesmen of equal merit with a common enemy but quite different ideologies. This notion naturally suited the Finnish state leadership, but it was also entirely acceptable for the German propaganda machine, which gladly brought to the fore the European objectives of this joint war. This theme was also one consciously cultivated by Hitler in his spontaneous speech to Mannerheim during the celebratory lunch, which was held in the two restaurant cars that had been transported to the rendezvous spot for that purpose. Before the meal, reciprocal presentations were organised by the retinues of both Mannerheim and Hitler, as well as a small-scale "Besprechung", or meeting, in the Field Marshal's saloon car. Ryti and the German commander of the Lapland forces, Colonel-General Eduard Dietl, were also in attendance.

To the hosts' relief, at no time during his visit did Hitler demand that Finland contribute more actively to the war effort. According to Ryti's notes, Hitler announced during the discussion that the Germans first intended to take the oil fields in the Caucasus, and thereafter to raze both Leningrad and Moscow to the ground. And

Fig. 8.4: Hitler and Mannerheim on the Marshal's birthday, 4 June 1942.

205

having praised the achievements of General Rommel in North Africa, he stated that the Italians had shown themselves to be completely incompetent soldiers, while he heaped praise on the Finns' heroic war efforts against the Soviet Union. Mannerheim contented himself with making the occasional interjection. When the conversation moved on to the Northern Front, Mannerheim requested the return of the Finnish troops that had, as agreed, been placed under German command in Lapland. This would soon be arranged.

Something that also drew attention was Hitler's calm and sober manner of speaking. This differed entirely from the passionate and irascible intonation which had become his trademark in his public appearances. Or, as an obviously surprised Mannerheim put it in a letter to his sister Eva Sparre, "The Chancellor of the Reich won plenty of sympathy through his straightforwardness and the unaffected way in which he behaved the whole time." This impression is also supported by an audio recording that was made, semi-unintentionally, of part of Mannerheim and Hitler's discussion. The microphone was discovered midway through their conversation and the recording was immediately cut short, but the tape would be kept for posterity in the Finnish Broadcasting Company's archives. Over time, its existence became common knowledge in Germany, and the actor Bruno Ganz used it while preparing for his role as Hitler in the feature film *Der Untergang* (2004; *Downfall*), about the dictator's last days in his bunker in war-torn Berlin. The movie became a global success, but in Germany it was difficult for many to accept the empathetic manner in which Ganz's Hitler spoke, which is hardly surprising given the tarnished legacy, to put it mildly, left by the Führer.

Three weeks after Hitler's surprise trip to Finland, Mannerheim made a return visit to the German headquarters in East Prussia, which the Germans also made copious use of for propaganda purposes. But contrary to the fears of the Finnish state leadership, neither of these top-level meetings caused any noticeable irritation on the Allies' side. This was probably due to both Ryti and Mannerheim continually keeping the British and American intelligence services informed that Finland's overarching war strategy was unchanged. Everything points to the fact that they counted on the information being conveyed onwards to Moscow. Nevertheless, they could scarcely have imagined that this happened through the conspiratorial assistance of the Soviet spies within the Western Powers' own administrations.

Mannerheim's legacy would obviously end up being quite different from Hitler's. In fact, the positive myths that formed around him received a powerful boost from all the honours and tributes that were showered on him on his 75th birthday. Mannerheim was most touched by the effusive speech that President Ryti made on behalf of the government, in which the decision to bestow upon him the honorary title of the Marshal of Finland was announced. At the same time, parliament sent word that it had decided to buy the house in Kaivopuisto for him that he had been renting from the Fazer family for nearly two decades. The military authorities' gift took the form of the announcement that, in future, their flag day would be celebrated on the Marshal's birthday, while the industry and banking circles gave a joint gift of an 18-million-mark donation to Mannerheim's National Foundation.

However, the most concrete demonstration of the Finnish people's appreciation of Mannerheim was that a number of cities, beginning with Helsinki, decided to name their main streets after him. The war situation effectively stopped any large civilian parties, but at the front the day was celebrated with double rations fortified with spirits and beer. This was done, incidentally, on Mannerheim's insistence, to ensure that the troops would at least have some sort of celebration on his birthday. In this respect, the day also resulted in an uproarious incident in Väinö Linna's great war novel *The Unknown Soldier* (1954). Enlivened by the special occasion, the machine gun company's men decide to imbibe a secretly produced batch of "kilju", an alcoholic drink made from a mash of yeast and sugar, which causes the company's commander, Lieutenant Vilho Koskela, to utter the *mot juste*, "Asialliset hommat hoidetaan, muuten ollaan kuin Ellun kanat"—"Let's do only what duty demands, otherwise we'll play like pigs in mud."

It was common knowledge that Mannerheim himself was not one to turn down a drink. On weekdays he would regularly drink two or three schnapps, a beer, a few glasses of wine for dinner and sometimes an evening nightcap. This level of consumption was undeniably sizeable for a person who was already over 70 years old, but since he was a tall fellow and in good shape, and had, moreover, drunk such quantities ever since his time in Russia, he did not seem to have appeared intoxicated, as far as we know. If one of his generals did not hold his drink so well, he quickly became the subject of derision. Mannerheim had a playful way of checking how steady his dining companions' hands were: he always had the schnapps glasses filled to the brim, a tradition he had brought back with him from Russia. Anyone who spilled his glass became, in due course, the target of pointed jokes or mocking glances.

In other respects, the daily routines at the headquarters were not particularly glamorous. At the start of the Continuation War, the Field Marshal lived in a private villa outside Mikkeli, but in autumn 1941 he moved into a stone house in the vicinity of the headquarters, which was based in the city's elementary school for the duration of both wars. When the risk of air strikes increased in March 1944, Mannerheim again housed himself outside the city, this time at Sairila Manor, 10 kilometres from Mikkeli. The Field Marshal's day began at 6.30am with a light breakfast, followed by an hour's ride in the environs of the city, and, during the warmer half of the year, a morning dip as well. At 9am he presented himself at the headquarters, whose whole personnel consisted of over 600 people. In Mannerheim's General Staff there served five officers, with whom Mannerheim and his two aides ate lunch at 12.30pm and dinner at 7.30pm at the Mikkeli Club (Mikkelin Klubi), a restaurant at the functionalist Hotel Kaleva in the centre of the city.

During these carefully planned breaks in what could be a twelve-hour-long working day, the burning news questions were discussed; jokes were sometimes cracked too, but they had to lend themselves to the moment. Setting the tone in all these discussions was obviously the Field Marshal himself, who had no shortage of anecdotes and memories to share with his colleagues. After dinner there followed a short time round the coffee table while the gentlemen smoked their cigarettes and cigars, which was not something unusual in the mid-1900s, when the large majority of the male population of Europe smoked regularly. This was also the case, of course, at the front, where the soldiers who fought for the Fatherland received a significantly larger ration of cigarettes than those on the home front. Mannerheim usually smoked long, slim La Planta cigars from Strengberg's tobacco factory in Pietarsaari, but only three a day.

After dinner, a group of Mannerheim's closest fellow officers and friends often gathered for evening tea and whisky at his home, especially if the Field Marshal's intimate friends, such as Rudolf Walden, were visiting. The ongoing war was entirely avoided as a topic of conversation. Instead, there arose long discussions about previous epochs in Finland's and Russia's history, during which Mannerheim would gladly also proffer lively memories from his childhood and adolescence or from his time in St Petersburg. A perennial fixture at these gatherings was the Field Marshal's personal physician, Lauri Kalaja; after the host had drawn the night's proceedings to a close, the doctor would go to his bedside and take his pulse. At this point, Mannerheim would usually take the opportunity to add critical postscripts to the evening's discussion, which Kalaja would then secretly note down.

Kalaja's subtlety was somewhat lacking, however, for the Field Marshal was obviously aware of this documentation. In autumn 1945, when there arose a risk that Mannerheim might become mixed up in the war-guilt process, he instructed Kalaja and his other close colleagues to destroy all such documents. Consequently, we will never know what Mannerheim told his doctor. But according to the publisher Heikki A. Reenpää, who later made Kalaja's acquaintance, at these late hours Mannerheim took pleasure in going over both large and small episodes in his life. Such reminiscences show that Mannerheim trusted his doctor implicitly, and he would also follow the latter's prescriptions to the letter, although he did so, too, out of necessity, since his health became increasingly fragile in the years 1943 and 1944.

As was typical, Mannerheim got a high fever immediately after Hitler's visit. In summer 1944, he was afflicted by a troublesome rash on his hands that forced him to wear gloves and that also made writing painful. Both these complaints were undoubtedly caused by the intense stress wrought upon Mannerheim by the heavy responsibility he bore for the defence and the entire future of Finland. However, Kalaja's medications and treatments gradually increased for other ailments as well. The Field Marshal was prone to inflammation of the respiratory passages and suffered from gastric ulcers. In the seven months between October 1942 and April 1943, he had such a serious bout of pneumonia that he believed he was going to die and wanted to rewrite his will. Kalaja successfully managed to keep the Grim Reaper at bay, however, and saw to it that Mannerheim, under his supervision, travelled to Switzerland for three weeks' convalescence, a trip which restored his health surprisingly well. At the turn of 1943 the pneumonia struck again, but on this occasion, too, the Field Marshal rose from his sickbed and retook command, like Colonel Döbeln in the Battle of Jutas—a heroic figure in a national poem by Johan Runeberg describing the war against Russia in 1808–09.

A Painful Withdrawal

Mannerheim's recovery coincided with a decisive shift in the war in the Baltic Sea region. In January 1944, the Red Army was able to break the siege of Leningrad, and over the next two months the front was pushed south-west towards the city of Narva in eastern Estonia. The Finnish Government became increasingly concerned about how they could extricate themselves from the war with their sovereignty intact. After German defeats in the Second Battle of El Alamein in late 1942 and the Battle of Stalingrad in early 1943, the Finnish state leadership and Mannerheim's General Staff became convinced that the Nazis were going to lose the war. The issue was, however, that Finland could not sever its relations with Germany and make its own peace agreement with the Soviet Union while the Wehrmacht still had the Baltic Sea region and northern Finland in a vice-like grip. No less dangerous, on the other hand, was waiting too long to break ties with Berlin, since this could lead to the Red Army also attacking Finland from the Baltics, resulting in even less favourable peace terms or, in the worst case, occupation.

In connection with Ryti's re-election as president in March 1943, a new coalition government was formed under the leadership of the National Coalition Party's Edwin Linkomies. In collaboration with the United States, he immediately started to gauge the possibility of declaring peace independently of Germany. The Nazis were extremely irritated by these efforts. In late summer 1943, it was leaked that a group of citizens had appealed directly to Ryti to begin peace negotiations with the Soviet Union as soon as possible. Aggravated by this, the Germans threatened serious reprisals and delayed negotiations for a new grain agreement that Finland desperately needed, as its own food production had been greatly reduced by the war. At the same time, the Western Powers also intensified their demands for Finland to enter into a peace deal with the Soviet Union, resulting in new peace overtures via Stockholm. At the end of November 1943, the Allied Powers agreed at a summit in Tehran that Finland would be forced to enter into a peace agreement that would restore its 1940 border and require the country to make significant reparations.

These demands were delivered to the Finnish Government just before Christmas 1943. Unaware that the Western Powers supported Moscow's peace conditions, the government chose not to accept them, for the Finnish forces continued to hold their positions far away in East Karelia. It realised that a return to the border of 1940 would be experienced as an act of treachery against the nation. The pressure, however, increased incessantly. In late January 1944, the American Government publicly urged Finland to initiate peace negotiations. The next month, the Red Army waged a campaign of heavy bombing against Helsinki and other densely populated urban areas in order to further force the Finnish hand.

The coercion worked. In late March 1944, the Finnish Government sent a delegation to Moscow to obtain more detailed information about the Soviets' peace demands. Besides a return to the border of 1940 and considerable reparations, these included the stipulation that the German troops in Lapland should be disarmed, which was seen as both unreasonable and dangerous, since it could facilitate a Soviet invasion. The Finnish Government rejected these demands in early April 1944, whereupon Stalin immediately gave orders to prepare for a large-scale offensive against the Finnish front in order to force Finland into a peace deal before the Soviet Union's decisive showdown with Germany. Moreover, the Western Allies were briefed that henceforth Finland would be called upon to make an unconditional surrender, in common with Germany's other satellite states.

The President and the government were obviously keen to hear Mannerheim's opinions on these peace efforts. In early February 1944, Mannerheim exhorted Ryti to quickly accept the Soviet demands. He saw that Germany had already lost the war and that

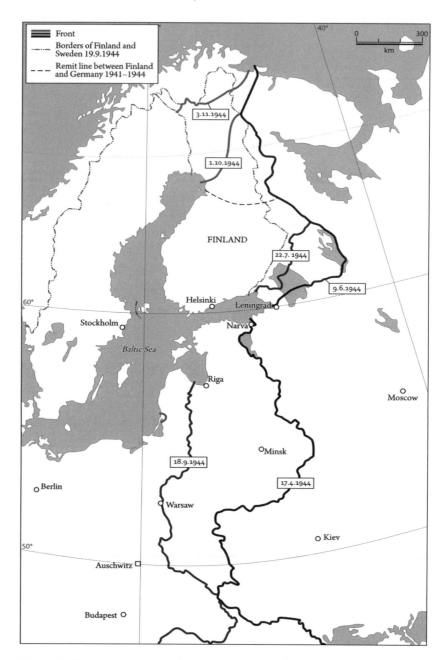

Fig. 8.5: The development of the Eastern Front between September 1943 and December 1944. The Finnish section was short, but at a strategically important position by the Gulf of Finland and Leningrad. Map by Hannu Linkola.

the Red Army now had a wholly different level of resources with which to break through the Finnish defensive positions. But he was unwilling to take a public stand on the matter. One justification for this was his failing health, which meant that he became tired more easily and took longer to make decisions. Another was surely the realisation that the Finnish people were going to find this political decision extremely difficult to swallow.

An address by Mannerheim might have helped, in the sense that his words carried weight with the nation. It was for this very reason that the Field Marshal had been asked to stand as a presidential candidate in spring 1943. He eventually agreed to do so on the assumption that a significant majority of the electoral college supported him. If he was to pilot the ship of state into harbour during stormy weather, then his popular support must be guaranteed. In a straw poll, however, it became apparent that less than half of the electors stood behind Mannerheim's candidature. Consequently, he dropped out of the race and Ryti won an overwhelming majority in the official vote. After this experience, Mannerheim consistently emphasised that his remit was defence, not national politics.

As such, it was hardly a surprise that, given this situation, the Field Marshal did not wish to have more responsibility. He had obtained almost all the honour and power that he could have hoped for, and he must have felt that his capacity for work had been reduced both by his age and ailments. At the same time, Mannerheim must clearly have been conscious of the fact that it would be easier to get the nation to accept the harsh conditions of the impending peace if he were president. This was also something about which many of his trusted friends and colleagues tried to convince him. Moreover, Mannerheim had no doubt been informed that many in the Allied camp saw him as an influential force who ought to be saved until such time when the really painful decisions had to be made.

In connection with the increasing attempts to advance peace between Finland and the Soviet Union in late autumn 1943, Moscow's Ambassador to Stockholm, Alexandra Kollontai, sent word via a Swedish diplomat that she had received an explicit promise from Stalin. This was, namely, that Mannerheim would never be held accountable for Finland's wartime policies, and it is very likely that this message also reached Mannerheim himself. That such an assurance was given indicates that Stalin would rather have come to a peace agreement with Mannerheim than with Ryti. As the Finnish question received a cursory discussion at the summit in Tehran, Stalin stated that he would "naturally" have preferred Finland to have had a government entirely devoid of Nazi sympathisers, but that he was nonetheless prepared to negotiate with "Ryti or the devil himself".

Stalin's criticism of Ryti was in many respects unfair, but it was partly because the latter had been forced to make positive comments in public about Hitler's Germany on a number of occasions during the Continuation War. Mannerheim, in contrast, had consciously avoided such statements. It is possible that Stalin also remembered that Mannerheim had shown himself understanding of Soviet security interests before the Winter War. Nevertheless, what counted most was probably the assumption that only Mannerheim had the necessary authority to get both the army and society to accept the severe peace conditions and the cutting of ties with Germany. Stalin's plans for Mannerheim after this happened were, however, another story. Stalin expert Kimmo Rentola has suggested that the intention was to gradually break down both the Field Marshal's and the Finnish social system's powers of resistance.

Both the Finnish Government and the country's increasingly vocal proponents of peace (known as the "Peace Opposition") had come to the conclusion that Mannerheim was a necessary backer for the peace process in March 1944. But despite their insistent attempts to get Mannerheim to agree to take the presidential office, he resolutely refused to do so. His rebuff contributed to the Soviets' peace conditions of the time being judged too dangerous and unreasonable to accept. Mannerheim himself took part in the meeting on 2 April 1944 in which Ryti and the government's standing committee for foreign affairs decided not to agree to the Soviet demands. The Field Marshal was actually willing to accept them, but he only expressed this vaguely and did not seriously try to influence the members of government.

On 9 June 1944, the Red Army began an enormous offensive (from the Finnish perspective) over the Karelian Isthmus, quickly breaking through a number of Finnish defensive lines. On the evening of 20 June, Soviet tanks rolled into Vyborg. But over the next three weeks, the Finnish forces successfully halted the Soviet offensive with the efficient support of the German air force, until the attack was finally called off in the middle of July. The Red Army had launched its large offensive in Belarus on 22 June. After this point the Soviet forces on the Finnish front no longer received reinforcements, which, combined with the increasingly effective Finno-German defence, meant that it was not worth the Soviet Union wasting more resources in forcing Finland to accept peace on the battlefield. It now judged the Finns ready to accept a political solution. On 14 July 1944, Moscow signalled, via Stockholm, that Stalin no longer demanded an unconditional surrender, and, a little over two months later, the two parties concluded a ceasefire agreement that brought Finland's three-year war against the Soviet Union to an end. The war had claimed the lives of 70,000 Finnish soldiers in total.

Nowadays, researchers are fairly unanimous that the rather unprofessional manner in which Mannerheim led his General Staff contributed to the abrupt collapse of Finnish defences on the

Fig. 8.6: The University of Helsinki's Main Building in flames after being struck by a bomb on the night of 26–27 February 1944.

Karelian Isthmus in June 1944. His Chief of General Staff, Erik Heinrichs, admitted as much in his large Mannerheim biography in the late 1950s. In spite of regular appeals from Ryti and from Mannerheim's military subordinates, he refused to strengthen the defences on the Karelian Isthmus with troops from East Karelia. The Field Marshal considered it unlikely that the Red Army would attack Finland at a time when its decisive battles against Germany were just around the corner. Additionally, he stressed that the captured areas of East Karelia could be used as articles of exchange in the forthcoming peace negotiations.

Matters were not improved by the fact that the fortification of the defensive lines on the Karelian Isthmus had advanced at a particularly sluggish pace; nor by the fact that, of the nearly 5,000 light anti-tank weapons that had arrived from Germany in April 1944, only a fraction were accessible at the front when the Red Army's tanks poured forth. The General Staff compounded these issues by erroneously interpreting reports from military intelligence that there were large concentrations of Soviet troops north of Leningrad, either as a diversionary tactic or in preparation for a large new offensive against the Germans on the Narva section of the Eastern Front.

On 12 June, just three days after the Soviet offensive had begun, the Finnish retreat became so panicked that Mannerheim appealed directly to Hitler for German assistance. And as proof that the brotherhood-in-arms was still intact, Hitler immediately gave the order that the Finns should get weapon and troop support as long as they continued to fight. Four days later there arrived the first fleets of the 70 fighter planes and dive bombers that the Germans would send to Finland. Over the next three weeks they would form a significant part of the air strikes that were directed against the Soviet armoured columns and supply lines. Alongside the aerial support, the Germans sent more than 10,000 new Panzerfausts (single-shot anti-tank grenade launchers) and, within a week, naval forces, an assault gun brigade and an infantry division had also come to help the Finnish cause.

The collapse at the front also increased the political pressure for a change of government and for new attempts to establish peace talks with the Soviet Union. Ryti tried one more time, in vain, to persuade Mannerheim to take up the office of president. In parallel with this, it was communicated via Stockholm to Moscow that the door was open for peace negotiations; but before Stalin's answer arrived, Hitler received information about these efforts. On 22 June he sent his foreign minister, von Ribbentrop, to Helsinki with an ultimatum: if the Finns wanted to receive military assistance in the future, Hitler must get an official promise that Finland would fight on Germany's side right to the very end. The next day Stalin's answer arrived: the Soviet Union declared that the prerequisite for peace negotiations was that the Finnish Government should announce that it was prepared to surrender.

It is not hard to imagine the anguished deliberations that tormented the Finnish Government in this situation. Mannerheim was consulted once again, and together with Prime Minister Linkomies he convinced Ryti beyond all doubt that German help was necessary. It was, however, out of the question that parliament or the government would accept a political agreement with Germany. As such, after consulting with leading legal experts, Ryti presented a personal guarantee to Hitler on 26 June 1944, one that was binding for neither the government nor parliament. This stated that no one in the government appointed by Ryti would begin peace negotiations with the Soviet Union without Germany's consent. As might be expected, the statement was heavily criticised by the Allies, but it ensured that the Germans' extensive weapon deliveries would continue, and it thereby strengthened the Finnish troops' morale at the same time.

While Mannerheim bore heavy responsibility for the poor preparation on the Karelian Isthmus, he also saw to it that German assistance arrived in time and continued until the offensive had been thwarted. Ryti's guarantee to Hitler was a necessary contribution to this fight for survival. The plan was obviously that Finland would break this promise as soon as the situation on the front had become more stable and the country had secured a better position for itself in advance of peace negotiations with Moscow. And this is precisely what came to pass. The Soviet offensive was called off in mid-July, after which Moscow indicated to the Finnish Government that the latter was no longer required to surrender. On 25 July, Mannerheim received, through intermediaries, a personal statement from Stalin, in which the Soviet leader declared his readiness to begin peace negotiations. On 27 July, a caveat was added to the message: before these discussions could start, Finland must undertake a regime change. The next day, Ryti and Minister of Finance Väinö Tanner finally convinced Mannerheim to agree to be appointed president through an emergency powers act, which concentrated even more authority in Mannerheim's hands and released the country from the personal promise that Ryti had made to Hitler.

What was the upshot of Mannerheim's actions during these fateful weeks and months in summer 1944? If his responsibility for the serious shortcomings in Finland's defensive readiness on the Karelian Isthmus are put to one side, after the setbacks of the first few weeks Mannerheim succeeded in uniting the Finnish field army into an opposition that was sufficient to stop the Red Army's offensive and pave the way for a political solution to the conflict. His younger colleagues at the General Staff would have certainly conducted the strict military dimension of the command better than Mannerheim. However, the question is whether the delicate balancing act between the political and military aspects of the crisis would have been achieved if Mannerheim had not used all his authority to convince Ryti and the government that the path they had chosen to follow was the only plausible one.

Mannerheim showed many symptoms of stress during these summer months. Both his subordinates at the General Staff and the country's ministers would later attest that this pressure often led to peevishness, capriciousness and an anguished decision-making process. But when this is brought up as evidence that he was no longer in command of the situation, it is worth bearing in mind that many other, significantly younger decision-makers were noted as having comparable psychosomatic weaknesses. Prime Minister Linkomies was forced to take extended sick leave at the start of the year, and Ryti fell ill with a difficult case of jaundice directly after Ribbentrop's visit in summer 1944. It was not only the state leadership that was suffering. When the goods wagons returned from the front filled with coffins, and when the civilian population of Karelia had to be evacuated once again, an increasing number of Finns began to ask whether all the sacrifices had really been worth it. In summer 1944, a total of 16,500 soldiers were killed in action. What was the decision-makers' responsibility for all this misery and suffering? Why had the Finnish Government not made a peace agreement back in spring 1944?

9

RESPONSIBILITY AND LEGACY

The President

On 4 August 1944, Mannerheim took the presidential oath in the debate chamber of the Parliament Building, after which he gave a short speech that began with the words: "As I, for the second time during a pivotal moment for the Fatherland, take up the duties of head of state, I do so deeply conscious of the responsibility that is imposed upon me." Among those present were around ten people who had been parliamentarians before during Mannerheim's short period as regent in 1918–19. The last quarter of a century had been a success story for Finland, right up until the outbreak of the Second World War. The subsequent years of conflict had naturally shaken and threatened the country's independence at a fundamental level, but the turmoil had also revealed that the Finnish people were consumed by a resistance and a will to survive that neither they themselves nor the wider world could have anticipated.

In summer 1919, Mannerheim had greatly looked forward to the prospect of being elected as President of the Republic of Finland. But when it finally happened twenty-five years later, it was through an emergency powers act passed by parliament, and the circumstances and prognosis for the future looked, in every respect, rather less promising. It is clear, therefore, that Mannerheim's decision to accept the post, despite his ill health and weighty responsibilities, did not come from a lust for power or a desire for revenge. Rather, he felt obliged, as the chief architect behind the brotherhood-in-arms with Germany, to straighten out the tangle that Finland had again ended up in. Furthermore, both the country's political elite

Fig. 9.1: The freshly appointed President Mannerheim inspects the guard of honour in front of Parliament House, 4 August 1944.

and the Allied Powers had, since spring 1943, given Mannerheim to understand that he was the best person to convince both his nation and the wider world that Finland ought to accept the harsh peace conditions.

In order to get this process underway, Mannerheim made sure that the key positions in government, which was appointed anew after the change in president, went to people whom he knew well and who were, moreover, authorities on Russia. Antti Hackzell was chosen to be prime minister and Carl Enckell was picked as foreign minister. Both had served as ministers and diplomats since the early 1920s, and, in common with Mannerheim, they had both lived in pre-revolutionary St Petersburg. But since Mannerheim did not want, under any circumstances, to break the bonds with Germany too abruptly, he chose to proceed with extreme caution. During the first two weeks, therefore, he did not disclose anything specific to Hackzell or Enckell about the timetable, or about how exactly the military co-operation would be wound up. This increased their misgivings that the Field Marshal was progressing far too slowly, and that, in the worst-case scenario, this could cause Moscow to lose patience and engage in a large new offensive.

On 17 August 1944, the Chief of the German General Staff, Wilhelm Keitel, visited the Finnish headquarters in Mikkeli to investigate why Mannerheim had assumed the office of president. And precisely as the Germans had suspected, Mannerheim then replied that he did not consider himself bound by the same personal assurances that his predecessor had given to Hitler. He was referring, of course, to Ryti's pledge that no one in his appointed government would begin peace negotiations with the Soviet Union without Germany's permission. It is important to note that Mannerheim delivered this message so courteously that Keitel, despite his irritation, did not make any threats of military consequences if the Finns independently struck a peace deal. Far away in the German headquarters, Keitel submitted such a tactful report to Hitler that it did not, contrary to expectation, cause an outburst of fury, but rather the resigned declaration that "Mannerheim is a good soldier but a wretched politician."

After Mannerheim's answer there followed a week of nervous waiting. Hitler was, according to Mannerheim, a hysterical person; they must, therefore, see how he was going to react before trying to arrange peace negotiations with the Soviet Union. Once the week had passed without any sign of revenge from the Germans, Mannerheim gave Finland's Envoy to Stockholm, G. A. Gripenberg, orders to deliver, through Swedish channels, an invitation to Moscow to start negotiations. Stalin's answer came a few days later: Finland must unequivocally make public its break with Germany and demand that the German troops leave its territory by 15 September at the latest. If the Germans opposed such a retreat, Finland would be forced to disarm them, after which a Finnish delegation would be invited to Moscow for negotiations about "a cease-fire or peace, or about both peace and a ceasefire".

After many days of anguished deliberation, Mannerheim decided to accept the conditions, even though the deadline for the Germans' retreat was totally unrealistic. On the morning of 2 September 1944, the Finnish Government sent this answer to Moscow with a proposal that hostilities should be suspended the next day, so that the Finnish Army could retire to the 1940 border. That same evening the government's proposal was accepted by parliament. Straight afterwards, Hackzell reported the decision in a radio broadcast, in which he expressed himself so vaguely about the termination of the brotherhood-in-arms that Moscow demanded a new announcement. Finland had to unambiguously stress that the prerequisite for peace negotiations was the disarmament of the German troops on its soil and their deliverance to the Allies, if they had not departed the country by the appointed date.

On the same day that Hackzell gave his radio speech, Mannerheim sent a personal letter to Hitler, in which he thanked him, in civil terms, for the favourable co-operation that Finland was now forced to break off for the survival of the nation. Germany would continue to exist even if it were defeated. This was not the case for the people of Finland, who, with certainty, "would be eradicated and banished" if the country was invaded, wrote Mannerheim, expressing hope that the good relations could be terminated as peacefully as possible. Hitler never answered Mannerheim's letter, of course, but a couple of days later he stated to a Japanese diplomat that the Finns had not betrayed the Germans, because they had given up only after all their strength had been fully depleted.

This understanding attitude also manifested itself in the termination of the brotherhood-in-arms that followed over the subsequent weeks. Except for a clumsy attempt to land at Suursaari Island in the Gulf of Finland, the Germans initiated a quick retreat from Finland without a lot of fuss. The retreat could have gone even more quickly had the Soviet Union not forced Finland to actively attack; but, after a couple of months of small-scale war in Lapland, the conflict became more of a staged war, which suited both parties admirably.

Alongside this conciliatory parting of the ways, which was strikingly different to the Germans' vindictive retreats in other parts of Europe, the Finnish Government hastened to meet the Soviet peace conditions. After Hackzell had issued a new communique, in which he clearly stated that the Germans would be disarmed, the ceasefire came into force on 5 September. Nine days later negotiations were started with Moscow, and on 19 September they concluded in an armistice agreement that was extremely harsh for Finland. Alongside a return to the border of 1940, Finland had to give up Petsamo and rent out Porkkalanniemi, a peninsula 30 kilometres west of Helsinki, for fifty years as a Soviet naval base. On top of all this, the country was bound to pay 300 million dollars in reparations, which, in proportion to its population, was a sum that was twice as large as Romania and Hungary were obliged to pay to the Soviet Union. Over the next three years, the Soviet-dominated Allied Control Commission, which had been granted considerable authority, oversaw Finland's adherence to the agreement.

When the peace delegation returned to Helsinki on 20 September, it immediately proceeded to give a report to Mannerheim, who had moved into the president's residence in Tamminiemi. The delegates' sorrowful and worn countenances told all, as did their debilitated health. While in Moscow, Prime Minister Hackzell had suffered a cerebral haemorrhage, from which he never recovered; Walden and Heinrichs were also the worse for wear, and both would soon undergo medical treatment as well. The big question was whether the Soviet Union really intended to respect the agreement, or whether its objective was still the occupation of Finland. As a precautionary measure, therefore, the Finnish headquarters began making secret preparations for a guerrilla war.

Mannerheim's view of the situation was deeply pessimistic when he met Paasikivi on the evening of 5 October. He stated that, in practice, the armistice signified a capitulation: "We are not in a position to defend ourselves." The discussion moved on to consider how the Field Marshal should handle the Control Commission's chairman, Colonel-General Andrei Zhdanov, who had arrived in Helsinki that same evening and would pay a visit to Tamminiemi two days later. Paasikivi advised Mannerheim to treat Zhdanov and the other Soviet delegates with great respect. The Bolshevik parvenus were much more uncertain of their prestige than the Russian elite of the Emperor's time.

Mannerheim followed this advice carefully. The energetic Zhdanov arrived in a long convoy of cars through the city to Tamminiemi and was introduced to Mannerheim and Walden, who were each clad in uniform and their distinguished decorations. The Finns escorted the guests to the dining room and began a polite conversation with Zhdanov in their pre-revolutionary Russian.

Mannerheim expressed regret that the countries had fallen into war with each other, and hastened to add that despite everything, Finland's loss had a favourable consequence, for the parties could now straighten out the conflict peacefully. At the same time, he reported progress in the war against the Germans in northern Finland and requested Soviet flank support from the Kola Peninsula.

This assistance never amounted to much, however. At that time, the Red Army was increasingly concentrating its forces in eastern Central Europe, which meant that it simply did not have enough resources to invade Finland. Zhdanov obviously revealed nothing of the sort. On the contrary, over the next winter he would, on multiple occasions, threaten the Finns with occupation if the conditions of the armistice were not met as agreed. Nevertheless, Zhdanov carefully avoided making such threats during the meeting with Mannerheim, of which he gave a surprisingly objective picture in his detailed report to Stalin, especially considering that his underlying attitude towards the old counter-revolutionary must have been critical. Some researchers have characterised Mannerheim's efforts in autumn 1944 as tottering. Certainly he acted slowly at times, but this caution most likely contributed to the successful transition, despite all the challenges, from the German-dominated brotherhood-in-arms to the Soviet-dominated regime of the Control Commission.

Due to the ongoing war with the Germans in northern Finland, Mannerheim would predominantly lead the country from his headquarters in Mikkeli during autumn 1944. He travelled to Helsinki on his personal train only to participate in important discussions, which were often organised in connection with the government's Presidential Sessions every Friday, but afterwards he quickly took himself back to Mikkeli and his accommodation at Sairila Manor outside the town. By early November, however, the country's political life had started to pulsate so strongly that the country needed a more dynamic government than the cabinet led by Urho Castrén, who had taken office in September following Antti Hackzell's strokes. One condition of the Moscow Armistice was that Finland's ban on communism should be lifted, and, at the end of October, the Finnish Communist Party began its activities anew. During this same period, many of the bourgeois politicians who had been engaged in the Peace Opposition were waiting impatiently to take on ministerial responsibilities. Alongside various domestic political issues, the most pressing concern was to establish an agreement with the Soviet Union about the substance and timetable of the war reparations.

Mannerheim, after a certain hesitancy, agreed that his old friend and Russia connoisseur, J. K. Paasikivi, should form the government. His doubt stemmed principally from a suspicion that Paasikivi would be too reasonable in comparison to the Russians, but when the political expectations surrounding the appointment increased, Mannerheim finally gave in. Moreover, Paasikivi succeeded in convincing the Field Marshal to accept a list of ministers that not only included three former members of the Peace Opposition, but also the Communist Yrjö Leino. The new government convened in mid-November. One of the Peace Opposition was the 44-year-old Agrarian League member, Urho Kekkonen. In his capacity as Minister for Justice, he was to take significant responsibility for all the large reforms and decisions that the government was expected to make.

Thus a gradual shift in power took place from the politically isolated Mannerheim to Paasikivi's government, whose close contacts with parliament and the Control Commission made it possible for many difficult questions to be quickly resolved. In December 1944 the reparations agreement was concluded, and, after a number of socio-political reforms, the government drove through a bundle of land provision laws. These included measures to provide the evacuated Karelians with replacement land. The new division of labour suited Mannerheim, although he had difficulty stomaching the fact that the Communists and their socialist umbrella organisation had an increasingly large influence. After their success in the parliamentary elections in March 1945, they obtained four ministerial positions in Paasikivi's new government.

At the turn of 1944–45, Mannerheim transferred the active leadership of the army to his trusted colleague Erik Heinrichs, whom he appointed commander of the defence forces. Mannerheim did, however, continue as commander-in-chief, and was a central actor in the discussions about the defence of the Gulf of Finland that were conducted with the Soviet Union over the winter of 1944–45. Just before Christmas, Mannerheim sent a letter to Zhdanov proposing that the coastal artillery should be preserved, even though the terms of the armistice obliged Finland to phase it out, and asserting that an effective defence of Finland's coast also served the interests of the Soviet Union.

When the suggestion failed to elicit enthusiasm, Mannerheim went a step further, and, in a discussion with Zhdanov in mid-January 1945, he advanced the idea that the countries could draw up a joint strategy for the defence of the western parts of the Gulf of Finland. And to emphasise that this was not just a passing fancy, Mannerheim reminded him that, even before the outbreak of the Winter War, he had recommended a solution that paid heed to the Soviets' security needs. Zhdanov's interest was piqued by the prospect of such large-scale co-operation. After asking Paasikivi for advice, Mannerheim quickly drew up a proposal together with Heinrichs and Lieutenant-General Oscar Enckell for Finno-Soviet co-operation in the defence of the Gulf of Finland's coast. It contained many components that would later form an integral part of the Agreement of Friendship, Co-operation and Mutual Assistance that the countries entered into in 1948.

Heinrichs had, in fact, already presented comparable ideas in a memorandum of September 1944, but then the Field Marshal had adjudged them to be in and of themselves unrealistic, if logical. A month earlier, similar thoughts had also been put forward to Mannerheim by the political scientist and international relations expert Yrjö Ruutu. A prominent notion in both proposals was that Finland should accept the Soviet Union's strategic interests, and make preparations to defend its own southern and western coasts against any attack on Leningrad and northern Russia that might be directed through Finnish territory. This was also the central message in Mannerheim's new suggestion. It quickly became apparent, however, that Stalin was not prepared to sign such an agreement before the countries had made a conclusive peace treaty. The initiative was consequently put on ice until the autumn of 1947.

This would be Mannerheim's last big achievement as a geopolitically inclined officer and statesman. In his analysis of these negotiations, Juhani Suomi has stated that Mannerheim's overarching aim was not a military agreement; rather, he wanted to prevent Finland's defences from being dismantled by deferring to the Soviet Union's security interests. If this bargaining was successful and resulted in some form of military arrangement, it would strengthen Finland's security, but only provided it was unified with measures which safeguarded the country's defensive capabilities.

In spring 1945, Mannerheim was again struck down by various ailments, which forced him to take sick leave and brought to the fore the question of his retirement. At the same time new problems appeared on the horizon. In May 1945, it was revealed that the White Guards had hidden weapons caches around Finland in autumn 1944, when the army had been demobilised and they themselves had been disbanded. Heinrichs was forced to resign as the defence forces' commander-in-chief, and there followed protracted court proceedings that would last until 1950. In late summer 1945, the Finnish Government was forced to comply with the Control Commission's demand for legal action against the country's wartime ministers. The idea of formal retribution had become difficult to disregard, since it was outlined both in article 13 in the Moscow Armistice, signed by Finland, and in the victorious powers' agreement in Potsdam about how Germany and its allies would be held accountable for the war.

Mannerheim was very suspicious of the proposal, and not only because it ran entirely contrary to the principles of the Western legal system to pass a retroactive law. There was quite clearly also the underlying concern that he and his wartime General Staff would be deemed responsible for the Finno-German brotherhood-in-arms. When his attempts to avert or water down the proposed bill failed, he decided to go on sick leave in September 1945, the very month that the law was to be ratified. He also gave the questionable honour of signing the law to his deputy Paasikivi.

Although Minister for Justice Urho Kekkonen consciously strived to prevent Mannerheim and his officer corps from going on trial, the preparations for the legal process demanded that the Field Marshal be interviewed. Mannerheim was permitted to acquaint himself with the questions in advance and formulated his answers to be as evasive as possible; this had the desired effect of shifting responsibility onto the politicians. The process nevertheless aggravated the frail Mannerheim's nerves, and after various twists and turns he travelled to Portugal in early November with Kalaja, his personal physician, to attend to his health.

The purpose of this convalescence was to keep Mannerheim at a safe distance when the politically motivated trial began, so that he would not run the risk of being prosecuted after all. With hindsight, it can be confirmed that at no stage did Moscow directly insist that he be held to account, but this was obviously not something that could be guaranteed at the time. As such, Mannerheim returned to Finland only after eight members of the wartime government, with Risto Ryti at their head, had stood on trial, and after the time limit for prosecution had expired at the turn of the year. At this point, however, the political landscape was filled with increasingly impatient calls for Mannerheim to resign. However, during the trial, increasingly incontrovertible evidence had come out that showed he had been actively involved in the preparations for the brotherhood-in-arms, so he chose to postpone his decision to resign until after the eight politicians' sentencing. This took place on 21 February 1946, and two weeks later, on 4 March, the government received Mannerheim's resignation, with a doctor's certificate enclosed. It was immediately accepted. Five days later, parliament used the Emergency Powers Act to elect Paasikivi president for the remainder of the term of office, in other words until 1950.

There is no doubt that Mannerheim, together with Ryti, had been primarily responsible for the decisions that led to the brotherhood-in-arms with Germany. Why, then, did Stalin let him go unpunished? It is hardly likely that the Soviet leader's vow in summer 1944, not to make Mannerheim the target of reprisals, counted for anything—he was notorious for breaking these sorts of promises in the blink of an eye. A more plausible explanation is that Moscow perceived that a trial against Mannerheim would have damaged Finno-Soviet relations more than was desirable. As Jukka Tarkka has pointed out, this judgement closely resembled the Americans' decision, at roughly the same time, to leave the Japanese Emperor Hirohito alone. In both cases, judiciousness carried the most weight.

Mannerheim never made a public comment about his exemption from the war-guilt trials. However, the threat of repercussions clearly left its mark on him: in late autumn 1946, during a stay at Finnish Envoy G. A. Gripenberg's residence in Stockholm, he complained to his trusted relative about a recurrent nightmare, in which he was arrested and sent to the Kremlin, where he had heated quarrels with Stalin about the war. "How does the dream end?" asked Gripenberg. "Always in the same way", sighed Mannerheim, "I am tortured", and then went on to give a detailed description of his sadistic treatment.

The Memoirs

On the evening Mannerheim resigned he was publicly thanked for his services in a radio speech by Paasikivi, who highlighted everything that the Marshal of Finland had done to liberate the country from the war. Now, Mannerheim could retire in good spirits: "Finland's people will never forget the extraordinary services he has performed for the Fatherland." The words beautifully summed up the public appreciation that Mannerheim always enjoyed, even though his timorous actions during the war-guilt process had dealt a blow to his reputation, especially among the wartime politicians who alone got the blame for the brotherhood-in-arms. But when the trial demanded by the victorious powers was finally over, the Marshal's inelegant exit was also carefully brushed to one side. It became framed as one of the regrettable episodes that the normalisation of relations with the Soviet Union had, unfortunately, entailed. Contributing to this atonement was the fact that those judged responsible for the war had, in the end, got off with much more lenient punishments than their counterparts in other countries that had allied with Germany. None of the politicians had received the death penalty, and soon their sentences would be reduced further. Risto Ryti served the longest prison term of all, but even he was released in May 1949.

Mannerheim, too, regarded the future with a new confidence. Straight after his resignation he threw himself into the maintenance of Kirkniemi Manor in Länsi-Uusimaa, which he had bought in August 1945 with the money he had received from parliament as a 75th-birthday gift. The money had really been intended for Mannerheim to buy the villa in Kaivopuisto where he had lived as a tenant since the mid-1920s. But when it became apparent that there was no right of redemption on the villa and that the housing regulations would have forced him to give up half his living space for use by others, Mannerheim elected instead to invest the sum in landed property. He eventually purchased Kirkniemi Manor and two adjoining properties, which had a combined total of 1,500 hectares. Among the property's distinguished previous owners there numbered two field marshals. While the manor house was in need of extensive repairs and new investment, it was nonetheless a grand country estate, with a main building consisting of fifteen rooms over two floors, constructed in the late 1790s.

In this way the Marshal came to return to the aristocratic manor life, which had been an integral part of his childhood and time in Russian service. In practice, Mannerheim only resided at the estate for short periods in the spring and summer, which meant that he otherwise gave instructions and supervised repairs and new builds at the manor via correspondence. He paid most attention to the main building's interior and the construction of a greenhouse and a new sauna. As a devotee of the latter, he was proud of this renovation, but he did not have chance to appreciate it all that often.

In connection with his purchase of Kirkniemi, in August 1945 the Marshal changed the large national fund collected for him in 1919 into a foundation, the General Gustaf Mannerheim's National Foundation, and donated the estate to it to increase its capital. Due to the Land Acquisition Act which was passed that same year, more than half of the estate's acreage had to be given up for new settlements, which were mainly established to ensure that the evacuated Karelian people would get replacement land. This obviously vexed the Marshal and caused him to make a number of requests to his successor Paasikivi for special treatment. But when it emerged that this had awoken strong protests, especially among the Communist Party's parliamentarians, Mannerheim let the matter lie.

Mannerheim's motive for changing the national fund into what is now called the Mannerheim Foundation was that deep down he feared becoming embroiled in the war-guilt process and, in the worst case, of losing the fund's proceeds. The inflation during the years of war had taken a heavy toll on the yield's real value, but it still guaranteed him a comfortable standard of living for the rest of his life. Besides his regular stays in hospital, he came to spend increasingly long periods of time in Sweden and Switzerland. The Swedish sojourns were occasioned primarily by Mannerheim's desire to have his acute gastric ulcer and other troublesome ailments tended to by Professor Nanna Svartz at the Karolinska Institute. But the Marshal otherwise enjoyed himself in Sweden, where, in addition to his relatives, he was partial to meeting old officer colleagues.

One problem, however, was that fewer and fewer of these were still alive. In late autumn 1945, Mannerheim stopped in Paris to meet his daughter Sophy on his journey home from Portugal, and there made the acquaintance of the 51-year-old Countess Gertrud Arco-Valley, whose elegance and wit he was instantly attracted to. Countess "Calle" had already been captivated by Mannerheim's charisma a few years earlier, in the well-known news broadcast of Hitler's visit to Finland. Mannerheim was similarly enamoured of her, and the two would take many long trips to the Continent

Fig. 9.2: Gertrud Arco-Valley (née Wallenberg) and Mannerheim in Central Europe, 1949.

together between 1947 and 1949, living the high life and staying in luxury hotels or pensions, mainly at her expense.

The Countess's extravagance can be explained by the fact that she was born a Wallenberg, and was sister of the Swedish industrialist powerhouses Marcus and Jacob Wallenberg. Marcus, in particular, had been of great service to Finland during the Second World War, having acted as an intermediary between the country's leadership and the Western Powers. Calle attempted to coax Mannerheim into settling down with her in Monte Carlo, but he turned her down diplomatically. What would the Finnish populace say if he chose to look after his health in Monte Carlo when people at home were still suffering from a shortage of almost all the basic necessities?

The Marshal's closest colleagues also quickly noticed that he had taken a genuine fancy to the Countess. The Wallenberg researcher Ulf Olsson's work on their relationship makes it clear that Mannerheim's letters to Calle were preserved, and that the correspondence reveals that Mannerheim's affection was reciprocated. The couple had found a common wavelength, and Mannerheim seemingly clung tightly to the glorious feelings they conjured together which were so very different from all the duties and troubles he had been forced to shoulder as commander-in-chief and president. But even though all this was mentally refreshing, Mannerheim's health could no longer cope with the jet-set lifestyle, which went completely against the strict diet and health advice his doctor had prescribed.

Indeed, the downside of these escapades was that Mannerheim often fell ill in their aftermath. There was, however, an auxiliary benefit to his time together with Calle, in that it gave the Marshal the opportunity to finally act on his long-held plans of writing his memoirs. Calle fervently urged him to set to work, but the frequent trips to the Continent obviously also provided the impetus for him to cast his gaze back over his life and distil his memories in book form. Mannerheim had previously been encouraged to do this by his friends in the 1930s, and had taken up the matter with the well-known historian Eirik Hornborg after the Winter War, earmarking him to be his ghost-writer. In summer 1946 he contacted Hornborg again, and, with his help, produced some passages of text.

But since the Marshal did not have the financial means to employ Hornborg, he instead arranged to produce his memoirs together with his former military colleagues Erik Heinrichs and Colonel Aladár Paasonen, during an extended stay at a sanatorium in Switzerland in spring 1948. To all intents and purposes, he ordered them to function as his ghost-writers. According to some sources, the Marshal had already started to dictate his memories to a Swedish-speaking secretary in summer 1947. In autumn 1948, the pair of ghost-writers returned to Mannerheim's sanatorium in Valmont, on the outskirts of Montreux, to, among other things, put together the manuscript from this earlier dictation. Despite the Marshal's health occasionally failing, the group's work advanced at a fast pace over the autumn and already by the following spring the bulk of the memoirs had started to take form.

Without a doubt it was Paasonen who did the lion's share of the work, for he put together two thirds of the whole manuscript. In their final form, the memoirs ended up being so comprehensive that they were later published in two volumes. But since neither Paasonen nor Heinrichs were historians nor particularly elegant writers in Swedish, the text had to be fundamentally revised by the librarian and polymath Emerik Olsoni, on whom it also fell to compose chapters about Mannerheim's ride through Asia and his time as president. Even with this done, the memoirs were, however, far from ready. Mannerheim still wanted to go through the whole text in minute detail, demanding numerous changes and adjustments as he did so. This meant that some sections of the manuscript went through five or six revisions during 1949.

As this editing work was ongoing, Mannerheim allowed parts of the text to be sent to some of his closest confidants for comments and amendments. First on the list was the diplomat G. A. Gripenberg, his relative and close colleague since the 1920s, who immediately protested at the strongly critical tone in which the Marshal discussed the Soviet Union and the entire Bolshevik era in Russia's history. Gripenberg also recommended toning down Mannerheim's biting criticism of Sweden's actions before and during the Winter War. If the book were to be published in such a form, stressed Gripenberg, it would cause difficulties for the Finnish Government. At first, Mannerheim was greatly irritated by these objections, but when he received similar comments about the book's foreword from Paasikivi and Carl Enckell, he took their advice to heart and trimmed the most critical diatribes against Finland's neighbours from the text.

After all these revisions, the manuscript was close to being ready at the start of 1950. That very spring, Mannerheim made a contract with the domestic publishers Holger Schildts and Otava, and also with the Swedish publisher Norstedts. With these agreed, the Finnish translation of the manuscript began. The memoirs might well have been published in autumn 1950 if the Marshal had not demanded that he be allowed to go through the text one more time with Paasonen. As a consequence, Mannerheim did not live to see the publication of the work. He passed away in late January 1951, and the first volume of his memoirs was only published in October that year, with the second volume coming out in early 1952.

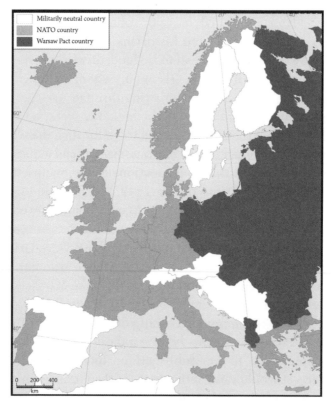

Fig. 9.3: Finland's geographical position in the Soviet-dominated post-war Europe was indeed challenging. Map by Hannu Linkola.

It was no coincidence that Mannerheim set about working on his memoirs with renewed energy precisely in April 1948. That same month, after a long drawn-out negotiation process in Moscow, Finland and the Soviet Union entered into a 15-year Agreement of Friendship, Co-operation and Mutual Assistance (also known as the YYA Treaty, from the Finnish *Ystävyys-, yhteistyö- ja avunanto-sopimus*). This followed, in many respects, the broad proposals Mannerheim and Heinrichs had outlined to Zhdanov in January 1945. Finland pledged to ward off any attack that would be directed against the Soviet Union through Finnish territory, but before military consultations could be considered, both parties had to agree to their necessity. Over the subsequent three years, however, relations between the Great Powers had changed so much that Mannerheim no longer regarded the arrangement at all positively. One obvious reason for this was the outbreak of the Cold War in spring 1946, and the establishment of Communist regimes loyal to the Soviets in all the countries the Red Army had captured at the end of the war. In common with many other Western-minded Europeans, Mannerheim feared that the Finno-Soviet YYA Treaty had the same aim: to pave the way for the transfer of power to the Communists in Finland, too.

Ultimately, of course, this never came to pass. Quite the reverse, in fact. The YYA Treaty in many ways stabilised Finland's relations with the East, and in so doing also facilitated the recovery of the country's domestic politics after the war. But for contemporaries this outcome was, of course, by no means self-evident, especially during 1948–49, when the Great Powers' conflict of interest in Central Europe was markedly intensified by the Communist coup in Czechoslovakia and the Soviet blockade of Berlin. All this meant that Mannerheim's requests to the West for the continued support of independent Finland came to be a running theme in his memoirs, even with the various redactions of the most flagrant anti-Bolshevik comments in the manuscript. Another oft-repeated theme in the work is his exhortation for national unity, which he returns to again in the epilogue: "The insight that I want, above all else, to impress upon the coming generation's consciousness is that discord in your own ranks cuts more deeply than the enemy's sword, and that internal conflicts open the door to outside interference."

The book became an instant success, with the expensive first edition of the two volumes selling over 60,000 copies, which at the time was a record in the history of Finnish publishing and brought in a healthy profit for the Marshal's foundation. The success was in part due to the memoirs' publication in the wake of Mannerheim's death and grandiose funeral. This gave a new boost to the cult of Mannerheim, which, with time, had breached further and further across the class divide. The success led to a shortened version of the work being published in German, French and Estonian in 1952, and in English two years later.

But despite all the revisions and political repercussions, the work also had its own lustre, beyond the fact that Mannerheim's life and achievements made for a dizzying tale. One of its real merits was Mannerheim's quite detailed description of his years in Russian service, which some of his editors feared gave a far too positive picture of Imperial Russia, but which was a glimpse into military events greatly appreciated by the general public. And certainly, in places, the text reflected the Marshal's personality, such as when a political turning point or noteworthy episode was summed up with a thought-provoking or witty closing remark.

At the same time, it is true that he skimmed over the less success-ful episodes in his life, such as his failure in the entrance examination to the Russian military academy and the regrettable break-up of his marriage with Anastasia Arapova. He had not wanted to divulge a single word about the marriage, but at his editors' insistence, he eventually dealt with it in a single sentence. The memoirs were over 800 pages in length and quite richly illustrated, yet they contained no reference to the birth and destiny of his two daughters. Something else that Mannerheim and his ghost-writers systemati-cally avoided acknowledging was the fundamental significance of Germany's military interventions for the development of Finland, both in 1918 and in 1941.

In contrast to what they left unsaid, the memoirs do contain many fine geopolitical observations and summaries, which can be inter-preted as the fruit of all the discussions that Mannerheim had con-ducted on the theme with Heinrichs and Paasonen over the years. These discussions, or rather these long expositions by the Marshal, would later also appear in Heinrichs's large biography *Mannerheim-*

gestalten (1957, 1959; The Figure of Mannerheim), and would come to point the direction for future analyses of Mannerheim's approach to national security policy. Typical of them is a clarity of vision about the driving forces behind the Great Powers' politics, where morality and justice seldom hold much sway over developments.

At the same time, there is no question that the memoirs' perspective on global progress was openly Western-oriented. This was not solely because of Mannerheim's Anglophile and Allied-minded personal history. Hardly surprisingly, Mannerheim's most industrious ghost-writer, Aladár Paasonen, also had a thoroughly pro-Western mindset, which was, of course, the reason that the first version of the manuscript was perceived as far too critical towards the Bolsheviks and the Soviet Union. Paasonen was linguistically gifted and analytically inclined, but Mannerheim's recruitment of him for the task caused a stir in well-informed government circles for other reasons. As the former Chief of Intelligence at the headquarters in Mikkeli, Paasonen had taken part in preparations for a guerrilla war against Soviet invaders after the arrival of peace, and later left Finland to work for the American intelligence agency, the CIA. Paasonen's connection to the CIA had already emerged when he began to work as Mannerheim's ghost-writer, which obviously increased mistrust towards the memoirs in a number of quarters.

Farewell and Retrospective

The memoirs demanded a great deal of the Marshal's attention and took a heavy toll on his strength during his final years. At the same time, they gave him an exceptional opportunity to look back over his life for the last time and to consider its significance in the long term. In autumn 1948, he pointed out to Heinrichs that the Second World War could have taken another course, if, for example, Roosevelt had died before Pearl Harbor. If that have happened, Japan could have attacked the Soviet Union instead, and, as a consequence, "America might not have intervened, and Russia would perhaps not have endured." The Finns have certainly had reason to wonder along similar lines about all the unforeseen twists and turns in Mannerheim's own life. Would things really have turned out the way they did for Finland without him?

237

That Mannerheim's careful compilation of his thoughts concluded with a systematic defence of himself and his actions in the memoirs was hardly surprising. It was, nonetheless, something that his old friend and successor in the post of president, J. K. Paasikivi, immediately paid attention to in his own diary entries. Mannerheim never acknowledged that he had done anything wrong, stated Paasikivi cuttingly. As might be expected, Paasikivi neglected to add that he was not inclined towards candid self-examination himself either.

When Erik Heinrichs published his expansive work on Mannerheim's achievements as a Finnish officer, eight years after the Marshal's death, he discussed in the conclusion why Mannerheim never spoke openly about his "disappointments, matters of pleasure and carefully guarded innermost thoughts". Even though, true to form, Heinrichs was careful not to jump to any quick conclusions, he pointed out something that is to this day often overlooked when Mannerheim's self-centredness is criticised. The Marshal had, quite simply, become so characterised by the heroic role he had played in public since early spring 1918 that he neither had the will nor the means to remove the armour that was integral to that character.

It was also inevitable that the sick and ageing Marshal's outlook on Finland's chances of survival in the Cold War climate should become increasingly pessimistic. After hearing one of his lamentations, Paasikivi replied sarcastically that, in that case, there was nothing else to do but go into the forest and blow one's brains out. But in contrast to this, Mannerheim also often expressed his gratitude that he had been able to experience such a long and dramatic life. He brought this to the fore in his private dealings with the relatives and friends he called on when he was in Finland or Sweden. At these moments, those around him still experienced a flicker of his gallant humour and self-deprecation, which was perhaps the best evidence that the erstwhile cosmopolitan gentleman kept his mental faculties almost up until his death.

At the end of August 1950, Mannerheim returned to Finland for the final time for his annual stay at Kirkniemi. A little over a month later, he became so seriously ill with pneumonia that he was transported, at his request, by military plane to the Karolinska Institute in Stockholm. After intensive treatment, he recovered enough to fly back to Switzerland just before Christmas. From there, he travelled on to the holiday resort of Lugano in northern Italy to celebrate Yuletide with Calle, which says something about his priorities, but which was hardly an ideal way to improve his health. In early January 1951, he returned to Valmont to continue revising his memoirs, only to suffer a complicated relapse of his gastric ulcer, which required a lengthy operation at a hospital in Lausanne. At first, it appeared that he would recover, but one afternoon three days later his condition dramatically worsened. Late that same evening, at 11.30pm Central European Time on 27 January, Mannerheim passed away.

It was already after midnight in Finland, and once the message about Mannerheim's death arrived on the morning of 28 January, flags were lowered to half-mast across the country. That same evening, Paasikivi gave a radio speech, in which he praised the Marshal's role in the defence of independent Finland. One of the most brilliant figures in Finland's history, stressed Paasikivi, has left us. And

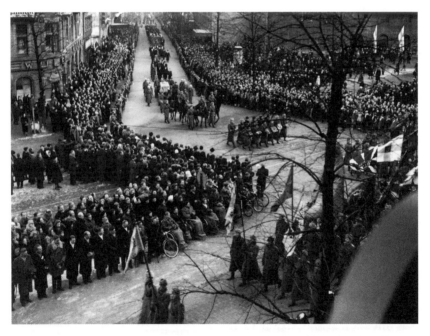

Fig. 9.4: Mannerheim's funeral procession passing by the Swedish Theatre in the centre of Helsinki, 2 February 1951.

in contrast to the often caustic diatribes against Mannerheim in Paasikivi's diary, his entry a few days later noted that it was good that the nation's mourning had given rise to such a patriotic spirit. With the exception of the communist press, the daily papers, in an unprecedented display of unity, expressed the sorrow of the nation and its gratitude towards its Marshal.

Then began preparations for the last farewell: Mannerheim's state funeral in Helsinki. On 2 February, Mannerheim's coffin arrived with military honours at the city's airport, after which it was conveyed to Helsinki Cathedral. The next day the public could pay their respects to the deceased at the closed casket. The stream of people seemed never-ending, and by the end of the day an estimated 40,000 mourners had filed past. The cathedral's doors were therefore kept open until only a few hours before the funeral on 4 February, which took place in the presence of the country's entire state leadership and social elite. Outside in Senate Square the guard of honour stood in position before the procession, and close to 100,000 people crowded along the city's streets to get a glimpse of the Marshal's cortège.

Inside the church four generals stood in a guard of honour at the coffin. The ceremony lasted a little less than an hour; it was conducted by Bishop Max von Bonsdorff, after which the Speaker of the Parliament, K. A. Fagerholm, gave a commemorative speech and the wreath-laying began. In the public consciousness, however, the indelible memory came to be the nearly 4-kilometre-long procession through the city to Hietaniemi's war graves. Those who witnessed the cortège would later tell how a peculiar silence swept over the crowd when the coffin, wrapped in the Finnish flag and resting on a gun carriage pulled by six horses, came into view. At that moment, Finland's people not only bid a last farewell to Mannerheim, but also to the mentality of the tough war years. The day was unusually cold and clear. At the same moment that the coffin was interred at Hietaniemi, a nineteen-shot salvo boomed over the whole Helsinki region.

A monumental granite gravestone, designed by Wäinö Aaltonen, was unveiled at the Marshal's last resting place in 1954. Flanked by Hietaniemi's thousands of war graves, this would become one of the nation's most important memorials, which perhaps more than anything else shows the esteem in which Mannerheim is held by posterity. Once the first weeks and months of mourning had passed, there gradually arose an animated discussion about Mannerheim's impact on Finland's history, one that has remained lively up to the present day, swinging at times from one extreme to the other.

How did Mannerheim's friends and closest colleagues look back on his life and personality? The question is not at all easy to answer, since they and their peers held the Marshal in such high regard that it was in practice extremely difficult to give frank opinions or engage in forthright analysis on the subject. Among those who came to this conclusion was his closest military co-worker Erik Heinrichs, who after penning his extensive work, *Mannerheim-gestalten*, was not satisfied with his slightly superficial characterisation of the Marshal. Ultimately, however, he found that he was unable to paint a portrait with more shadows and contrasts. In fact, Heinrichs had already provided his most personal reflection on Mannerheim in an article for a commemorative publication brought out by Finland's Association of the Nobility (*Aatelisliitto*) in 1953. In this he stated that Mannerheim's success stemmed, above all, from an extraordinary willpower, or "soulpower", as the Marshal himself had put it, in a conversation with Heinrichs just after the Winter War had ended, when discussing the qualities that made a competent officer.

G. A. Gripenberg, Mannerheim's relative and colleague in the diplomatic corps for many years, also had an article in the same commemorative publication. As would be expected, he gave a warmer account of the Marshal than Heinrichs, who had regularly been subjected to Mannerheim's military discipline. According to Gripenberg, Mannerheim had a superb ability to inspire devotion and admiration among his subordinates; he would respond to this appropriately, without allowing things to lead to an equal friendship or intimate openness. He does not appear to have been capable of such expressions of emotion, which some people have interpreted as a manifestation of an unfriendly, hard-boiled personality. However, it should be considered whether that sort of empathy and openness would have been desirable, or whether it was even possible, for an officer and a political actor at his level. How much evidence is there that, say, Paasikivi or Kekkonen would have laid bare their innermost thoughts and feelings about their motives and objectives in life?

From Gripenberg's short profile of Mannerheim, it appears that the Marshal had two qualities that he retained until his death. One was his meticulous need for order, which expressed itself in the fact that every object in his surroundings or luggage had to have its exact appointed place. The habit obviously had its origins in Mannerheim's military training and service, in which there were carefully planned timetables that required such an orderliness. But it also made its mark on his everyday behaviour, to the extent that even in the autumn of his life he would make minute lists before trips, detailing what to take with him and where his various accessories had been stowed. The result was a minor work of art, where everything "fitted in like pieces in a jigsaw puzzle" and was so tightly packed that nothing could become disordered during transportation.

The second quality of Mannerheim that Gripenberg particularly emphasised was his keen interest in and strong feeling for external qualities and verbal communication. The most concrete example of this was Mannerheim's genuine curiosity about how people carried themselves: their gait, their posture and their gesticulation. Presumably this interest was borne out of his background as a cavalryman and inveterate horse enthusiast. Mannerheim appears to have sized up his fellow men with the same physiological eye—and perhaps also attitude—with which he inspected horses; incidentally, there are examples of him doing just this in the diary of his ride through Asia. Mannerheim's precision with words is easy to ascertain from his letters, but Gripenberg noted that it was even more pronounced in conversations, when the Marshal could, with the help of quick replies, courteous questions or personal anecdotes, steer the conservation in the desired direction.

Paasikivi, too, summed up his impression of Mannerheim immediately after the Marshal passed away, but since he did so in his diary, the final judgement was much harsher. According to Paasikivi, in reality Mannerheim was a "highly ambitious, conceited and egocentric" person, who had been so fixated on his posthumous reputation during his final years that he went out of his way to avoid making unpopular decisions. The characterisation was in many respects apt, but reveals just as much about how profoundly irritated Paasikivi was by the hero worship that had been directed towards Mannerheim in his homeland since 1918. Moreover, it is worth remembering that Paasikivi had expressed significantly more positive opinions about his nearly coeval compatriot during the latter's lifetime, not least immediately before and during the Second World War, when they in essence often came to the same geopolitical conclusions.

Consequently, the first reflections on Mannerheim's life were broad in scope, encompassing everything from effusive praise to verbal attacks. The most biting critique came, unsurprisingly, from the political far left, which, after it had regained the right to function in public lost no time in airing all the accusations that had been directed against Mannerheim from Bolshevik quarters during both the Finnish Civil War and the Second World War. Many of these condemnations typically extrapolated a comprehensive explanation for Mannerheim's whole personality and life from a particular incident in his history or from one of his character traits. Such is the way people often pass judgement on each other. But what is completely ignored is that Mannerheim had such a long and improbably eventful life that it, by its very nature, also contained many contradictions and moments of weakness. On these occasions he did not behave with much consideration and morality at all.

Many of Mannerheim's dominant characteristics were inherited and formed during his youth and his years of Russian service. These included a large ego and the realisation that he had chanced to have many aces in his hand: a privileged background, an attractive appearance, a hardy physique and last, but not least, an unparalleled ambition. If he had lacked just one of these qualities, then sooner or later he would likely have been so crushed by all the challenges and setbacks he encountered that his life would have been a much more ordinary and perhaps also a significantly shorter tale. And how he got the better of these situations and ultimately managed to turn them to his own—and in many cases, to Finland's—advantage was also bound up with his singular ability to "read the game"; that is, his capacity to identify the different contexts in which he functioned and to act accordingly. To put it differently, he often succeeded in taking risks at the right time, or, alternatively, avoided doing so when it would not have been to his benefit.

All the same, it is impossible to overstate the extent to which Mannerheim's achievements over his lifetime gained their direction and driving force from the different cultures, civilisations and epochs in which he came to exist during his 83-year-long life. At the time he was born, no more than six decades had passed since Finland had been wrenched loose from Sweden, a state of affairs which clearly made its mark on his childhood environment. And when, due to a combination of circumstance and happenstance, he embarked on a military career, it was just at the very moment when the whole of Europe began to drift into the destructive maelstrom that would result in both the First and the Second World War. The result was that Mannerheim the cavalryman and nineteenth-century gentleman came to take part in more wars than perhaps any other Nordic man in the 1900s, even living to see the deployment of atomic weapons and the Soviet Union ruling two thirds of the European continent.

The other great upheaval in European history that also coincided with Mannerheim's lifetime was the breakthrough of parliamentary democracy and communism, as well as the rise and fall of their counter-reaction, fascism. Although Mannerheim gradually came to accept representative democracy, he was absolutely not a great admirer of it, which was not solely a consequence of his noble back-ground and lifelong loyalty to the Emperor. Democracy as a form of governance is founded on the reconciliation of fundamentally different viewpoints about which way society should be run. This sort of decision-making process requires patience and the willing-ness to compromise. It also, therefore, requires sufficient time to work effectively, but on those occasions when Finland was dragged into two world wars, he felt, prompt decisions were needed. This obviously had a negative impact on Mannerheim's opinion of par-liamentarianism, while also contributing to the fact that parliament's attitude towards him remained reserved, even if it did elect him as President of the Republic in 1944.

No life, however, is dictated solely by hereditary and environ-mental factors, but also by the prevailing social contexts. Every individual's story contains numerous unexpected events; these are impossible to predict, and their consequences are often altogether too haphazard to be worth the trouble of seeking reasonable explanations for them. So, too, was it with Mannerheim's life. He ended up in a number of life-threatening situations, but out-lived

nearly all of his contemporaries. And even when he failed completely and appeared to have lost control of his life, by chance
there emerged a new opportunity for him to push forward. It
should be added that this was fortunate not only for his own destiny, but also for that of Finland.

10

POSTERITY

The Field of Research

Mannerheim's memoirs were by no means the first written summation of his life. Already during his lifetime several written tributes, biographies and minor political hatchet jobs were published about him, which all, in one way or another, laid the foundations for the interpretations, opinions and myths that would later come into existence and that still surround him today. Within a decade of the Marshal's death, the first academic studies of his military and political achievements had also been published. And since it was in the government's interest to defend his legacy, the cult of Mannerheim has also received steady support from official quarters, which in turn has contributed to the fact that the public's interest in his character has stayed high and has constantly taken new shapes and forms.

How, then, has the historiography of Mannerheim developed over the decades? Kai Donner and Herman Gummerus, both distinguished researchers in their academic fields, published biographies of him in 1934 and 1937 respectively, but neither were able to distance themselves from the cult of personality that had emerged around the White General in bourgeois quarters in the wake of the Finnish Civil War. In practice, their biographies did not markedly differ from the festschrifts published in honour of his 70th and 75th birthdays in 1937 and 1942. The latter anniversary took place during wartime, when there was a pressing need for a depiction of Mannerheim that crossed class boundaries, and so he was idealised as someone who always put Finland first.

Straight after the Winter War, a rather heavily edited version of Mannerheim's diary entries from his ride through Asia between

1906 and 1908 was published in multiple languages. The aim was, quite clearly, to bolster both his own heroic reputation and that of the Finnish people who had fought valiantly in the Winter War. Every vestige of his physical fragility and selfish motives was, therefore, censored, which meant that it was not until 2010 that the general public had a chance to acquaint themselves with the real hardships Mannerheim endured on his ride through Asia. This was when Harry Halén's complete and meticulously edited version of the diaries was published, also containing many of the photographs that Mannerheim had taken during the trip.

The years immediately after the Second World War saw the publication of historical works discussing the conflict from a Finnish perspective. None of these, however, could be characterised as serious academic research. In 1948, Professor of History Arvi Korhonen did anonymously publish a comprehensive English-language account of Finland's fortunes during the war years, but although it contains much thought-provoking analysis, the book's primary purpose was to exonerate Finland's badly tarnished reputation in the West. As such, Korhonen neglected to mention anything that would have laid bare how systematically Mannerheim and Ryti embraced the Finno-German brotherhood-in-arms. And since Mannerheim's memoirs were also written in the same vein, it would not be until the late 1950s that the war years and the Marshal's role in them would be subjected to a more source-critical study.

The German researcher Michael Jonas has described this conscious repression of the actual scope of the brotherhood-in-arms as a kind of memoir cartel. Mannerheim's ghost-writers, Aladár Paasonen and, in particular, Erik Heinrichs, kept in touch with many of the wartime actors who published their own memoirs in the 1950s, with the purpose of preventing the recollections becoming so conflicting that the true nature of the brotherhood-of-arms might be disclosed. A number of publications were aligned with Mannerheim's memoirs in this way, including German liaison officer Waldemar Erfurth's account, Der finnische Krieg (1950; The Finnish War), and the memoirs of Helsinki Ambassador Wipert von Blücher. Von Blücher also offered a fitting exculpatory metaphor: Finland had, during the Second World War, been dragged involuntarily along, like driftwood, in the Great Powers' political torrent.

Despite the best efforts of Heinrichs and Paasonen, during the 1950s a number of the generals who had served under Mannerheim did publish their own accounts of the war years, which revealed that the headquarters' actions had not, by any means, been blameless. This forced Heinrichs to make admissions along similar lines in his large work, *Mannerheim-gestalten* (1957, 1959; The Figure of Mannerheim). By this stage, the so-called memoir cartel had already started to fall apart, and in 1957 the American historian C. Leonard Lundin published *Finland in the Second World War*, in which the extent of the brotherhood-in-arms was explored in far more detail than ever before. Even though Lundin was subjected to fierce criticism from a cohort of domestic historians, a criticism that Arvi Korhonen would summarise in the work *Barbarossa-suunnitelma ja Suomi* (1961; Operation Barbarossa and Finland), it was a watershed moment. The rhetoric of innocence that had framed Finland's conflict as a "separate war" since its outbreak in 1941 had been irreparably undermined.

Three years after Korhonen's work, British historian Anthony Upton published *Finland in Crisis, 1940–1941* (1964), which used a variety of sources to demonstrate that the Finnish state leadership had actively engaged in the preparations for war. A few years later, the American historian Hans Peter Krosby published *Suomen valinta 1941* (1967; Finland's Choice, 1941), the title of which already reveals the message of the study. During the 1970s and 1980s, there were also a number of well-researched studies published in West and East Germany, which further helped dismiss the separate war thesis. It was hardly surprising that foreign researchers took the initiative in this regard. The Finno-German brotherhood-in-arms was, of course, a sensitive topic throughout the whole Cold War for both domestic and foreign political reasons, which clearly contributed to the cautiousness of the Finnish academic community.

One of the researchers who stuck most persistently to the separate war narrative was Stig Jägerskiöld, whose monumental Mannerheim biography extends to eight volumes (1964–81) and was published in both Swedish and Finnish. It is, in all probability, the most exhaustive overview of the Marshal's life that will ever be produced, and not merely because of its size. Until the 1980s, Jägerskiöld had exclusive access to Mannerheim's private correspondence and archive, which the Marshal had had transported during the war to Östergötland in Sweden, for safekeeping at Grensholm Manor, owned by his brother's children. Mannerheim had the most politically sensitive material in this Grensholm collection sealed for fifty years, after which it could be returned to the National Archives of Finland, provided that the country was still free and was no longer threatened by Bolshevism. These documents were ultimately returned in autumn 1994.

They did not, however, remain sealed for that entire time. Heinrichs had already gone through them in the 1950s, and later Jägerskiöld, too, was able to acquaint himself with their contents. But since Mannerheim had selected documents that supported his own interpretation of his achievements during the Second World War and ordered that the rest be destroyed, the information they contained did not significantly upset the picture that his own memoirs had given of developments. Jägerskiöld was also so impressed by his object of research that many of his interpretations ended up being clearly uncritical and sometimes simply contradictory. This is not just in respect of Jägerskiöld's descriptions of Mannerheim's actions and motives during 1917–19 and 1939–45; it also, to a large extent, concerns his account of Mannerheim's Russian career. Jägerskiöld's expansive Mannerheim biography can therefore be described as a monumental painting, with clean lines and fine details, but lacking the shadows and dark tones required for a more in-depth portrait of the Marshal.

In spite of these reservations, Jägerskiöld's biography has been a bountiful source for this book, as has the Mannerheim biography by the British researcher J. E. O. Screen, which was published in two stages. The first part, spanning Mannerheim's Russian career, was published in English in 1970; Screen completed the biography with a corresponding work on Mannerheim's years in Finland in autumn 2000, and a year later the two parts were published as a Finnish translation in a single volume. One undoubted merit of Screen's work is that he keeps a significantly greater distance from his subject than, for example, Jägerskiöld, and this comes across extremely clearly in Screen's nuanced analyses of Mannerheim's motives and priorities as a Russian officer and political actor in Finland between 1917 and 1919. An important reason for this is that Screen, in contrast to Jägerskiöld and most Finnish researchers, also had a good grasp of Russian. As such, he was more capable than other Mannerheim researchers of positioning Finland in a wider context: that is, as a pawn in the politics of the Great Powers. Jonathan Clements's English-language biography of Mannerheim from 2009 also offers a similarly broad perspective, largely due to the fact that he followed the same approach as Screen.

A peculiar feature of the academic literature on Mannerheim is that, thus far, no Finnish historian has written a complete and empirically documented biography of the Marshal. The officer Erik Heinrichs's *Mannerheim-gestalten* only covers the Marshal's years in Finland, and, moreover, lacks methodical documentation. Tuomo Polvinen and Ohto Manninen have both published many commendable studies in which they analyse in detail Mannerheim's activities as a Finnish officer and as a statesman specialised in national security policy. Neither, however, have gathered their knowledge into a comprehensive academic account of the Marshal's life and accomplishments. Nor can Martti Turtola's Mannerheim biography from 2016, nor this very book, be characterised as academic studies in the strictest sense. They are both concise overviews, primarily based on other secondary literature.

One explanation for this rather striking omission in the body of Finnish research is that Mannerheim's role in Finland's twentieth-century history has loomed so large that even much shorter episodes from his career have been regarded as sufficiently challenging topics of investigation. There is also an abundance of such studies, which makes it entirely possible to get a multifaceted picture of a certain period in Mannerheim's life by first ploughing through Jägerskiöld's and Screen's biographies, then familiarising oneself with Mannerheim's published letters and diaries, before finally immersing oneself in the research that touches on the epoch or theme in question. Another factor that has probably also deterred researchers from putting together a fully sourced biography of Mannerheim is that biographical studies began to be seen as a rather limited genre among historians after the Second World War, due to the grotesque cults of personality that sprang up in the communist and fascist dictatorships. The biography has, however, retained its popularity and social significance in the Anglo-Saxon world, and there are clear signs that it is experiencing a renaissance elsewhere, too.

It should also be noted that Jägerskiöld's and Screen's biographies are by no means the only life histories of Mannerheim to have been published outside of Finland. Already straight after the Winter War, two similar biographies were published in London—one authored by the Finnish-born art historian Tancred Borenius and the other by Mannerheim's old colleague from the Chevalier Guards, Paul Rodzianko. Both texts are prone to eulogising and, with the exception of Screen and Clements, this tendency towards lionising narratives has been prevalent in the majority of other foreign biographies and works about Mannerheim. The most extreme example is probably the Russian author Leonid Vlasov, who, between 1994 and 2007, published ten or so richly illustrated works about Mannerheim's career and life as a Russian officer. The books contain many exaggerations and outright fictitious elements, but they are partly based on unique archive material, which means that in certain respects they are important additions to Screen's depiction of Mannerheim's years in Russian service.

During the Soviet era, Russian interest in Mannerheim understandably focused on his role as commander of the counter-revolutionary forces in Finland and as a central actor in the Finno-German brotherhood-in-arms between 1941 and 1944. But as Vlasov's prolific output demonstrates, there was also a latent interest in Mannerheim's life in the Russian Empire, which has resulted in many other books being published about him since the 1990s. Of these, Aleksei Shkvarov's doctoral thesis is particularly worthy of mention: it analyses Mannerheim's entire military career in Russia in the context of the Russian Army's development and fortunes until 1918. The Finnish translation of the work was published in 2010, and is likewise an important addition to Screen's biography. But in common with most of the other foreign Mannerheim researchers, Shkvarov lacks the aspect that made Screen unique, namely a superb knowledge of Finnish. This enabled the latter to familiarise himself with the extensive and empirically detailed research that has been published in that language.

Stig Jägerskiöld made some use of Finnish-language research, but there is no doubt that his knowledge of the language was decidedly more limited than Screen's. This has also been the weakness of most other works and documentaries that have come out in Sweden about

Mannerheim over the years. Relatively recent examples of this are the biographies by veteran Swedish diplomat Dag Sebastian Ahlander and journalist Herman Lindqvist, published in 2016 and 2017 respectively. They are both well written, but many of their interpretations and explanations would have been given added nuance by engaging with the abundant Finnish-language research on Mannerheim that has come out since the 1980s.

As such, another way to view the extensive body of Mannerheim research is as a collection of national discourses, each one guided by the specific culture of history in its country of origin. The interest surrounding Mannerheim in Sweden and Russia is clearly influenced by the close ties he had to both countries over his long life, the strength of which was evidenced by the fact that he spoke better Swedish and Russian than Finnish. Therefore the Swedish literature on Mannerheim emphasises his Swedish family connections and warm feelings towards the country, while in Russia he is looked upon, first and foremost, as a product of the empire. A telling expression of this latter perspective is that the subtitle of Shkvarov's biography is "Born to Serve the Tsar" (*Syntynyt tsaarin palvelukseen*). In turn, the English and German-language research typically emphasises Mannerheim's imperialistic experiences and network of contacts on the Continent and in Great Britain.

As would be expected, the Finnish research on Mannerheim is also characterised by a number of fixed national ideas and deeply rooted notions about his role in the country's history. Fundamentally, it reflects the researchers' attitudes to what is often called the great patriotic story, that is to say, the all-embracing conception of what driving forces and turning points have directed the country's development. Despite the fact that extremely few Finnish researchers today are of an explicitly nationalistic mindset, a sizeable number of them tend to conceive of Finland's twentieth-century history as the predestined fulfilment of the nation's maturation into an independent republic. This has also shaped their outlook on Mannerheim, whose close ties to Sweden and Russia and disinclination towards Finnish nationalism have been either repressed or described as a troublesome deviation from the patriotic narrative.

What are the blind spots and subjective aspects of this work? This is naturally a question that I, as the author, cannot answer myself.

As a Swedish-speaking Finn from Helsinki and a former curator of the Mannerheim Museum, I most probably have a number of fixed ideas about Mannerheim of which I am unaware. Inserted into an appendix to the French author Marguerite Yourcenar's magnificent novel about the Roman Emperor Hadrian (1951; *Memoirs of Hadrian*), are text fragments and thoughts that she noted down when she wrote the book. In these she debated how she would describe and relate to the man of antiquity. She wished to disregard everything that prevented this understanding in her epoch, and instead to focus her powers of insight on what might unite people across thousands of years. "Keep your shadow outside of the picture", Yourcenar reminded herself when she tried to make contact with people "who just like us chewed on olives and drank wine; who fought in the headwind and the torrential rain or in the summer sought shade under the trees; who enjoyed their lives, thought their thoughts, grew old and died". This, in a nutshell, ought to be the guiding star for all historians.

Politics of Mannerheim's Legacy

As has already been made clear, Mannerheim's legacy came to influence post-war domestic and foreign politics in a variety of ways. A representative example in this respect were the closing statements in the war-guilt trials in 1945 and 1946, in which the defence were forbidden from mentioning two topics: the Winter War, and Mannerheim's central role in the decision-making process that led to, shaped and ended the Continuation War. Although Mannerheim's real wartime influence remained taboo in the political debate long into the 1950s, it had an indirect impact when the power struggle before the 1956 presidential elections became increasingly fraught. One of the primary candidates—and the eventual victor—was the Agrarian League's strongman Urho Kekkonen, who would go on to be Finland's longest-serving president, remaining in power until 1981. During the war, he had been part of the Peace Opposition; and, in his capacity as Minister for Justice from 1944 to 1946, he had borne responsibility for the drafting and enforcement of the war-guilt legislation. This gave rise to resentment against him, not only among the eight politicians who were sentenced, but also within wider bourgeois circles. A particular source of criticism was how Kekkonen, through his actions, had gained great appreciation in Moscow and had then effectively made use of this to further his political career.

To accuse Kekkonen of cuddling up to Moscow was, however, impossible, since doing so would have implied criticism against the Soviets' influence over Finnish politics. In the run-up to the 1956 presidential elections, therefore, Kekkonen's adversaries instead focused on his role in the war-guilt process. Just before Christmas 1955, the journalist Yrjö Soini published the work *Kuin Pietari hiili-valkealla* (Like Peter at the Charcoal Fire), in which Kekkonen's role in this legal action was brought up to portray him as an opportunist without principles or morals. The title referenced Saint Peter and his three-fold denial that he knew Jesus. To emphasise Kekkonen's careerist behaviour, Soini contrasted the politician's extremely pro-German statements at the start of the Continuation War with his fervent efforts to put such politicians as the Social Democrat Väinö Tanner on trial, despite the fact that Tanner's attitude towards the brotherhood-in-arms had been guarded and distanced throughout the war. The book became an instant bestseller, with over 24,000 copies sold in the first two months after publication.

A common feature in the arguments of Soini and his peers was that they stuck tightly to the separate war thesis. The rehabilitation of the eight men judged responsible for the war was, in other words, concurrently a criticism of Kekkonen and the other politicians who had sided with the Peace Opposition at the end of the Winter War, and who had then gained high positions in politics after the

Fig. 10.1: Marshal Mannerheim on the eve of the Continuation War. Satirical cartoon by Heikki Paakkanen 1991.

255

Continuation War. This all contributed to the fact that the discussion of Mannerheim's role in the Continuation War also came to encompass Kekkonen's political reputation for a number of decades. The more it was revealed in the research that Mannerheim and the political leadership had, from an early date, systematically agreed to ally themselves with Germany, the more difficult it was to maintain that the sentences in the war-guilt trials had been totally unjust. And, as this happened, it was not only the attempts to rehabilitate those judged responsible that began to seem questionable. Kekkonen's actions as organiser of the legal process against them also began to appear more justified and acceptable.

Unsurprisingly, Kekkonen showed an active interest in research that was, in one way or another, about the war years, and picked suitable junctures at which to either criticise or praise studies, depending on the picture they painted of the Finno-German brotherhood-in-arms. With this, he also indirectly took a position on the posthumous depiction of Mannerheim, which surely, in part, contributed to the decline of the Marshal's reputation during Kekkonen's twenty-five years as president. Nonetheless, it would be decidedly wrong to single out Kekkonen for blame for the slow stagnation of Mannerheim's legacy. Kekkonen's opinion of him had been quite critical since autumn 1944, but he carefully avoided making any disparaging public statements about the Marshal, since it was neither in his nor the state's best interests to do so. Rather, the increasingly muted attention given to Mannerheim was because the younger generation, in the mid-1960s, were weary of the bombastic patriotism and the Winter War spirit that had been a feature of most of their childhoods and adolescence in the post-war period.

The last big political demonstration of the Finnish nation's gratitude towards Mannerheim was, therefore, the unveiling of the Marshal's equestrian statue in Helsinki in early summer 1960. The idea for a horse-riding sculpture of this sort had been born straight after the war in 1918, and in the late 1930s, a prestigious equestrian statue committee was set up to co-ordinate the fund-raising and make arrangements for the artistic work. Mannerheim felt little enthusiasm towards this project. Ever the cavalryman, he remained sceptical about the possibility of finding a domestic sculptor who would be able to design a credible horse and rider successfully. At least equally important, however, was that he probably realised that the statue would cause political offence within the labour movement, which certainly did not want to pay tribute to the victorious commander from the civil war.

During wartime the project was put on ice, but straight after the Marshal's death a new equestrian statue committee was set up and, with fresh energy, took up the task of realising the artwork. After many changes, the sculptor Aimo Tukiainen's proposal was chosen in 1954, and he spent the next five years busily constructing the statue. At the same time, it was decided that the statue should be erected in Helsinki's new centre, at the crossroads of Mannerheiminkatu and Arkadiankatu, that is, between three of the city's landmark buildings: the Parliament House, and two celebrated examples of functionalist

Fig. 10.2: President Kekkonen lays a wreath at the newly unveiled equestrian statue of Mannerheim, 4 June 1960.

architecture from the late 1930s, the Main Post Office and the Glass Palace (Lasipalatsi). This junction had clear political symbolism, being almost the exact place where Mannerheim had been greeted by the Mayor of Helsinki when he rode into the city at the head of the Whites' victory parade on 16 May 1918. However, its selection was not explained in any such terms; instead, the emphasis was put on the fact it was a prestigious location with sufficient space around it.

A few years after the statue's unveiling, the architect Alvar Aalto put forward a new city plan for the whole area. Its idea was that all the planned cultural buildings along Töölönlahti should stand in a straight line behind the Mannerheim statue. Even though it was never realised in its entirety, the proposal was, nevertheless, carried out in one important instance, namely in the location of Finlandia Hall, a congress centre constructed directly in line with the equestrian statue. In the 1990s, the contemporary art museum Kiasma was built right next to the statue, which led to protests in many quarters. But due to the area's new architectural form, the museum in fact constituted a fine background for the equestrian statue, which ended up being one of the last figurative statues of Finnish statesmen to be erected in Helsinki.

The equestrian statue was unveiled with the utmost pomp and circumstance on 4 June 1960, Mannerheim's birthday. President Kekkonen gave an inauguration speech to an audience that included the government, the diplomat corps, the upper echelons of the military leadership, hundreds of Knights of the Mannerheim Cross and a large number of injured veterans and guests of honour. A crowd numbering in the tens of thousands also thronged around the statue to catch a glimpse of the historic event. In his speech Kekkonen praised, as expected, Mannerheim's efforts for the Fatherland, but went on to emphasise that the equestrian statue should be seen as a monument to all the soldiers who, under the Marshal's leadership, had fought and fallen for the country's freedom. After the unveiling, the President received a march-past of a 5,000-strong parade troop. Mannerheim's two daughters were also invited, but, owing to traffic congestion and misunderstandings, they only arrived once the statue had already been unveiled. This was undeniably an embarrassing blunder, but it was also reminiscent of their relationship with their father: they had met each other far too infrequently.

However, the daughters did take part in the grand dinner that was arranged for honoured guests that evening at Kalastajatorppa restaurant, in the west of Helsinki.

As expected, the erection of the equestrian statue was the cause of great irritation in the communist and people's democratic labour movement. Its daily papers played host to a lively debate about the statue's propaganda message, and proposed that a monument to the Red Guards should also be built. Some of the contributors characterised the statue as an expression of the vengeful and warmongering attitude towards the Soviet Union which many on the far left presumed had begun to manifest itself in Finland after Stalin's death in 1953. The interpretation was in many respects exaggerated, but it was undeniably true that the statue project had gained new life following Stalin's demise and the thawing of tensions between the Great Powers that occurred in the era of the new Soviet leader, Nikita Khrushchev. Despite the vague threats in the press debate that the statue ought to be destroyed, the far left's party leadership did not deliver any such demands in public, even though, naturally enough, they stayed away from the equestrian statue's unveiling ceremony.

It is, however, worth remembering that these sullen objections to the Mannerheim cult, which was particularly effusive at that moment, probably represented about a quarter of the population, that is, those who sympathised with the Communists, the Finnish People's Democratic League or the left wing of the Social Democratic Party. Due to its close proximity to the Soviet Union, Finland remained, throughout the Cold War, on the fringes of Western civilisation, and self-censorship prevailed in public discourse around communism. This clearly benefitted the Finnish Communist Party, which performed fairly well in elections and played an active role in domestic politics until the 1980s. It was also clearly detrimental to Mannerheim's legacy, given the strong aversion to him felt by those on the left.

Alongside the equestrian statue project in Helsinki, four other Mannerheim statues were also constructed in different parts of the country. The crowning glory, however, was erected in Switzerland: in 1955, a 7-metre-high obelisk to the Marshal was unveiled on the shore of Lake Geneva in Montreux, commemorating both the fact that he had lived out his final years in the region and that it was the place of his passing.

The equestrian statue in Helsinki was not the only one to generate controversy, however, for Evert Porila's statue of Mannerheim also received negative attention. It had been intended to be constructed in the centre of Tampere in the late 1930s, but this was delayed when the Winter War broke out. After the Second World War, the left saw the statue as a political provocation, since Mannerheim was depicted as the White Commander at the battle for Tampere in 1918. Consequently, in 1956 the statue was instead constructed on a hill in the eastern outskirts of the city where Mannerheim had directed the operations. But this, too, irritated left-wing locals so much that the statue became the target of serious vandalism on at least two occasions. These displays of anti-Mannerheim sentiment, which are particularly characteristic of Tampere, peaked on 4 June 1967, the 100th anniversary of the Marshal's birth, when the statue was emphatically tarred and feathered.

The equestrian statue in Helsinki avoided this kind of fate. What is more, its delegation so exceeded its fund-raising target that it used the leftover money to purchase the Marshal's childhood home, Louhisaari Manor in Southwest Finland, which it then donated to the state. The manor was converted into a cultural museum under the care of the Finnish Heritage Agency. In this way, with the support of the state, a whole series of Mannerheim monuments was created, each of which tells, in its own fashion, a chapter of his life's story. At Louhisaari Manor, visitors can get to know the Marshal's family history, with its close ties to Sweden and roots in the old estate society. From 1974, his achievements as an officer have been open for inspection in his office at the headquarters in Mikkeli, which was housed in the city's former elementary school. In early summer 2001, it reopened in expanded form as the Headquarters Museum. In summer 1959, the Marshal's hunting lodge in Loppi was opened to the public. Originally built for him as a 75th-birthday present in East Karelia, it was moved to the Kanta-Häme region of Finland in 1944–45.

Mannerheim's mausoleum in Helsinki's Hietaniemi cemetery is, naturally, the symbolic endpoint in this string of state-sponsored or state-preserved sites of remembrance. But for a more vivid picture of Mannerheim and his life, the Mannerheim Museum in southern Helsinki is the best destination, as it had been his home since 1924, and was opened to the public less than a year after his death. The Mannerheim Foundation subsequently bought a large part of the home's personal artefacts from his heirs, and in 1957 also purchased the building and the plot from the Fazer family. In this way, a reasonably authentic home museum came into being. Mannerheim's young aide from the war years, Rafael Bäckman, was even appointed as the museum's first curator.

The state's support for the museum's operations was apparent from the fact that the first visitor, in November 1951, was President Paasikivi, who over the years had held countless discussions with Mannerheim there. The museum, accordingly, came to receive state backing early on in its existence, and up to the present day it has regularly functioned as an esteemed destination on state visits and as a general introduction to the history of independent Finland for foreign diplomats and officers. Unsurprisingly, members of the latter two professions are usually especially impressed by the Marshal's exceptionally extensive collection of high orders, which serves as a reminder of how many wars he fought in and how many different allies he fought besides during his life.

After the fall of the Soviet Union, it also became politically acceptable for Russian politicians and diplomats to visit the museum, which contributed to many of them later showing a lively interest in Mannerheim, and particularly in his Russian career. Certain Russians had already visited the museum in Soviet times, such as the KGB officer Sergei Ivanov, who worked in Helsinki between 1984 and 1990, and who concluded his career as President Putin's Chief of Administration. A few months before his dismissal in late summer 2016, Ivanov took part in a ceremonial unveiling of a plaque to the Russian Lieutenant-General Mannerheim in central St Petersburg. His presence was an indication that he may well have been involved in the erection of the sculpture. However, the memorial immediately generated protests in Russia's communist and ultra-nationalist circles, as well as from the city's war veterans, who in no way remembered Mannerheim as a Russian officer, but instead as a Finnish counter-revolutionary and as Hitler's ally in the siege of Leningrad between 1941 and 1944. In the end, the political pressure became so great that the authorities declared that the artwork had been put up without legal consent and had it taken down that same autumn. Some have drawn the conclusion that Ivanov's departure from his position as Chief of Administration was a consequence of this minor controversy, but it was most likely due to a difference of opinion about how the Kremlin should handle the Ukraine crisis.

But as has been noted, Mannerheim's legacy has also been met with plenty of opposition in Finland. During the second half of the 1960s, this led to pacifist student radicals and left-leaning citizens in general adopting the Communists' traditional characterisation of Mannerheim as the White Butcher and as Hitler's lackey. Integral to the spirit of the times was the questioning of all conservative institutions and values, which meant that the church and the military became the focus of various denunciations. Both Jesus and Mannerheim were the targets of coarse abuse on stage and in diverse cabarets. After the initial shocked reactions within bourgeois circles, these provocations gradually lost their impact, and by at least the early 1980s, the discussion surrounding Mannerheim had become more balanced once again.

In the 1990s there was another twist in Mannerheim's legacy, but this time in the opposite direction. A buoyant wave of nationalistic feeling swept across Eastern Europe in the wake of the Soviet Union's disintegration, and this was soon reflected in Finnish depictions of Mannerheim. In this context, he suddenly became an object of uncritical admiration once again. At the extreme end of this resurrection of the wartime cult of Mannerheim were several far-right or fascist groups that strongly admired the Marshal's anti-communist disposition and his visions of a Finnish East Karelia. But just as with the counter-cultural activity in the 1960s and 1970s, the upsurge in nationalism was ultimately a fringe movement articulating its political passions, which meant that its social influence was relatively limited.

Moreover, in the 1990s, the acceptance of different views of Mannerheim increased as Europe's political map was reshaped. As new members of the European Union, many Finns wanted to highlight the common European traits in their culture, which meant some adjustments to the country's historical narrative. One facet of this was to highlight the bona fide European Mannerheim's role in the patriotic story. For the state this did not cause any great difficulty, since the authorities' respect for Mannerheim had remained intact throughout the Cold War. And in the officer corps, of course, his heroic reputation had never been questioned, as representatives of the military authorities have self-evidently found it useful to present themselves as principally responsible for upholding his tradition.

In parallel with these institutional stewards of Mannerheim's posthumous reputation, many new associations, subcultures and networks have emerged during the last few decades, all with their own specific interest in Mannerheim's political legacy. Some of these are focused on, for example, his Russian epoch, others on his geopolitical perspectives or his broad linguistic knowledge. This world of "Mannerheimiana" is thus distinctive in its readiness to interpret the Marshal's personality and life's work in an increasing range of contexts.

The Myths of Mannerheim

Something that has also moderated the political passions around Mannerheim is that in popular culture he has started to appear, to an increasingly great extent, as a mythical figure. His historical achievements certainly still interest many, but they no longer necessarily dictate posterity's view of him. Even in the Marshal's lifetime there appeared a motley web of anecdotes, rumours and slander about him. These started to assume a life of their own and gave rise to a rich variety of Mannerheim literature, portraits and other interpretations of him: as a rider and a soldier, as a gourmet and a wine connoisseur, as a dandy and a ladies' man, as a homosexual and a Russian, as a cosmopolitan and a traveller, as an orator and a master of the pithy expression. The reason for this multitude of identities is simple: nothing feeds collective fantasies more than power and public presence.

There are those who are irritated by this slow shift from non-fiction to fiction. But it is important to realise that Mannerheim's transformation from a historic to an increasingly mythical person is, in a certain respect, a necessary condition of keeping the memory of and the interest in Mannerheim alive. There is no need, therefore, to regard the Mannerheim of fantasy as a misrepresentation, but rather

Fig. 10.3: Monumental. Pekka Vuori's apt summation of the mythology around Mannerheim, 1994.

as a stimulating complement to the picture of him provided by the historical research. The most expressive manifestation of this can be found, naturally enough, in the visual arts, where, as far back as the 1960s there appeared depictions of the Marshal that portrayed him as a problematic cult figure. Most striking in this respect was J. O. Mallander's photo montage "White Out", from 1972, in which Mannerheim has been retouched out of a postcard of the equestrian statue, leaving only a big white blank space in his absence.

In surveys of the fictional literature on Mannerheim, it is traditional to refer to Paavo Rintala's trilogy of novels, *Mummoni ja Mannerheim* (1960–62; My Gran and Mannerheim). In these books the Marshal's egotistic, elitist perspective and hawkish verbosity is contrasted with a working-class woman's toil and worldly wisdom. A clear literary bedfellow to this deconstruction of Mannerheim is Hannu Salama's scandal-wracked novel, *Juhannustanssit* (1964; The Midsummer Dances), in which a drunkard yells in the night about Jesus having group sex with Simon Peter and a prostitute. After the furore that the book's publication caused, it undoubtedly became more difficult to provoke outrage with literary works. Since then, Mannerheim fanatics and critics alike have increasingly found an outlet for their innermost feelings in their own cliques.

It was not, therefore, until the twenty-first century that the next ambitious attempts to portray Mannerheim in fiction were made. These took the form of novels by Jari Tervo and Hannu Raittila. Tervo's *Troikka* (2008; The Troika) is set in 1920s Tampere, where the assassination of Mannerheim had been planned, demonstrably on Moscow's orders. In contrast, Raittila's *Marsalkka* (2012; The Marshal) allows the reader to meet the ageing Mannerheim in Switzerland, where he is reflecting on his whole life while editing his memoirs. Neither novel seeks to cast Mannerheim's character as saintly or demonic. Instead, they aim to capture his life in a precise historical and cultural era, and in a particular emotional landscape, which despite their literary nature has also made them of value to historical researchers.

In the early 2000s, an ambitious project was undertaken to produce an English-language feature film about Mannerheim for the international public. Finnish-born Hollywood director Renny Harlin was recruited, who up to that point had made his name as a director of fast-paced action films. At first, the idea was met with great enthusiasm and financing of the expensive production looked to have been arranged, but as time went on the project encountered one difficulty after another, which ended in the production company plunging into bankruptcy in 2013. Although it is regrettable that the initiative petered out, its demise surely caused many Mannerheim supporters to breathe a sigh of relief. There is plenty to suggest that the end result would in any case have only been a half-measure. It was a little like the gnawing anxiety that surrounded the destiny of Mannerheim's equestrian statue. Goodwill and a patriotic mindset seldom count for much when it comes to creating great art.

While this project was still in the works, the tabloid press had a field day covering two other Mannerheim films. In early spring 2008, the animation film *Uralin perhonen* (The Butterfly from Ural) was released, in which a marionette Mannerheim assumed a variety of roles: a centaur riding across Asia, a corset-wearing homosexual who has sex with a Kyrgyz, and a blood-dripping butcher of Tampere workers. The radical author Hannu Salama was partly responsible for the manuscript. It was four decades since he had been convicted of blasphemy for his aforementioned novel, *Juhannustanssit*, but the reaction on this occasion was more of a troubled smile than unbridled outrage. This was not simply because the beautiful animation film was so fanciful that even the most narrow-minded viewers realised that it was playing with the myths of Mannerheim. It was also because the film's director, Katariina Lillqvist, explained openly that it was based on various malicious stories and ditties about Mannerheim that had circulated in working-class Pispala ever since the last remnants of the Red Guards had surrendered there to Mannerheim's White Army during the Battle of Tampere in 1918.

Four years later, in 2012, an even stranger Mannerheim film premiered. *The Marshal of Finland* was shot in Kenya with only Black actors, which unsurprisingly caused irritation in the culturally con-servative circles that held on tightly to the patriotic narrative about Mannerheim. But in other respects, this low-budget film became more the subject of sarcastic comments about its unintentional com-edy and thinly veiled racism. The Black Mannerheim's uniform was ill-fitting and his horse looked like a donkey. Some could not help associate the grotesque production with the Belgian author Hergé's classic cartoon, *Tintin au Congo* (1946; Tintin in the Congo), in which the native Africans are duped into buying glass beads and other Western trinkets and baubles.

It is fascinating to imagine how Mannerheim's character might be depicted fifty or a hundred years in the future. Supposing that inde-pendent Finland still exists, the Marshal will certainly be celebrated together with the nation, and the two narratives will continue to be intertwined. But it is almost as likely that the country's sovereignty and national identity will, sooner or later, give way to new state-building and collective communities, which will then reflect on opinions of the nation's pre-eminent hero. In an unofficial poll of the nation in autumn 2004, Mannerheim was chosen by a large majority as the foremost Finn of all time. Such an outcome is, however, not at all guaranteed in a future Finland, entwined in new political structures and linguistic communities. How Mannerheim is understood, and how much interest there is in him, will, in other words, largely depend on how things go for the Finland and the Finns of the future.

That said, posterity's changing interpretations of and connections to Mannerheim are one thing, but the verifiable events of his life are quite another. The task of the professional historian is to actively fight against the provincialism of contemporaries; that is, to be constantly on guard against projecting present-day values and opinions on a past that was, in many respects, very different. If we really want to understand and explain how people thought and acted in earlier times, we must treat them just as fairly and impartially as we do our contemporaries, and avoid the temptation to let our perspectives be shaped by hindsight. Mannerheim is, without question, a challenging case in this respect, and not only because he lived such a long and action-packed life, full of contradictions and remarkable twists. His life was so strikingly different from that of his contemporary countrymen that comparisons easily become distorted or directly misleading. At the same time, it is completely impossible to understand Finland's twentieth-century history without him. In all probability it is this very paradox that most fascinates us about Gustaf Mannerheim and his dramatic life as a nineteenth-century aristocrat in twentieth-century geopolitics.

BIBLIOGRAPHY

Note on Mannerheim's memoirs: the references below are to the Swedish-language version, which has been published over two volumes. The memoirs have been translated into English, but were significantly abridged in the process. The reader can find this abridged translation available as a single volume: *The Memoirs of Marshal Mannerheim*, trans. Eric Lewenhaupt (London: Cassell, 1953).

Chapter 1: Childhood and Adolescence

Alapuro, Risto. *Suomen älymystö Venäjän varjossa* [Finland's Intelligentsia in Russia's Shadow]. Helsinki: Tammi, 1997.

Backmansson, Hugo. *Teckningar ur kadettlifvet* [Sketches of Cadet Life]. Helsinki: Tilgman, 1892.

Churchill, Winston. *My Early Life: A Roving Commission*. London: Fontana/ Collins, 1972 (8th impression).

Enckell, Carl. *Finska kadettkåren 1812–1887* [The Finnish Cadet Corps, 1812–1887]. Hamina: Tryckeri- och tidnings-aktiebolagets tryckeri, 1890.

Engman, Max. *Ett långt farväl: Finland mellan Sverige och Ryssland efter 1809* [A Long Farewell: Finland between Sweden and Russia after 1809]. Stockholm: Atlantis, 2009.

———— *Språkfrågan: Finlandssvenskhetens uppkomst 1812–1922* [The Language Question: The Genesis of Finland-Swedishness, 1812–1922]. Helsinki & Stockholm: Swedish Literature Society in Finland & Atlantis, 2016.

Gripenberg, G. A. "Försök till karakteristik av marskalk Mannerheim" [An Endeavour to Characterise Marshal Mannerheim]. In *Marskalken av Finland, friherre Gustaf Mannerheim: Krigaren, statsmannen, människan* [Finland's Marshal, Baron Gustaf Mannerheim: The Soldier, the Statesman, the Person]. Helsinki: Söderström, 1953.

Jensen, Alfred. *Slavia: Kulturbilder från Volga till Donau* [Slavia: Cultural Representations from the Volga to the Danube]. Stockholm: Bonniers, 1896.

Jussila, Osmo. *Suomen suuriruhtinaskunta 1809–1917* [The Grand Duchy of Finland, 1809–1917]. Helsinki: WSOY, 2004.

Jägerskiöld, Stig. *Den unge Mannerheim* [The Young Mannerheim]. Helsinki: Schildt, 1964.

Keskisarja, Teemu. *Hulttio: Gustaf Mannerheimin painava nuoruus* [The Ne'er-Do-Well: The Troubled Youth of Gustav Mannerheim]. Helsinki: Siltala, 2016.

Luntinen, Pertti. *The Imperial Russian Army and Navy in Finland, 1808–1918*. Helsinki: Finnish Historical Society, 1997.

Mannerheim, C. G. E. *Minnen: Del I, 1882–1930* [Memoirs: Part I, 1882–1930]. Helsinki: Holger Schildts Förlag, 1951.

———— *Brev från sju årtionden* [Letters from Seven Decades]. Edited by Jägerskiöld, Stig. Helsinki: Söderström, 1984.

Meinander, Henrik, "Kalejdoskopet August Schauman" [August Schauman, Kaleidoscope]. In *Svärdet, ordet och pennan: kring människa, makt och rum i nordisk historia* [The Sword, the Word and the Pen: On People, Power and Place in Nordic History]. Edited by Kuvaja, Christer, and Östman, Ann-Catrin. Turku: Turku Historical Society, 2012.

Pieterse, Arnolds, and Starmans, Peter. *Suomalais-alankomaalaisia suhteita: Ennen ja nyt* [Finno-Dutch Relations: Then and Now]. Translated by Määttänen, Leena. Helsinki: Arnolds Pieterse and Peter Starmans, 2012.

Ramsay, Anders. *Från barnaår till silfverhår: Skildringar af Anders Ramsay* [From Child's Play to Going Grey: Accounts of Anders Ramsay]. Parts I–VIII. Helsinki: Söderström, 1904–07.

Savolainen, Raimo. *Suosikkisenaattorit: Venäjän keisarin suosio suomalaisten senaattoreiden menestyksen perustana 1809–1892* [Chosen Senators: The Russian Emperor's Favouritism and the Success of Finnish Senators, 1809–1892]. Helsinki: Hallintohistoriakomitea, 1994.

Schauman, August. *Nu och förr* [Now and Then]. Helsinki: G. W. Edlunds Förlag, 1886.

Screen, J. E. O. "Utgivarens inledning: Carl Enckell och Finska kadett-kåren" [Editor's Introduction: Carl Enckell and the Finnish Cadet Corps]. In Enckell, Carl, and Screen, J. E. O., *Finska kadettkåren*

1887–1903: Fortsättning af arbetet under samma rubrik för åren 1812–1887, med kort öfversigt öfver denna period [The Finnish Cadet Corps, 1887–1903: A Sequel to the Work under the Same Title for the Years 1812–1887, with a Short Outline of that Period]. Helsinki: Swedish Literature Society in Finland, 1990.

———— *Mannerheim*. Translated by Turtia, Kaarina. Helsinki: Otava, 2001.

Screen, J. E. O., and Syrjö, Veli-Matti. *Keisarillinen Suomen kadettikoulu 1812–1903: Haminan kadetit koulussa ja maailmalla* [The Imperial Finnish Cadet School, 1812–1903: Hamina's Cadets in School and the Wider World]. J. E. O. Screen's text translated by Tiilikainen, Heikki. Helsinki: Tammi, 2003.

Chapter 2: The Empire's Man

Buchanan, Meriel. *Petrograd: The City of Trouble, 1914–1918*. London: W. Collins, 1918.

Charmley, John. *Churchill, The End of Glory: A Political Biography*. London: Houghton Mifflin Harcourt, 1993.

Davies, Norman. *Europe: A History*. Oxford: Oxford University Press, 1996.

Engman, Max. *Pietarinsuomalaiset* [The Finns of St Petersburg]. Juva: WSOY, 2004.

Gay, Peter. *The Cultivation of Hatred, Volume III: The Bourgeois Experience: Victoria to Freud*. London: W. W. Norton, 1993.

Iroshnikov, Mikhail, Protsai, Liudmila, and Shelayev, Yuri. *The Sunset of the Romanov Dynasty*. Moscow: Terra, 1992.

Jussila, Osmo. *Suomen suuriruhtinaskunta 1809–1917* [The Grand Duchy of Finland, 1809–1917]. Helsinki: WSOY, 2004.

Jägerskiöld, Stig. *Den unge Mannerheim* [The Young Mannerheim]. Helsinki: Schildt, 1964.

Lieven, Dominic. *Towards the Flame: Empire, War and the End of Tsarist Russia*. London: Allen Lane, 2015.

Luntinen, Pertti. *Sota Venäjällä, Venäjä sodassa* [War in Russia, Russia at War]. Helsinki: Finnish Literature Society, 2008.

Mannerheim, C. G. *Minnen: Del I, 1882–1930* [Memoirs: Part I, 1882–1930]. Helsinki: Holger Schildts Förlag, 1951.

———— *Päiväkirja Japanin sodasta 1904–1905 sekä rintamakirjeitä omaisille* [Diary from the Russo-Japanese War, 1904–1905 and Personal Letters from the Front]. Helsinki: Otava, 1982.

―――― *Brev från sju årtionden* [Letters from Seven Decades]. Edited by Jägerskiöld, Stig. Helsinki: Söderström, 1984.

Polvinen, Tuomo. *Valtakunta ja rajamaa: N. I. Bobrikov Suomen kenraaliku-vernöörinä 1898–1904* [The Realm and the Borderland: N. I. Bobrikov as Governor-General of Finland, 1898–1904]. Helsinki: WSOY, 1984.

Porthan, Lennart, and Frenckell, Arthur. "Hästsporten i Finland" [Equestrian Sports in Finland]. In *Idrotten i Finland i början av tjugonde seklet* [Sport in Finland at the Beginning of the Twentieth Century]. Edited by Wilskman, Ivar. Helsinki: Helios, 1904.

Screen, J. E. O. *Mannerheim*. Translated by Turtia, Kaarina. Helsinki: Otava, 2001.

Shkvarov, Aleksei. *Kenraaliluutnantti Mannerheim: Syntynyt tsaarin palveluk-seen* [Lieutenant-General Mannerheim: Born to Serve the Tsar]. Translated by Ikonen, Susan. Helsinki: Teos, 2010.

Stråth, Bo. *Europe's Utopias of Peace, 1815, 1919, 1951*. London: Bloomsbury, 2016.

Uola, Mikko. *Marskin ryyppy: Marskalkamme juomakulttuuria Chevalier-kaartista ylipäällikön ruokapöytään* [The Marski's Snifter: Our Field Marshal's Drinking Culture from the Chevalier Guards to the Commander-in-Chief's Dinner Table]. Helsinki: Finnish Literature Society, 2002.

Vlasov, Leonid. *Mannerheim i Petersburg 1887–1904* [Mannerheim in St Petersburg, 1887–1904]. Translated by Ekberg, Henrik. Helsinki: Gummerus, 1994.

Wilson, John Dover. *Milestones on the Dover Road*. London: Faber, 1969.

Wolff, Charlotta. *Kejsarens man: Constantin Linder och hans värld 1836–1908* [The Emperor's Man: Constantin Linder and His World, 1836–1908]. Helsinki: Siltala, 2016.

Chapter 3: The Officer's Journey

Clark, Christopher. *The Sleepwalkers: How Europe Went to War in 1914*. London: Allen Lane, 2012.

Franck, Martin. "En husars minnen av general Mannerheim från första världskriget" [A Hussar's Recollections of General Mannerheim from the First World War]. In *Marskalken av Finland, friherre Gustaf Mannerheim: Krigaren, statsmannen, människan* [Finland's Marshal, Baron Gustaf Mannerheim: The Soldier, the Statesman, the Person]. Helsinki: Söderström, 1953.

Jägerskiöld, Stig. *Gustaf Mannerheim 1906–1917* [Gustaf Mannerheim, 1906–1917]. Helsinki: Holger Schildts Förlag, 1965.

Korpisaari, Harri. *Itsenäisen Suomen puolesta: Sotilaskomitea 1915–1918* [For an Independent Finland: The Military Committee, 1915–1918]. Helsinki: Finnish Literature Society, 2009.

Luntinen, Pertti. *Sota Venäjällä, Venäjä sodassa* [War in Russia, Russia at War]. Helsinki: Finnish Literature Society, 2008.

Mannerheim, C. G. E. *Minnen: Del I, 1882–1930* [Memoirs: Part I, 1882–1930]. Helsinki: Holger Schildts Förlag, 1951.

———— *Brev från sju årtionden* [Letters from Seven Decades]. Edited by Jägerskiöld, Stig. Helsinki: Söderström, 1984.

———— *Dagbok förd under min resa i Centralasien och Kina 1906–07–08* [Diary from My Expedition in Central Asia and China, 1906–07–08]. Volumes I–III. Edited by Halén, Harry. Helsinki & Stockholm: Swedish Literature Society in Finland & Atlantis, 2010.

———— *Matka Kiinaan: Tiedusteluraportti 1906–1908* [The Journey to China: Intelligence Report, 1906–1908]. Translated by Halén, Harry. Helsinki: Finnish Literature Society, 2013.

Meri, Veijo. *C. G. Mannerheim: Suomen marsalkka* [C. G. Mannerheim: Finland's Marshal]. Helsinki: WSOY, 1988.

Nolan, Mary. *The Transatlantic Century: Europe and America, 1890–2010*. Cambridge: Cambridge University Press, 2012.

Sandberg, Peter (ed.). *C. G. Mannerheims fotografier från Asienresan 1906–1908—Photographs by C. G. Mannerheim from His Journey across Asia, 1906–1908*. Helsinki: Schildt, 1990.

Screen, J. E. O. *Mannerheim*. Translated by Turtia, Kaarina. Helsinki: Otava, 2001.

Shkvarov, Aleksei. *Kenraaliluutnantti Mannerheim: Syntynyt tsaarin palvelukseen* [Lieutenant-General Mannerheim: Born to Serve the Tsar]. Translated by Ikonen, Susan. Helsinki: Teos, 2010.

Vlasov, Leonid. *Kvinnorna i Mannerheims liv* [The Women in Mannerheim's Life]. Translated by Geust, Carl-Fredrik. Espoo: Schildt, 2002.

Chapter 4: The Chain Reaction

Ahti, Martti. *Salaliiton ääriviivat: Oikeistoradikalismi ja hyökkäävä idänpolitiikka 1918–1919* [The Outlines of a Conspiracy: Right-Wing Radicalism and the Aggressive Eastern Policy, 1918–1919]. Espoo: Weilin+Göös, 1987.

Alapuro, Risto. *State and Revolution in Finland*. Berkeley: University of California Press, 1988.

Churchill, Winston. *The World Crisis: The Aftermath*. London: Butterworth, 1929.

Franck, Martin. "En husars minnen av general Mannerheim från första världskriget" [A Hussar's Recollections of General Mannerheim from the First World War]. In *Marskalken av Finland, friherre Gustaf Mannerheim: Krigaren, statsmannen, människan* [Finland's Marshal, Baron Gustaf Mannerheim: The Soldier, the Statesman, the Person]. Helsinki: Söderström, 1953.

Heinrichs, Erik. *Mannerheim-gestalten I: Den vite generalen 1918–1919* [The Figure of Mannerheim I: The White General, 1918–1919]. Helsinki: Schildt, 1957.

Hemmer, Jarl. *A Fool of Faith*. New York: Liveright Publishing Corporation, 1935.

Hentilä, Marjaliisa, and Hentilä, Seppo. *Saksalainen Suomi 1918* [German Finland, 1918]. Helsinki: Siltala, 2016.

Jägerskiöld, Stig. *Mannerheim 1918*. Translated by Rapola, Sirkka. Helsinki: Otava, 1967.

———— *Riksföreståndaren: Gustaf Mannerheim 1919* [The Regent: Gustaf Mannerheim, 1919]. Helsinki: Schildt, 1969.

Ketola, Eino. "Lokakuun vallankumoukseen 1917, Suomen kautta ja Suomen avulla" [The October Revolution 1917, Finland as a Conduit and Abettor]. In *Lenin ja Suomi: Osa II* [Lenin and Finland: Part II]. Edited by Numminen, Jaakko. Helsinki: Valtion painatuskeskus, 1989.

Korpisaari, Harri. *Itsenäisen Suomen puolesta: Sotilaskomitea 1915–1918* [For an Independent Finland: The Military Committee, 1915–1918]. Helsinki: Finnish Literature Society, 2009.

Kuisma, Markku. *Metsäteollisuuden maa: Suomi, metsät ja kansainvälinen järjestelmä 1620–1920* [The Country of the Wood Industry: Finland, Forests and International Relations, 1620–1920]. Helsinki: Finnish Historical Society, 1993.

———— *Sodasta syntynyt: Itsenäisen Suomen synty Sarajevon laukauksista Tarton rauhaan 1914–1920* [Born of War: The Birth of Independent Finland from the Sarajevo Gunshots to the Treaty of Tartu, 1914–1920]. Helsinki: WSOY, 2010.

Kulha, Keijo K. *Marski ja hänen varjonsa: Kahden miehen kolme sotaa ja rauhaa* [The Marski and His Shadow: Two Men, Three Wars and Three Peace]. Jyväskylä: Docendo, 2016.

Lackman, Matti. *Suomen vai Saksan puolesta? Jääkäreiden tuntematon historia: Jääkäriliikkeen ja jääkäripataljoona 27:n (1915–1918) synty, luonne, mielialojen vaihteluita ja sisäisiä kriisejä sekä niiden heijastuksia itsenäisen Suomen ensi vuosiin saakka* [For Finland or Germany? The Jaegers' Unknown History: The Birth, Character, Mood Swings and Internal Crises of the Jaeger Movement and the 27th Jaeger Battalion (1915–1918), and Their Reverberations in the Early Years of Finnish Independence]. Helsinki: Otava, 2000.

Luntinen, Pertti. *The Imperial Russian Army and Navy in Finland, 1808–1918*. Helsinki: Finnish Historical Society, 1997.

Mannerheim, C. G. E. *Minnen: Del I, 1882–1930* [Memoirs: Part I, 1882–1930]. Helsinki: Holger Schildts Förlag, 1951.

———— *Brev från sju årtionden* [Letters from Seven Decades]. Edited by Jägerskiöld, Stig. Helsinki: Söderström, 1984.

Manninen, Ohto (ed.). *Itsenäistymisen vuodet: Osat I–III* [The Inception of Independent Finland: Parts I–III]. Helsinki: Painatuskeskus, Valtionarkisto, 1992–93.

Polvinen, Tuomo. "Lenin ja kansallisuuskysymys" [Lenin and the Question of Nationality]. In *Lenin ja Suomi: Osa III* [Lenin and Finland: Part III]. Edited by Numminen, Jaakko. Helsinki: Valtion painatuskeskus, 1990.

Polvinen, Tuomo, Heikkilä, Hannu, and Immonen, Hannu. *J. K. Paasikivi: Valtiomiehen elämäntyö I, 1870–1918* [J. K. Paasikivi: The Life's Work of the Statesman I, 1870–1918]. Helsinki: WSOY, 1989.

Ruotsila, Markku. *Churchill and Finland: A Study in Anticommunism and Geopolitics*. London: Routledge, 2005.

Rystad, Göran. "The Åland Question and the Balance of Power in the Baltic during the First World War". In *In Quest of Trade and Security: The Baltic in Power Politics, 1500–1990, II: 1890–1990*. Edited by Rystard, Göran, Böhme, Klaus-Richard, and Carlgren, Wilhelm M. Stockholm: Lund University Press, 1995.

Screen, J. E. O. *Mannerheim*. Translated by Turtia, Kaarina. Helsinki: Otava, 2001.

Strengell, Gustaf. *Hemmet som konstverk* [The Home as a Work of Art]. Helsinki: Holger Schildts Förlag, 1923.

Stråth, Bo. *Europe's Utopias of Peace, 1815, 1919, 1951*. London: Bloomsbury, 2016.

Uino, Ari. *Nuori Urho Kekkonen: Poliittisen ja yhteiskunnallisen kasvun vuodet (1900–1936)* [The Young Urho Kekkonen: The Years of Political and Social Growth (1900–1936)]. Helsinki: Kirjayhtymä, 1985.

Chapter 5: The Gentleman

Ahti, Martti. *Kaappaus? Suojeluskuntaselkkaus 1921, fascismin aave 1927, Mäntsälän kapina 1932* [Coup? The White Guards Incident 1921, the Spectre of Fascism 1927, the Mäntsälä Rebellion 1932]. Helsinki: Otava, 1990.

von Bonsdorff, Bengt. "Mannerheimin kodin taidetta" [The Artwork in Mannerheim's Home]. In *Marsalkan koti: Mannerheim-museon vuosikymmenet* [The Marshal's Home: The Mannerheim Museum through the Decades]. Edited by Norrback, Märtha. Helsinki: Otava, 2001.

Heinrichs, Erik. "Mannerheim som överbefälhavare" [Mannerheim as Commander-in-Chief]. In *Marskalken av Finland, friherre Gustaf Mannerheim: Krigaren, statsmannen, människan* [Finland's Marshal, Baron Gustaf Mannerheim: The Soldier, the Statesman, the Person]. Helsinki: Söderström, 1953.

Joffe, Eleonora. *Mannerheim: Chevalier-kaartin kasvatti* [Mannerheim: Product of the Chevalier Guards]. Translated by Pikkupeura, Arja. Helsinki: Otava, 2006.

Jägerskiöld, Stig. *Mannerheim mellan världskrigen* [Mannerheim between the World Wars]. Helsinki: Schildt, 1972.

Kulha, Keijo K. *Marski ja hänen varjonsa: Kahden miehen kolme sotaa ja rauhaa* [The Marski and His Shadow: Two Men, Three Wars and Three Peace]. Jyväskylä: Docendo, 2016.

Kuusanmäki, Jussi. "Malitiosa desertio: Mannerheimin avioero 1919" [Malitiosa desertio: Mannerheim's Divorce in 1919]. *Kanava* 31, nos. 4–5 (2003): 308–11.

Lähteenmäki, Maria. *Mahdollisuuksien aika: Työläisnaiset ja yhteiskunnan muutos 1910–1930-luvun Suomessa* [A Time of Possibilities: Working-Class Women and Social Change in Finland, 1910s–1930s]. Helsinki: Finnish Historical Society, 1995.

Mannerheim, C. G. E. *Minnen: Del I, 1882–1930* [Memoirs: Part I, 1882–1930]. Helsinki: Holger Schildts Förlag, 1951.

——— *Brev från sju årtionden* [Letters from Seven Decades]. Edited by Jägerskiöld, Stig. Helsinki: Söderström, 1984.

Meinander, Henrik. *Nationalstaten: Finlands svenskhet 1922–2015* [The Nation-State: Finland's Swedishness, 1922–2015]. Helsinki: Swedish Literature Society in Finland, 2016.

Müller, Jan-Werner. *Contesting Democracy: Political Ideas in Twentieth-Century Europe*. New Haven, CT: Yale University Press, 2011.

Norrback, Märtha (ed.). *Marsalkan koti: Mannerheim-museon vuosikymmenet* [The Marshal's Home: The Mannerheim Museum through the Decades]. Helsinki: Otava, 2001.

Pallaste, Tuija. "Rakkaudella, Gustaf" [With Love, Gustaf]. *Helsingin Sanomat*, Kuukausiliite, June 2013. https://www.hs.fi/kuukausiliite/art-2000002659106.html (accessed 27 July 2022).

Ranki, Kristina. *Lukeva Mannerheim: Poimintoja Marsalkan kirjastosta* [Reading Mannerheim: Selections from the Marshal's Library]. Helsinki: Mannerheim Museum, 2013.

Rosén, Gunnar. "Suomen Punaisen Ristin tiennäyttäjä" [The Pioneer of the Finnish Red Cross]. In *Richard Faltin: Sotakirurgi ja Punaisen Ristin työntekijä* [Richard Faltin: War Surgeon and Red Cross Worker]. Edited by Rosén, Gunnar. Helsinki: Otava, 1967.

Screen, J. E. O. *Mannerheim*. Translated by Turtia, Kaarina. Helsinki: Otava, 2001.

Selén, Kari. *Sarkatakkien maa: Suojeluskuntajärjestö ja yhteiskunta 1918–1944* [The Land of Frieze Jackets: The White Guard and Society, 1918–1944]. Helsinki: WSOY, 2001.

Vlasov, Leonid, and Vlasov, Marina. *Gustaf Mannerheim ja valkoiset emigrantit: Historia kirjeissä* [Gustaf Mannerheim and the White Emigrants: A History in Letters]. Translated by Mallinen, Jukka. Helsinki: Schildt, 2007.

Wolff, Charlotta. *Kejsarens man: Constantin Linder och hans värld 1836–1908* [The Emperor's Man: Constantin Linder and His World, 1836–1908]. Helsinki: Siltala, 2016.

Chapter 6: Storm Warning

Götz, Norbert. *Ungleiche Geschwister: Die Konstruktion von nationalsozialistischer Volksgemeinschaft und schwedischem Volksheim* [Unequal Siblings: The Construction of the National Socialist People's Community and the Swedish People's Home]. Baden-Baden: Nomos, 2001.

Ilmjärv, Magnus. "Kahden diktatuurin välillä" [Between Two Dictators]. In *Historian kosto: Suomen talvisota kehyksissään* [The Revenge of History: Framing Finland's Winter War]. Edited by Meinander, Henrik. Helsinki: Siltala, 2015.

Jakobson, Max. *Paasikivi Tukholmassa: J. K. Paasikiven toiminta Suomen lähettiläänä Tukholmassa 1936–39* [Paasikivi in Stockholm: J. K. Paasikivi's Actions as Finnish Envoy to Stockholm, 1936–39]. Helsinki: Otava, 1978.

BIBLIOGRAPHY

Mannerheim, C. G. E. *Minnen: Del II, 1931–1946* [Memoirs: Part II, 1931–1946]. Helsinki: Holger Schildts Förlag, 1952.

——— *Brev från sju årtionden* [Letters from Seven Decades]. Edited by Jägerskiöld, Stig. Helsinki: Söderström, 1984.

Nolan, Mary. *The Transatlantic Century: Europe and America, 1890–2010.* Cambridge: Cambridge University Press, 2012.

Nummela, Ilkka. "Haupitseilla ja haulikoilla" [With Howitzers and Shotguns]. In *Historian kosto: Suomen talvisota kehyksissään* [The Revenge of History: Framing Finland's Winter War]. Edited by Meinander, Henrik. Helsinki: Siltala, 2015.

Polvinen, Tuomo, Heikkilä, Hannu, and Immonen, Hannu. *J. K. Paasikivi: Valtiomiehen elämäntyö II, 1918–1939* [J. K. Paasikivi: The Life's Work of the Statesman II, 1918–1939]. Helsinki: WSOY, 1992.

Rentola, Kimmo. *Stalin ja Suomen kohtalo* [Stalin and the Fate of Finland]. Helsinki: Otava, 2016.

Screen, J. E. O. *Mannerheim*. Translated by Turtia, Kaarina. Helsinki: Otava, 2001.

Selén, Kari. *C. G. E. Mannerheim ja hänen puolustusneuvostonsa* [C. G. E. Mannerheim and His Defence Council]. Helsinki: Otava, 1980.

Soikkanen, Timo. *Kansallinen eheytyminen—myytti vai todellisuus? Ulko- ja sisäpolitiikan linjat ja vuorovaikutus Suomessa vuosina 1933–1939* [Solidifying National Unity—Myth or Reality? Finland's Foreign and Domestic Policies and the Interaction Between Them, 1933–1939]. Turku: University of Turku, 1983.

Turtola, Martti. *Torniojoelta Rajajoelle: Suomen ja Ruotsin salainen yhteistoiminta Neuvostoliiton hyökkäyksen varalle vuosina 1923–1940* [From the River Torne to the Sestra: Finland and Sweden's Secret Co-operation in Case of a Soviet Attack, 1923–1940]. Helsinki: WSOY, 1984.

——— *Erik Heinrichs: Mannerheimin ja Paasikiven kenraali* [Erik Heinrichs: General to Mannerheim and Paasikivi]. Helsinki: Otava, 1988.

——— *Mannerheim*. Helsinki: Tammi, 2016.

Vihavainen, Timo. "Stalin ja geopolitiikka" [Stalin and Geopolitics]. In *Historian kosto: Suomen talvisota kehyksissään* [The Revenge of History: Framing Finland's Winter War]. Edited by Meinander, Henrik. Helsinki: Siltala, 2015.

Wegner, Bernd. "Die Welt aus der Balance: Europa im internationalen System der 1930er-Jahre" [The World out of Balance: Europe and International Relations in the 1930s]. In *Stabilität durch Gleichgewicht?*

Balance of Power im internationalen System der Neuzeit [Stability through Equilibrium: The Balance of Power in Modern International Relations]. Edited by Jonas, Michael, Lappenküper, Ulrich, and Wegner, Bernd. Paderhorn: Brill/Schöningh, 2015.

Åselius, Gunnar. "Tukholmalainen perspektiivi" [The Stockholm Perspective]. In *Historian kosto: Suomen talvisota kehyksissään* [The Revenge of History: Framing Finland's Winter War]. Edited by Meinander, Henrik. Helsinki: Siltala, 2015.

Chapter 7: The Winter War

Cannadine, David. *In Churchill's Shadow: Confronting the Past in Modern Britain*. London: Allen Lane, 2002.

Heinrichs, Erik. *Mannerheim-gestalten II: Marskalken av Finland* [The Figure of Mannerheim II: The Marshal of Finland]. Helsinki: Schildt, 1959.

Jokipii, Mauno. *Jatkosodan synty: Tutkimuksia Saksan ja Suomen sotilaallisesta yhteistyöstä 1940–41* [The Birth of the Continuation War: Research on the Military Co-operation between Germany and Finland, 1940–41]. Helsinki: Otava, 1987.

Jonas, Michael. "Hitlerin horisontin laitamilla" [On the Fringes of Hitler's Horizon]. In *Historian kosto: Suomen talvisota kehyksissään* [The Revenge of History: Framing Finland's Winter War]. Edited by Meinander, Henrik. Helsinki: Siltala, 2015.

Jägerskiöld, Stig. *Fältmarskalken: Gustaf Mannerheim 1939–1941* [The Field Marshal: Gustaf Mannerheim, 1939–1941]. Helsinki: Schildt, 1975.

Kinnunen, Tiina, and Kivimäki, Ville (eds.). *Finland in World War II: History, Memory, Interpretations*. Leiden: Brill, 2012.

Laaksonen, Lasse. *Eripuraa ja arvovaltaa: Mannerheimin ja kenraalien henkilösuhteet ja johtaminen* [Discord and Authority: The Personal Relationships and Leadership Styles of Mannerheim and His Generals]. Helsinki: Gummerus Ajatus, 2004.

Maisky, Ivan. *The Maisky Diaries: Red Ambassador to the Court of St James's, 1932–1943*. Edited by Gorodetsky, Gabriel; translated by Sorokina, Tatiana, and Ready, Oliver. New Haven, CT, and London: Yale University Press, 2015.

Polvinen, Tuomo. *J. K. Paasikivi: Valtiomiehen elämäntyö III, 1939–1944* [J. K. Paasikivi: The Life's Work of the Statesman III, 1939–1944]. Helsinki: WSOY, 1995.

Rautkallio, Hannu. *Mannerheim vai Stalin: Yhdysvallat ja Suomen selvi-*

ytyminen 1939–1944 [Mannerheim or Stalin: The United States and Finland's Survival, 1939–1944]. Helsinki: Otava, 2014.

Rentola, Kimmo. *Stalin ja Suomen kohtalo* [Stalin and the Fate of Finland]. Helsinki: Otava, 2016.

Rose, Jonathan. *The Literary Churchill: Author, Reader, Actor*. New Haven, CT, and London: Yale University Press, 2014.

Screen, J. E. O. *Mannerheim*. Translated by Turtia, Kaarina. Helsinki: Otava, 2001.

Sclén, Kari (ed.). *Mannerheim: Puheet 1918–1947* [Mannerheim: Speeches, 1918–1947]. Helsinki: WSOY, 2008.

Turtola, Martti. *Mannerheim*. Helsinki: Tammi, 2016.

Wahlbäck, Krister. *Jättens andedräkt: Finlandsfrågan i svensk politik 1809–2009* [The Giant's Breath: The Finnish Question in Swedish Politics, 1809–2009]. Stockholm: Atlantis, 2011.

Chapter 8: Brothers-in-Arms

Baryshnikov, Nikolay. *Leningradin piiritys ja Suomi 1941–1944* [The Siege of Leningrad and Finland, 1941–1944]. Translated by Kettunen, Aleksei. Helsinki & St Petersburg: Johan Beckman Institute, 2003.

Danielsbacka, Mirkka. *Sotavankikohtalot: Neuvostovangit Suomessa 1941–1944* [The Fate of POWs: Soviet Prisoners in Finland, 1941–1944]. Helsinki: Tammi, 2016.

Heinrichs, Erik. *Mannerheim-gestalten II: Marskalken av Finland* [The Figure of Mannerheim II: The Marshal of Finland]. Helsinki: Schildt, 1959.

Hurmerinta, Ilmari, and Viitanen, Jukka. *Suomen puolesta: Mannerheim-ristin ritarit 1941–1945* [Fighting for Finland: Knights of the Mannerheim Cross, 1941–1945]. Helsinki: Ajatus, 1994.

Jonas, Michael. *Kolmannen valtakunnan lähettiläs: Wipert von Blücher ja Suomi* [The Third Reich's Envoy: Wipert von Blücher and Finland]. Translated by Lappalainen, Otto, and Ovaska, Mervi. Helsinki: Ajatus, 2010.

Mannerheim, G. *Minnen: Del II, 1931–1946* [Memoirs: Part II, 1931–1946]. Helsinki: Holger Schildts Förlag, 1952.

Meinander, Henrik. *Finland 1944: Krig, samhälle, känslolandskap* [Finland 1944: War, Society, Emotional Landscape]. Helsinki: Söderström, 2009.

Nevakivi, Jukka. *Ždanov Suomessa: Miksi meitä ei neuvostoliittolaistettu?* [Zhdanov in Finland: Why Weren't We Sovietised?]. Helsinki: Otava, 1995.

Polvinen, Tuomo. *J. K. Paasikivi: Valtiomiehen elämäntyö III, 1939–1944* [J. K. Paasikivi: The Life's Work of the Statesman III, 1939–1944]. Helsinki: WSOY, 1995.

Rautkallio, Hannu. *Mannerheim vai Stalin: Yhdysvallat ja Suomen selviytyminen 1939–1944* [Mannerheim or Stalin: The United States and Finland's Survival, 1939–1944]. Helsinki: Otava, 2014.

Rentola, Kimmo. *Stalin ja Suomen kohtalo* [Stalin and the Fate of Finland]. Helsinki: Otava, 2016.

Saarenheimo, Eero. "Salainen äänite: Mannerheimin ja Hitlerin keskustelu kesäkuun 4 päivänä 1942" [The Secret Recording: Mannerheim and Hitler's Discussion on 4 June 1942]. In *Historiantutkimuksen apuna: Yleisradion julkaisusarja II* [Aiding Historical Research: The Finnish Broadcasting Company's Publication Series II]. Helsinki: Yleisradio, 1966.

Screen, J. E. O. *Mannerheim*. Translated by Turtia, Kaarina. Helsinki: Otava, 2001.

Suomi, Juhani. *Mannerheim: Viimeinen kortti? Ylipäällikkö-presidentti* [Mannerheim: Finland's Last Chance? The Commander-in-Chief President]. Helsinki: Siltala, 2013.

Turtola, Martti. *Mannerheim*. Helsinki: Tammi, 2016.

Uola, Mikko. *Marskin ryyppy: Marskalkamme juomakulttuuria Chevalier-kaartista ylipäällikön ruokapöytään* [The Marski's Snifter: Our Field Marshal's Drinking Culture from the Chevalier Guards to the Commander-in-Chief's Dinner Table]. Helsinki: Finnish Literature Society, 2002.

———— *Eritahtiset aseveljet: Suomi ja muut Saksan rinnalla taistelleet 1939–1944* [Brothers-in-Arms, Out of Step: Finland and Germany's Other Allies, 1939–1944]. Jyväskylä: Docendo, 2015.

Vehviläinen, Olli. *Finland in the Second World War: Between Germany and Russia*. New York: Palgrave, 2002.

Vihavainen, Timo. "Sodan ja vaaran vuodet" [The Years of War and Peril]. In *Yleisradion historia 1926–1996, I–III* [The Finnish Broadcasting Company's History, 1926–1996, I–III]. Helsinki: Yle, 1996.

Visuri, Pekka. *Mannerheimin ja Rytin vaikeat valinnat: Suomen johdon ratkaisut jatkosodan käännekohdassa* [Mannerheim's and Ryti's Difficult Choices: The Finnish Leadership's Decisions at the Turning Point of the Continuation War]. Jyväskylä: Docendo, 2013.

BIBLIOGRAPHY

Chapter 9: Responsibility and Legacy

Ekberg, Henrik. *Gustaf Mannerheim: bolsjevismens svurne fiende* [Gustaf Mannerheim: The Sworn Enemy of Bolshevism]. Raasepori: Västnyländska kultursamfundet, 2022.

Gripenberg, G. A. "Försök till karakteristik av marskalk Mannerheim" [An Endeavour to Characterise Marshal Mannerheim]. In *Marskalken av Finland, friherre Gustaf Mannerheim: Krigaren, statsmannen, människan* [Finland's Marshal, Baron Gustaf Mannerheim: Soldier, Statesman, Person]. Helsinki: Söderström, 1953.

———— *Dagbok 1943–1946, I–III* [Diary, 1943–1946, I–III]. Stockholm: Kungliga samfundet för utgivande av hanskrifter rörande Skandinaviens historia, 2019.

Heinrichs, Erik. "Mannerheim som överbefälhavare" [Mannerheim as Commander-in-Chief]. In *Marskalken av Finland, friherre Gustaf Mannerheim: Krigaren, statsmannen, människan* [Finland's Marshal, Baron Gustaf Mannerheim: The Soldier, the Statesman, the Person]. Helsinki: Söderström, 1953.

Liinamaa, Matti. "Mannerheimin muistelmat Emerik Olsonin kirjeenvaihdossa" [Mannerheim's Memoirs in Emerik Olsoni's Correspondence]. In *Mannerheimiana: Champion of Liberty -yhdistyksen julkaisu* [Mannerheimiana: Publication of the Champion of Liberty Association], 3/2006. Helsinki: Champion of Liberty, 2006.

Manninen, Ohto. "Mannerheimin muistelmien synty" [The Genesis of Mannerheim's Memoirs]. In *Scripta Mannerheimiana: Puheenvuoroja Mannerheim-kirjallisuudesta & valikoiva bibliografia* [Scripta Mannerheimiana: Speeches on Mannerheim Literature and a Selective Bibliography]. Edited by Meinander, Henrik. Helsinki: Helsingin yliopiston kirjasto, 1996.

Meinander, Henrik. *Den nödvändiga grannen: Studier & inlägg* [The Necessary Neighbour: Essays and Contributions]. Espoo: Schildt, 2001.

———— *Kekkografi och andra historiska spånor* [Kekkography and Other Reflections on Finnish History]. Helsinki: Söderström, 2008.

———— *Finland 1944: Krig, samhälle, känslolandskap* [Finland 1944: War, Society, Emotional Landscape]. Helsinki: Söderström, 2009.

Nevakivi, Jukka. *Ždanov Suomessa: Miksi meitä ei neuvostoliittolaistettu?* [Zhdanov in Finland: Why Weren't We Sovietised?]. Helsinki: Otava, 1995.

Olsson, Ulf. *Berättelsen om Gertrud "Calle" Wallenberg: Mannerheims sista kärlek* [Tales of Gertrud "Calle" Wallenberg: Mannerheim's Last Sweetheart]. Stockholm: Atlantis, 2014.

Reenpää, Heikki A. "Mannerheimin muistelmien syntyminen" [The Creation of Mannerheim's Memoirs]. In *Mannerheimiana: Champion of Liberty -yhdistyksen julkaisu* [Mannerheimiana: Publication of the Champion of Liberty Association], 3/2006. Helsinki: Champion of Liberty, 2006.

Screen, J. E. O. *Mannerheim*. Translated by Turtia, Kaarina. Helsinki: Otava, 2001.

Soikkanen, Timo. *Yrjö Ruutu, Näkijä ja tekijä: Itsenäisyyden, eheyttämisen ja uuden ulkopolitiikan juurilla* [Yrjö Ruutu, Seer and Doer: The Origins of Independence, Unity and a New Foreign Policy]. Helsinki: WSOY, 1991.

Suomi, Juhani. *Mannerheim: Viimeinen kortti? Ylipäällikkö-presidentti* [Mannerheim: Finland's Last Chance? The Commander-in-Chief President]. Helsinki: Siltala, 2013.

Tarkka, Jukka. *Hirmuinen asia: Sotasyyllisyys ja historian taito* [A Terrible Matter: War Guilt and the Art of History]. Helsinki: WSOY, 2009.

Turtola, Martti. *Erik Heinrichs: Mannerheimin ja Paasikiven kenraali* [Erik Heinrichs: General to Mannerheim and Paasikivi]. Helsinki: Otava, 1988.

Chapter 10: Posterity

Ahlander, Dag Sebastian. *Gustaf Mannerheim*. Lund: Historiska media, 2016.

Bergholm, Tauno. *Mannerheim kaskujen kuvastimessa* [Mannerheim Reflected in Anecdotes]. Helsinki: Ajatus, 1997.

von Blücher, Wipert. *Gesandter zwischen Diktatur und Demokratie: Erinnerungen aus den Jahren 1935–1944* [Envoy between Dictatorship and Democracy: Memories from the Years 1935–1944]. Wiesbaden: Limes, 1951.

Borenius, Tancred. *Field-Marshal Mannerheim*. London: Hutchinson, 1940.

Clements, Jonathan. *Mannerheim: President, Soldier, Spy*. London: Haus Publishing, 2009.

Donner, Kai. *Fältmarskalken friherre Mannerheim* [The Field Marshal Baron Mannerheim]. Helsinki: Söderström, 1934.

Erfurth, Waldemar. *Der finnische Krieg, 1941–1944* [The Finnish War, 1941–1944]. Wiesbaden: Limes, 1950.

Gummerus, Herman. *Fältmarskalk Mannerheim* [Field Marshal Mannerheim]. Helsinki: Schildt, 1937.

Heinrichs, Erik. *Mannerheim-gestalten I: Den vite generalen 1918–1919* [The Figure of Mannerheim I: The White General, 1918–1919]. Helsinki: Schildt, 1957.

———— *Mannerheim-gestalten II: Marskalken av Finland* [The Figure of Mannerheim II: The Marshal of Finland]. Helsinki: Schildt, 1959.

Ignatius, Hannes. *Gustaf Mannerheim*. Helsinki: Otava, 1918.

Ilvas, Juha. "Mannerheim in Art and Popular Imagery". In *Mannerheim: An Officer of the Imperial Russian Army, Marshal of Independent Finland*. Edited by Vihavainen, Timo, et al. Helsinki: St Petersburg Foundation of Finland, 2005.

Jonas, Michael. *Wipert von Blücher und Finnland: Alternativpolitik und Diplomatie im "Dritten Reich"* [Wipert von Blücher and Finland: Alternative Politics and Diplomacy in the "Third Reich"]. PhD dissertation. University of Helsinki, 2008.

Konttinen, Riitta. *Suomen marsalkan ratsastajapatsas* [The Equestrian Statue of Finland's Marshal]. Helsinki: Marshal Mannerheim Heritage Foundation, 1989.

Korhonen, Arvi. *Finland and World War II, 1939–1944*. New York: The Ronald Press, 1948.

———— *Barbarossa-suunnitelma ja Suomi* [Operation Barbarossa and Finland]. Porvoo: WSOY, 1961.

Krosby, Hans Peter. *Suomen valinta 1941* [Finland's Choice, 1941]. Translated by Ihanainen, Erkki, and Pakkala, Ulla. Helsinki: Kirjayhtymä, 1967.

Kruskopf, Erik. *Stadens stoder: Om offentlig skulptur i Helsingfors* [The City's Statues: Public Sculpture in Helsinki]. Espoo: Schildt, 2000.

Lehmus, Kalle. *Tuntematon Mannerheim* [The Unknown Mannerheim]. Helsinki: Weilin+Göös, 1967.

Lindqvist, Herman. *Mannerheim: Marsken, masken, myten* [Mannerheim: Marski, Mask, Myth]. Stockholm: Albert Bonniers Förlag, 2017.

Lundin, Charles Leonard. *Finland in the Second World War*. Bloomington: Indiana University Press, 1957.

Peltonen, Ulla-Maija. "Keksitty Mannerheim—muistamisen ja kertomisen politiikkaa" [The Imagined Mannerheim—The Politics of Memory and Narrative]. In *Menneisyys on toista maata* [The Past Is Another Country]. Edited by Knuuttila, Seppo, and Piela, Ulla. Helsinki: Finnish Literature Society, 2007.

———— "Yhdistävä ja erottava sankaruus: C. G. E. Mannerheim"

[Unifying and Divisive Heroism: C. G. E. Mannerheim]. In *Kirjoituksia sankaruudesta* [Writings about Heroism]. Edited by Peltonen, Ulla-Maija, and Kemppainen, Ilona. Helsinki: Finnish Literature Society, 2010.

Piotrovsky, Mikhail. "Our Mannerheim". In *Mannerheim: An Officer of the Imperial Russian Army, Marshal of Independent Finland*. Edited by Vihavainen, Timo, et al. Helsinki: St Petersburg Foundation of Finland, 2005.

Rodzianko, Paul. *Mannerheim: Krigaren och människan* [Mannerheim: The Soldier and the Man]. Helsinki: Söderström, 1942.

Screen, J. E. O. *Mannerheim: The Years of Preparation*. London: C. Hurst, 1970.

Shkvarov, Aleksei. *Kenraaliluutnantti Mannerheim: Syntynyt tsaarin palvelukseen* [Lieutenant-General Mannerheim: Born to Serve the Tsar]. Translated by Ikonen, Susan. Helsinki: Teos, 2010.

Toivonen, Hannu. "Isosetäni Mannerheim" [My Great-Uncle Mannerheim]. *Seura*, 17 December 2012. https://seura.fi/ilmiot/historia/isosetani-mannerheim/ (accessed 10 August 2022).

Turtola, Martti. *Mannerheim*. Helsinki: Tammi, 2016.

Upton, Anthony. *Finland in Crisis, 1940–1941: A Study in Small-Power Politics*. London: Faber & Faber, 1964.

INDEX

INDEX

INDEX